A YEAR WITH ST. JOHN OF THE CROSS

365 DAILY READINGS AND REFLECTIONS

LEONARD DOOHAN

ISBN-13:
9780991006779

ISBN-10:
0991006771

The front cover photo is of the Carmelite Monastery in Segovia where St. John of the Cross lived and where he is now buried.

The Author

Dr. Leonard Doohan is Professor Emeritus at Gonzaga University, Spokane. He has written 24 books and many articles and has given over 350 workshops throughout the USA, Canada, Europe, Australia, New Zealand, and the Far East. Doohan's recent books include *Spiritual Leadership: the Quest for Integrity* (2007), *Enjoying Retirement: Living Life to the Fullest* (2010), *Courageous Hope: The Call of Leadership* (2011), *The One Thing Necessary: The Transforming Power of Christian Love* (2012), and *Spiritual Leadership: How to Become a Great Spiritual Leader—Ten Steps and a Hundred Suggestions* (2014). Doohan has given courses and workshops on John of the Cross all over the world and his published tapes have been used throughout the English speaking countries.

Visit leonarddoohan.com

ABBREVIATIONS OF THE WORKS OF ST. JOHN OF THE CROSS

A = Ascent of Mount Carmel

N = Dark Night

C= Spiritual Canticle

F = Living Flame

P = Poetry

S = Sayings of Light and Love

Pr = Precautions

L = Letters

Other books on John of the Cross by Leonard Doohan:

The Contemporary Challenge of John of the Cross

John of the Cross: Your Spiritual Guide

The Dark Night is Our Only Light: A Study of the Book of
the *Dark Night* by John of the Cross

John of the Cross—The Spiritual Canticle: The Encounter of
Two Lovers. An Introduction to the Book of the
Spiritual Canticle by John of the Cross

John of the Cross: The Living Flame of Love

These books are available from amazon.com

An Opportunity for Study, Reflection, and Renewal

John of the Cross, like Teresa of Avila, insisted on solid biblical, theological, and spiritual foundations for growth in Christian life. This book's daily readings offer opportunities for study of John's life, ministry, spiritual direction, and his many works of poetry and prose. Each day gives four key concepts that link the readings with contemporary situations, thereby creating occasions for reflection, interpretation, and application. Finally, three daily challenges focus the reader's attention on action items that can lead to growth and personal renewal. Love is based on knowledge and the more we know John of the Cross and his works the more we are drawn into an enthusiastic dedication to the challenges he presents to deepen our spiritual lives in union with the Lord.

Many writers on John feel that the best introduction to John is to read his poetry and let it inspire and enthuse the reader. Should readers wish to begin with the poetry then by all means start with chapter eight and with a daily reading of one or two stanzas of John's poems. However, the approach I have found helpful, both personally in in courses and workshops I have given, and which I have chosen here, is to start with John's life and all aspects of his ministry. I have always been convinced that when someone knows John better as a person; his life, the extent of his dedication in ministry, his tireless service in spiritual direction, such a one cannot help being enthusiastically overwhelmed with what a wonderful person John is and how many aspects of his life are very like our own. If one follows this up with an awareness of the difficult situations in which John lived and struggled—situations not unlike the problems we face in our contemporary world—he or she discovers how relevant for us is John's approach and teachings. Too many people do not know John well enough to appreciate, or want to appreciate, his teachings. If we get to know him well, we are sure to want him as a friend and guide. I hope readers will find this approach helpful.

I have quoted extensively from John of the Cross' writings so that readers have direct contact with his thought. However, this book is best used as a companion to John's own writings, and I would remind readers how important it is to stay in direct contact with them. So, I have given references throughout indicating appropriate readings for the day. When used as a companion to John's writings, this handbook of readings and reflections can become a personal formation program.

Friends who have read this book have commented on how it is a compendium or like an encyclopedia on all things about John of the Cross. Several have said that this is the kind of book they have been waiting for. One suggested, 'If you want an introduction to John of the Cross and his writings, you don't need any other book except this one.'" I realize daily dedication to follow the readings, reflections, and challenges will require firm and persevering commitment. I hope the book will contribute to deepening your knowledge of John's life and teachings, increase your enthusiasm for John as your friend and guide, and open your heart to respond to his challenges to follow Christ in this journey of love.

How to Use This Book

Give as much time as you can to the readings and reflections, thinking and praying about them. These reflections are based on John of the Cross' writings. Where appropriate, a reference to the source of the reflection is given.

Reflect slowly and quietly on the four reflection points.

Plan to implement the suggestions under *CHALLENGES FOR TODAY*. Some of the questions and challenges will be repeated, sometimes asked from a different perspective, sometimes coming later and looking for a deeper response.

Do not worry if some readings do not challenge you or seem complicated at the time. Just move on!

Write down your own thoughts and reminders. There is lots of extra space. Next year you can re-read your own comments, assess your progress, and redirect your commitment.

Start whenever and wherever you like, day 1 is any day you choose. Then keep going! The book is divided into sections and you can read the sections in whichever order you choose. If you are in a formation program, read the sections of this book that correspond to the focused readings of your program.

You may decide to share the reflections with close friends who, like you, see John of the Cross as their spiritual guide. You could decide to form a group to help each other, even sharing on Facebook or Twitter to urge each other on.

One of the main uses of the book is to help readers who do not have ready access to a spiritual director. These readings and reflections my help fill that gap. For many, spiritual direction is a luxury and finding a competent spiritual director as difficult as John of the Cross suggested it would be. Many need to find alternative solutions and substitutions. I hope these readings and reflections will help.

Reader Comments

"Thank you so much for the excellent work. Your insights and reflection questions are wonderful."

"The clarity of the book, along with its depth without being complex, makes this work a real treasure."

"What a great idea and a superb execution, a work that will be helpful to so many."

"I recently purchased the Kindle edition of your book on St. John of the Cross. I have been reading from it each day as part of my prayer time. To sum it up in a word: wow!"

A YEAR WITH ST. JOHN OF THE CROSS: 365 DAILY READINGS AND REFLECTIONS

Table of Contents

A contemporary sculpture of John of the Cross in the museum
of the monastery of Ubeda where John died

Introduction
John of the Cross in
Everyday Life

DAY 1 *THANK YOU*

Thank you for joining me for this year of readings and reflections from St. John of the Cross. I am delighted to share with you this opportunity to immerse ourselves in the spiritual challenges of one of the greatest figures in all the history of spirituality. I really got to know John of the Cross when I studied for several years with the greatest living scholar of John, Fr. Federico Ruiz Salvador. His exceptional knowledge, enthusiasm, and perceptive interpretation persuaded many, including myself, of John's historical importance, theological and spiritual brilliance, and relevance for our contemporary lives. These convictions intensified for me over 35 years of teaching classes and offering workshops in many countries throughout the world, where people responded with enthusiasm to John's vision and challenges. Among spiritual writers, John is clearly the most influential for me, and he has become a very special spiritual guide. I hope these readings and reflections will not only contribute to your knowledge of John's vision and teachings, but also be a source of your enthusiasm for him as they always have been for me.

1. We often choose favorite spiritual writers and some are helpful while others get us nowhere. Have we chosen well?
2. In this book we will get to know John and see how his life and teachings go together, and both are remarkable.
3. We need to spend time with someone if we really want to get to know him or her. Let us give quality time to St. John, knowing he can lead us to the Lord.
4. We will be building a relationship with John; let's start slowly and develop it carefully.

CHALLENGES FOR TODAY
- Which spiritual writer has influenced you the most?
- What image of John of the Cross do you have now?
- Are you willing to give this project sufficient time?

DAY 2 *A YEAR WITH JOHN OF THE CROSS*

In this year with St. John of the Cross we will read and reflect on his life, ministry, spiritual direction, spirituality, as well as selections from all his works, short and long. The readings and reflections in this book will introduce us to all these, as well as comments from many leading writers and commentators on John. This year will be an opportunity to immerse ourselves in the spirituality of John of the Cross. Throughout the year we should keep in mind the importance of appreciating the entire spiritual system of John, which is reflected in all of his works. Likewise we should see the links between John's various works, know something of the historical background and times of John, and be sensitive to his use of mystical language. When reading John's works we must avoid entering them with prejudice from former false understandings of John. We should read his writings directly, often, and reflectively, and try to enter into dialogue with John. We should appreciate the unique focus and message of each of his works, remember the central significance of his poetry, and above all be sure to interpret his message for today.

1. This year is an opportunity for each of us to respond to John's call and challenge like never before—to dedicate ourselves to life with God in Christ.
2. Perhaps in the past we may have dabbled a little with John's life and works. This year can be an integrated approach.
3. If we are faithful to these daily readings and reflections they can transform our approach to spirituality.
4. Let us prepare our hearts for the reflections that lie ahead.

CHALLENGES FOR TODAY
- Pray for openness to the challenges of this year.
- Ask God to prepare you for the unexpected.
- Think about sharing these reflections in a group.

DAY 3 *JOHN OF THE CROSS IN EVERYDAY LIFE*

These readings and reflections are for everyone who longs for a deeper spirituality. Too often John is mistakenly seen as elitist—a misunderstanding that has done a lot of harm, misinterpreted John, and excluded so many people of good will from the opportunities intended for them. John may have started by focusing on the members of the Carmelite Reform, but over time God's Church recognized John's gifts for everyone, declaring John a doctor of the universal Church. Why? Because John's teaching is part of the universal call to holiness. You will find John's teachings and their guidance and challenges in this selection of readings and reflections. Scholars today focus less on the intentions of a writer and more on the response of readers. This reader response criticism is what identifies an author's true audience, and we know that more people read John of the Cross today than ever before. Thus, readers throughout the world have found in John answers to their needs and now claim John as their mentor and guide.

1. Let us give ourselves enthusiastically to these readings.
2. What spiritual needs do we have and who do we know can respond to them? Maybe John is our answer.
3. Let us hope that these readings and reflections may well lead us where we have always wanted to go.
4. As we begin our readings and reflections perhaps we will find John has answers we have been seeking.

CHALLENGES FOR TODAY
- Pray for openness to the Holy Spirit.
- Let John speak for himself; don't merge his ideas with others' views.
- Pray the Lord will keep your heart open to challenge.

DAY 4 *TAKE COURAGE TO BEGIN THIS JOURNEY WITH JOHN OF THE CROSS*

When undertaking our spiritual journey with John of the Cross we must not feel burdened by thoughts of the impossibility of making even the first steps. We are not struggling to move forward step by step. Rather we must be aware that God is drawing us to divine life. So, John urges us to have an attitude of confident response, for "God is the principal agent in this matter, and . . . acts as the blind man's guide who must lead it by the hand to the place it does not know how to reach" (F. 3.29). The primary activity for us who seek God is not to place any obstacles in the way of God's work of drawing us to union in love. So, this year, as we reflect on John's call and challenges, let us take courage. Our responsibility includes letting God draw us in small steps, never allowing ourselves to go back, never overdoing it at first— just moving steadily and consistently in the one direction that matters. In these efforts, John can be our guide. "Our goal will be, with God's help, to explain all these points, so that everyone who reads this book will in some way discover the road that they are walking along" (A. Prologue.7).

1. We all know that beginnings are always hard.
2. We have probably tried before and not done too well. Let us just move slowly, peacefully, confidently, step by step.
3. Teresa of Avila spoke about making this journey with "a determined determination."
4. Let us pray for perseverance in sticking with this commitment to journey with John for a year.

CHALLENGES FOR TODAY
- Half-hearted responses will not help you on this journey.
- Remember Jesus' stories about a man who started to build a tower and couldn't finish it, and a king who started a war and couldn't get organized. Make sure you desire to finish a job that you want to start.
- Pray for others who begin this journey with John in these readings and reflections.

DAY 5 EMPHASIZE RECOLLECTION

If we wish to undertake this spiritual journey with John of the Cross as guide, we must maintain a spirit of deep recollection. "Recollection" refers to the discipline of collecting ourselves around a central thought. It helps us to gather together the scattered aspects of life and unite them in a meaningful whole. Reading John's writings requires education and sensitivity born of deep recollection, nurtured in silence, what John calls a "deep and delicate listening" (F. 3.34). John acknowledges that some people are just not ready for the material he wishes to present. Only a total immersion in the desire for the will of God and longing for God's love will enable us to appreciate John's channeling of God's call to spiritual life and enrichment. John waited to write some of the commentaries until he felt God had endowed him with gifts of knowledge and fervor. We will need the same gifts to read them with profit. Four practices or attitudes can help us in developing a spirit of recollection: stillness of body, being open to inspiration by the Spirit, concentrating on being present to Christ, and silence in God. Each of these practices comes from ordinary events of each day. They come together in times of reflection.

1. Each day we should have times when we just sit still and do nothing.
2. Reflection also requires that we be people who can prepare themselves to be inspired, otherwise we are just left with empty quiet time.
3. Recollection requires focused attention. Can we give quality time to others, to the events of the day, to the issues of the world around us?
4. Recollection needs silence and this is not easy in our noisy world. Some quiet time each day is critical for spiritual health.

CHALLENGES FOR TODAY
- Try to be fully present to the people and events of this week.
- Remember recollection is not possible when your mind is cluttered with all kinds of issues.
- Give importance to stillness and silence.

DAY 6 DESIRE WHAT GOD WANTS OF YOU

It is important as we spend a little time each day with John of the Cross that we maintain a clearly focused commitment. A key attitude in one who makes this journey is to want to reach the goal of a deeper spirituality. A lot of people say they want to pursue a deeper spiritual life and seek union with God but they do not have the necessary attitudes. We must match our longing with readiness to be drawn by God. Perhaps the one great attitude needed to benefit from this year with John of the Cross is that we who seek this transformation must above all desire that God be everything for us. This is a time when we who pursue God give ourselves totally with fidelity and stability, wanting nothing except what God wants and doing nothing except what God wants. John tells us; "What does it profit you to give God one thing if He asks of you another? Consider what God wants, and then do it" (S. 95). God must be everything to the person who approaches this stage. It is a fundamental attitude of directing the whole of life to God and centering all one does on God alone.

1. Let us begin to make our own the challenge that John gives later in the journey: "Everything I do I do with love, and everything I suffer I suffer with the delight of love" (C. 28.8).
2. The end of our journey will include the total union of our desires with God's, so let's start by wanting this now.
3. Let us be honest with ourselves and say whether we really want the end of this journey.
4. We are beginning a difficult climb; are we ready to accept the struggles that lie ahead?

CHALLENGES FOR TODAY
- How much of your life is given to God?
- What do you want to do with the rest of your life?
- What does God want of you in these days?

DAY 7 *ACCEPT GOD'S CALL*

We can easily think that the experiences John describes are unreal and the teachings too extraordinary for most human beings. Or at least we can conclude that reading some of his writings is a waste of time for us who will never attain what John describes. John is aware of this possible response and warns readers against it. But, we should begin with awareness of God's goodness and of the human call to greatness and to union with God in love. We can always thwart our challenge to spiritual growth by insisting on a reduced ideal of our calling. John reminds us that God "declared that the Father, the Son, and the Holy Spirit would take up their abode in anyone who loved Him" (F. Prologue.2). So, in approaching John's life and works, let us gratefully appreciate this call to humanity and be enthused by it, even though we may still be at an earlier stage in the spiritual life. When God calls us it isn't for some task God wants from us. God calls us to be who we are destined to be. God's call is not to do something but to be someone. As we begin these readings and reflections let us open our hearts to God's transformation within us.

1. Call is not about the end but to the process that leads to the end.
2. Let us express our gratitude for God's involvement in this year's journey.
3. When we reflect on John's life we will see that from the earliest times in his journey the end is already evolving.
4. God's call always includes the gifts needed for response.

CHALLENGES FOR TODAY
- Try to make more dedicated effort on this journey than on any other you have previously tried.
- In prayer offer yourself to God in emptiness ready to be filled with God's grace.
- Pray you will not thwart God's will in this commitment.

DAY 8 *KEEP AN EYE ON DAILY LIFE*

We do not read John merely to gain clearer understanding of how people understood his teachings in the sixteenth century, but to gain insight into what those teachings mean for us in our own time and place. So, we need to read John with an eye on our own situations—personal, ecclesial, and societal. Some spiritualities come and go, and it is appropriate that some die as they become irrelevant to changed situations. John and his teachings are as relevant today, or maybe more relevant, than ever, but we must interpret his language, concepts, dynamic development, and insights to our own situations. So, in reading any of John's works, we should never be locked in to one interpretation. It is important that we always let God speak to us according to the divine will for us. John gave the guidance for our approach to all his works in the prologue to the *Spiritual Canticle.* "As a result, though we give some explanation of these stanzas, there is no reason to be bound to this explanation" (C. Prologue.2). We will find other explanations and applications of his message as times and circumstances change. So, we shall always keep an eye on our present circumstances as we read John, interpreting his teachings in light of our contemporary needs.

1. We must make John's teachings as relevant to our changed lifestyles as they were for the nuns and friars of the Carmelite Reform.
2. These readings and reflections will give us the foundation from which to explore and discover John for today.
3. If we do not interpret John's message it becomes fossilized.
4. John's disciples included many laity from all walks of life who gave his vision a sense of daily reality.

CHALLENGES FOR TODAY
- As you read John do not leave his challenges in the past but make them relevant today.
- Pray for discernment to know how and when to interpret John for your daily life.
- You might well discuss with others how relevant John's particular teachings are for today.

DAY 9 PERSEVERE IN THIS JOURNEY

I would like to ask each of you to give serious thought to the depth of your commitment for this particular journey with John of the Cross during the course of an entire year. I believe it will be an enriching year if you are able to persevere. Many reasons will arise that seem legitimate excuses for dropping out or taking a break for a few weeks. It will be difficult, as John pointed out; "[W]e are not writing on pleasing or delightful theme addressed to the kind of people who like to approach God along sweet and satisfying paths" (A. Prologue.8). However, I hope you will be able to continue with equal enthusiasm throughout the course of the year. If you are able to do so, I think you will learn a lot about John and his life and teachings. I am equally convinced you will learn a lot about yourself and your strengths and weaknesses. There is also every likelihood that you will become enthusiastic for John of the Cross' vision of life. I have journeyed with John as a guide for many years, and I do not think there is anyone quite like him as a guide. If you are able to persevere I believe you will find this year one of the most enriching years in your spiritual journey.

1. We often need others' help to persevere over the long haul.
2. Often we give ourselves to a spirituality only to drift away to another approach.
3. Many spiritualities today are lightweight; John's is substantial.
4. Let us always be aware that God is drawing us to life.

CHALLENGES FOR TODAY
- Organize your day to make sure this commitment has its fixed place and time.
- Get to know John like never before.
- See each day as spending time with a friend.

DAY 10 JOURNEY WITH FRIENDS

When I was much younger I used to love to climb mountains in the Alps of Northern Italy. It was, and is, a wonderful experience. However, serious climbing is not something a person should do on his or her own. It is always better to climb with a guide and more enjoyable when you can also do it with friends. Let us think about the possibility of making this year's journey with some close friends who share our hopes and dreams for spiritual growth. We could use e-mail once a week to share our reflections, or a posting on Facebook, or a daily tweet focusing on a day's reflection. Sharing a thought from John with close friends can be mutually supportive. For example, "The power and the tenacity of love is great for love captures and binds God himself" (C. 32.1) Friends can be very supportive of each other during this year, keeping each other focused, and urging each other along the year.

1. We should decide what supports we need to make this year a success.
2. Let each of us list some of our personal goals for this year.
3. Let us identify our weaknesses that could hinder the year's program.
4. We should mark our calendars with times to reassess our progress.

CHALLENGES FOR TODAY
- Who has the same interests as you?
- How have you prepared for this year?
- Is there someone else you can support in this year's undertaking?

DAY 11 *CHOOSE A TIME FOR YOUR DAILY READING*

In the ancient world there were three uses of the word "time," namely, tempus, chronos, and kairos. The first is simply historical time that relates to historical events. Every day will have its events that are part and parcel of life; this is who we are as human beings living in history. The second word for time, "chronos," is measured time that eats up our lives with its demands, as the Greek god Chronos devoured his six children to prevent them from inheriting his throne and bringing in a new era. Chronos gives the impression of consuming anything so that he can keep things the way they were. This kind of time stifles growth and blocks us from entering a new way of living. The third concept of time is "kairos" which means time of grace, of gift, of opportunity, and of blessing. This year will include the first two, but it is primarily the time of gift, of blessing, and of opportunity for each of us. Within each day with its events and consumption we must create space for blessing. Let us set aside a special time each day when we can read, reflect, and accept challenge.

1. We all drift to "chronos" more than we would like.
2. Let us think about times in our spirituality that have been moments of "kairos."
3. Let us find a time in each day when we can be free enough to reflect on the day's readings.
4. Can we create special places where we will engage in our daily readings and reflections?

CHALLENGES FOR TODAY
- Which kind of time do you emphasize most?
- What stifles your use of time?
- What do you think is a waste of time in your life?

The church built over the birth home of John of the Cross.

1
The Life and Times of John of the Cross

St. John of the Cross was a great poet, theologian, mystical doctor, philosopher, and literary and poetical genius. From earliest times, his life was filled with trials and suffering. He certainly was a great mystic who lived in deep union with God; yet at the same time he was a great practical reformer, builder, leader, director, and writer. His mysticism was not achieved through withdrawal from real life, but while struggling with injustice and persecution. John was a wonderful model of uncompromising dedication to God and the life of prayer amidst the pressures of daily life. We begin our reflections by thinking about his life and how he is an extraordinary model for us.

DAY 12 *JOHN OF THE CROSS*

John of the Cross was born into a family that had, and always would retain, clearly defined values regarding family life, love, poverty, sharing, and the priorities of spiritual life over all else. John's parents, Gonzalo and Catalina, made all their decisions motivated by what was the most loving thing to do. Their decisions were often very hard and implied a lot of pain and hardship, but they never sacrificed their values for an easier, more comfortable life. Gonzalo and Catalina created a family environment in which John learned to cherish the approaches they modelled for their three sons, Francisco, Luis, and John. Gonzalo had enjoyed status, privilege, wealth, and security, but he lost it all when his family rejected him because he chose the genuine love for a poor orphan girl instead of the artificiality of maintaining family wealth and bloodlines. In hardship, poverty, malnutrition, and sickness, Gonzalo and Catalina built their life together on love and shared the wealth of their goodness with anyone in need.

1. The future John of the Cross was born in Fontiveros, a small Castilian town not far from Avila. He lived from 1542-1591.
2. John was born into a family where love and sharing were more important than accumulation of material goods.
3. Do we have the same sets of priorities that molded John of the Cross and gave him a foundation for life?
4. We can appreciate the challenge to imitate John and always make decisions based on what is the most loving thing to do.

CHALLENGES FOR TODAY
- Which of the values that John's family nurtured would be good for you?
- Re-examine some of the decisions you have recently made to see if you are proud of them.
- Which values have you learned from your parents, and which are you passing on to your own family?

DAY 13 *COPING WITH STRUGGLES*

John's mother, Catalina, had to cope with lots of pain and struggles while setting the future direction for her family. Soon after John's birth, her husband, Gonzalo, died after a prolonged and painful illness. Then her son, Luis, also died, probably from malnutrition. The family lived in poverty, intensified by famine and drought and the resulting higher food prices. When Catalina decided to beg from Gonzalo's family she experienced the same rejection that he had and returned empty handed to Fontiveros. With no improvements in the family's situation any time soon, she left her home and the tombs of her husband and son, and went in search of work, first in Arévalo and then in Medina del Camp. Catalina, who wove silk scarves, found a little work, enough to buy food, but immediately the family immersed itself in charitable activities for those more needy than themselves, especially abandoned orphans.

1. From early life John learned to deal with pain, struggles, poverty, rejection, social injustice, and death in the family.
2. John is an example for us in these troubling economic times. His family dealt with unemployment, uprootedness, the need to travel in search of work, and mistreatment by the wealthy.
3. What importance do we give to helping the needy in our contemporary troubled times?
4. John lived in a single-parent family with its special needs. Let us be sensitive to those today who must endure such difficulties.

CHALLENGES FOR TODAY
- What are the present difficulties that you must face?
- Who do you know whom you can help in times of hardship?
- What have you learned from the struggles of your parents?

DAY 14 *EARLY FORMATION*

John's mother, Catalina, sent him to a boarding school where orphans learned a trade and were fed and clothed by the support of generous benefactors. In the trade schools John learned a lot of skills he could put to good use later in renovating dilapidated buildings in the early times of the reform. John moved from the boarding school to one of the city's hospitals where he developed a love for the sick, an ability to beg for financial support for them, and learned excellent administrative skills from the hospital's sponsor. In the evenings John began studying at the local Jesuit College where he found he had a love for study and a lot of success at it. Catalina and her family continued their dedicated service to the poor, sick, and needy. John followed in their footsteps. John also learned from his earliest years the importance of simple, honest, dedicated work, purity in relationships and love, and the enriching values of family and friendship.

1. Early in life, John learned how one can grow spiritually in the midst of poverty, deprivation, and constant hardship.
2. Do our lives show the same concern for the poor and the sick that John's did?
3. John's family is a model for us all in moving from self-centeredness to other-centeredness.
4. Let us look for opportunities to have the same kind of formative influence on our families as Catalina did on hers.

CHALLENGES FOR TODAY
- Are there aspects of your life that are centered on the needs of the sick and the poor?
- John loved study and his books evidence great knowledge of Scripture and theology. Does your spirituality have solid foundations?
- Who today is an example for you to follow with the virtues John learned from his mother?

DAY 15 JOHN'S THREE VOCATIONS

John consciously gave himself to three vocations—human, religious, and literary. Born in 1542, John lived through many of the experiences that characterize modern struggles, whether personal or family. He worked in many trades, hospital ministry, studied in his free time, was chosen as student leader in university, and worked with the ups and downs of organizations—civic and ecclesiastic. He learned from all these experiences and put them to good use. He also appreciated the struggles and sacrifices of individuals and families. His religious vocation started in 1563 and included novitiate, early formation, theological studies, religious crises, and commitment to reform. John is not a born reformer but life needs a suitable environment to develop, and if a determined person cannot find it he or she creates it. That is what John did. John's literary vocation started early with his *Sayings*, but got a major focus during his formative experience in the prison in Toledo. From 1578-1586 his writing developed slowly but continuously.

1. We understand vocation as the acceptance of a call, conscious of having the qualities to respond.
2. Unfortunately, John does not write in the last five years of his life, so his most intense personal experiences are outside the scope of his writings.
3. When we look at John's life we find that he is a very contemporary person.
4. We often think that spiritually dedicated individuals live outside the pressures of contemporary life. John certainly did not.

CHALLENGES FOR TODAY
- If the environment you are in is unsuitable for spiritual growth can you change it?
- What are the components of your vocation?
- What do you appreciate most about St. John of the Cross?

DAY 16 JOHN'S ENVIRONMENT

John lived life to the full. He had links with all the key places and events of Spain of his time. Unlike Teresa of Avila he did not have contact with the great people of his day, except for Teresa herself and the scholar, Luis de León. However, John did not live as a hermit, even though he loved solitude. Rather, he travelled extensively and had a lot of contact with the real world. John is the kind of person who does not look but sees everything, unlike the modern tourist who looks at everything and sees nothing! John's writings reflect well the environment of his day, even better than contemporary writings that claim to be doing precisely that! John lived in some of the most beautiful cities of Spain—Avila, Salamanca, Toledo, Segovia, Granada, Cordoba, and he loved the beauty of the countryside.

1. If we know the places where John lived when he wrote, it can help us understand aspects of his writings.
2. Regarding how the environment influenced John's works, we can do two things. Contemplate the views that he contemplated when he wrote. Contemplate the places from which he contemplated the views.
3. Knowing about Toledo helps us understand John's prison poetry. Knowing about the history of Granada while John was writing in Los Martires is also important.
4. Religion needs incarnation in real environments. John does that for us.

CHALLENGES FOR TODAY
- How does the environment in which you live affect you?
- Does your appreciation of the beauty of the world aid your spirituality?
- Are you a "spiritual" tourist?

DAY 17 *CHOOSING WELL*

John spent thirteen years in Medina del Campo, from age nine to twenty-two. His dedication, hard work, hospital ministry, and service of the poor, led to John being known and respected by many people in Medina del Campo. Leaders offered him many opportunities. However, John had clear ideas about what he wanted to do. One day in 1563, unknown to those interested in his future, John entered the Carmelite monastery. A year later he was professed and immediately asked to live by the more primitive rule of the order, the one that preceded the many adaptations and dispensations that had been introduced due to religious and social problems in the fifteenth century. By the age of twenty-two, John had learned several trades, worked in the hospital, gained a good knowledge of administration and organizational skills, studied in the university, entered a religious order, and sought permission to live a more rigorous form of religious life. He discovered that no situation, no ministry, no institution, no amount of study, no form of religious life can of themselves lead one to God. One must make a deliberate choice for this.

1. Medina del Campo was a Castilian town of about 30,000 inhabitants, a favorite place of the Catholic monarch, Isabella.
2. It seems John was attracted to the Carmelites by their dedication to prayer and their Marian piety.
3. Let us examine our own lives and ask whether we have made good choices regarding our commitment to God.
4. What attracts each of us to the kind of life we have chosen?

CHALLENGES FOR TODAY
- What leads you to God?
- John had a clear sense of the direction he wanted his life to take. Do you?
- This week make a deliberate choice to re-dedicate yourself to God.

DAY 18 *STUDYING SPIRITUALITY*

In 1564 John arrived in the great university city of Salamanca to begin his studies of theology and philosophy. But he also found that learning about God in Scripture and theology does not necessarily bring one closer to God or help one experience God. So John passed through a creative crisis regarding the essential role of contemplation in his life and the importance of the pursuit of God. John was well-known among the students for his prolonged prayer, penances, and continued observance of the rigors of religious life. In the late summer of 1567 he returned to Medina del Campo to celebrate his first Mass as a priest. There he met Mother Teresa of Avila who asked him to work with her in the reform of the male branch of the Carmelites. John told her that he was thinking of going to the Carthusians, but Mother Teresa insisted that his desire for contemplation, solitude, and penance could be found in the reform movement if he would give it a chance.

1. John complemented the prescribed program with further studies in prayer, spirituality, and contemplation.
2. Salamanca was the place to be, and the place where careers were developed. John was not interested in careerism.
3. Mother Teresa was fifty two years old when she first met John of the Cross who was only twenty-five. She immediately appreciated both his depth of spirituality and his leadership abilities.
4. In Salamanca John struggled with the direction of his life and experienced questions concerning his vocation.

CHALLENGES FOR TODAY
- Do you study your faith and spiritual commitment enough?
- Have you struggled with the role of contemplation in your life?
- Does your spirituality have solid foundations or is it one built on religious trivia.

DAY 19 RELIGIOUS RENEWAL

John accepted Mother Teresa's invitation to join the reform and the first new foundation officially opened in Duruelo in November 1568. The first little group organized their lives in times of prayer, community, and ministry in the surrounding area. So, John found an initial realization of his dream for a more rigorous and contemplative focus to spiritual life. Duruelo offered penance, sacrifice, simplicity, solitude, and community, and a chance to focus on the wholehearted pursuit of the love of God. Soon others came to join the reformed group, and John began his life's work of forming others in the spirit of the reform.

1. From early in the reform, John became a spiritual director for so many. When we read his great commentaries they are filled with practical advice based on the many real situations with which he had to deal.
2. We see that in John's life his many sacrifices and penances are all means to the end of the pursuit of the love of God.
3. John encourages us to follow him and leave aside everything so that the inner life of God's love can be allowed to grow on its own, unhindered by our false values.
4. Although the new life in Duruelo focused on personal renewal, John and his companions saw the need to also include a ministerial dimension in their work of service to those nearby.

CHALLENGES FOR TODAY

- Can you create an environment in which you can realize your spiritual dreams and longings?
- What roles do penance, sacrifice, simplicity, and solitude play in your life?
- John's priorities were clear. What are your priorities?

DAY 20 ENDURING PERSECUTION

Not everyone was supportive of Mother Teresa's reform, and both Teresa and John had their critics. There were also clashes of ideas and visions, as well as problems with the competing authorities of the day. Some of these difficulties came to a head when Teresa and John were superior and chaplain of the monastery of the Incarnation in Avila—a community that was not initially part of the reform. The Carmelite friars in Avila felt they had had enough, and in December 1577 they took John prisoner and sent him to Toledo where he was declared a rebel and placed in the monastery's prison. John ended in a small cell, originally a lavatory for an adjoining guest room, and he stayed there for nine months, weak from illness, deprived of the liturgy, suffering from hunger, frostbite in winter, searing heat in summer, and profound abandonment. On Monday, Wednesday, and Friday he was given only bread and water, and on Wednesday every member of the community joined in a communal public lashing of John. With no end in sight, John decided to escape and did so in August 1578.

1. John's treatment in prison was certainly cruel and inhumane. We would probably consider it torture.
2. John endured deprivation, hunger, cold, and abandonment, as well as human degradation, solitary confinement, fear of poisoning, and perverse psychological pressures.
3. John never criticized his tormentors, but viewed his experiences in light of God's ongoing call to him to love.
4. While in this loveless situation John wrote extraordinary love-filled poetry, and he emerged transformed in love.

CHALLENGES FOR TODAY
- How do you deal with suffering inflicted by others?
- What pain and sacrifice have you endured for love of God?
- Is there someone who you think is persecuting you now?

DAY 21 ABANDONED BY HIS OWN

Teresa was in Avila when she heard about John's imprisonment and immediately wrote to King Philip, informing him about what had happened, telling the king what an extraordinary dedicated monk John was, and pleading for the King's intervention to release John. She also told Philip that she had no confidence in the Calced friars and believed they would treat John badly. A few weeks later she wrote to the archbishop of Évora, an influential prelate at the time, repeating what she had said to the king about John. In March she wrote to Fr. Gracián, a friar of the Carmelite reform, expressing her distress at the way John was treated by the Calced and the seeming lack of support from the Discalced. "In every letter that she wrote her anxiety about him comes out and her suspicion that the leading friars of the reform, among them Gracián, were not doing all they could to secure his release. 'I don't know how it is,' she wrote to him in August, 'that the saint is so unfortunate that no one remembers him'" (See Brenan, pp. 28-29). John seemed to have vanished and no one seemed to care.

1. Teresa wrote, "God's treatment of his friends is terrible . . . [but] he did the same to his own Son."
2. Sometimes the friends we expect to help us do not. What is our response?
3. Religions often persecute and abandon those who hold different views.
4. How do we think John felt never hearing from the only people who could help him?

CHALLENGES FOR TODAY
- Let us think about those who are expecting help from us.
- Have you ever thought of gain from someone's downfall?
- Give examples of when you have gone out on a limb to help someone in need.

DAY 22 *JOHN'S DRAMATIC, DARING ESCAPE*

John was imprisoned in the Carmelite priory in Toledo, a huge building some ninety feet above the rocky river bed of the Tagus, not far from the Alcantara gate. John asked his jailor for a needle and thread to mend his habit, but instead tied a stone to the thread and let it hang down from the window so he could judge the height of his window from the wall below, and then calculated whether he could reach it if he cut up two rugs into strips and tied them together. At the same time, whenever free, he loosened the padlock on the door until he was sure it would fall out with a good push. On the 16th of August 1578, John decided the time had come. At first it seemed the plan might not succeed, for there were several guests in the next room. Once John thought they were asleep, around 2 am, he made his move. A good push forced the screws out of the padlock and John then took the strips of rug and tied them together and then lowered himself to the narrow ledge below, just a couple of feet from the sheer drop to the valley of the river Tagus. He was now free and gradually made his way to the Discalced Carmelite monastery of nuns where the prioress allowed him into the safety of the enclosure on the pretext of hearing the confession of a sick nun. The next day his escape was discovered and a search undertaken, but John was smuggled to the home of one of the canons of the cathedral and rested there, just a hundred yards from his prison cell.

1. It is nice to see how practical mystics can be! John planned a daring escape, the prioress quickly made a series of equally daring decisions.
2. Although John was obedient to the Church and its leaders, he was not passive to their faults and thus decided to escape.
3. What a difference between the first mean jailor and the second sympathetic one. We can do any job with justice and goodness.
4. One of the first things John did after his escape was to dictate a series of poems that he had composed in prison.

CHALLENGES FOR TODAY

- How do you explain John's escape in light of his commitment to obedience?
- Can you be both an everyday mystic and a very practical person?
- What do you think of the prioress who helped John?

DAY 23 *FACING THE STRUGGLES OF LIFE*

We cannot achieve anything significant in life without struggles, what in spirituality we call asceticism. "[I]n the thought of John of the Cross, asceticism is at the base of all mysticism, which is as much as to say that it is the prelude to love. He tells us that it requires a stronger love and a stronger desire to put to flight lesser loves, lesser desires" (See Cristiani, p. 158). So, to face life's struggles and enter the night of sense, we must have strong love, like that implied in the denials John lists on his diagram of Mount Carmel. This love is a gift from God that brings us satisfaction and enables us to face the challenges of this journey and its difficult climbs. With this love to support us we can persevere in this adventure and experience happiness amidst the trials, difficulties, and hardships.

1. This struggle leads to fulfillment: it is the struggle to strip ourselves of all false attachments and all false loves.
2. We see asceticism is not a goal in itself, it is a means to love.
3. Can we sacrifice lesser loves in our pursuit of God's love?
4. Can we appreciate our spiritual journey as an adventure?

CHALLENGES FOR TODAY
- Think about your own present day struggles.
- Which lesser loves are obstacles to your growth?
- To which passions are you a slave?

DAY 24 *ENJOYING THE OUTDOORS*

When John lived in Los Martires, Granada, or El Calvario, he enjoyed the beauty of the countryside and liked his community to enjoy the outdoors too. When he was superior he often took the friars into the fields and hills, especially as far as the foothills of the Sierra Nevada. John loved the surroundings, the plants and trees, the green hills and snow-covered summits. Stanzas 1-22 of the *Spiritual Canticle* form an ode to the beauty of nature. He wanted his friars to appreciate nature like he did. "When they arrived at the place he had chosen, they would pause in contemplation of the magnificence of the countryside. . . . Sometimes, also, he would get them engaged in some quiet game or sport, and then withdraw to spend the time before they were to eat in prayer" (See Cristiani, pp. 205-206).

1. "St. Francis and St. John are assuredly the two saints who have most savored the beauty of nature" (Gilles Mauger).
2. In his treatment of others, John shows his deep and consistent humanity.
3. John was a person of self-denial, while at the same time organizing feasts and holidays for his brethren, making sure that while he fasted they had abundant and more appealing fare.
4. In Granada John had the smallest room in the monastery, but from its tiny window he would spend much time looking at the flowers by day and the stars by night.

CHALLENGES FOR TODAY
- Do you treat other people better than you treat yourself?
- Can you enjoy nature like Saints Francis and John?
- Are you well-known among your friends and acquaintances for your simplicity, thoughtfulness, and humanity?

DAY 25 *LIFE AND MISUNDERSTANDING*

After John's dramatic escape from the Toledan prison he spent about a month in hospital, and in spite of his ill health he insisted on attending a meeting of the friars of the reform in Almodóvar. Then his ministry took him to Beas, El Calvario, and Baeza. In June 1580, Pope Gregory XIII granted the request of the Discalced to become a separate province, and Fr. Jerónimo Gracián was elected provincial. Within the year, tensions developed between Grancián's emphasis on Teresa's vision of life and ministry and Nicolás Doria's—the future provincial's—emphasis on austerity and observance. John was caught in the middle of this. However, he continued his ministry to the nuns and friars of the reform, travelling over 16,000 miles –with all the hardships and discomfort of travel in those days, not to mention natural dangers and banditry. Fr. Doria became uneasy and suspicious of John's role in the Gracián matter and in the nuns desire to free themselves of Doria's control. Doria and his council turned against John, even initiating a revengeful attempt to disgrace and humiliate John. Through all these misunderstandings John maintained peace, calm, and a spirit of obedience.

1. It is amazing how John maintains balance between manual work, extensive travels, pressure-filled decisions, tension in community, and spiritual direction and contemplation in solitude.
2. In the midst of his many trials, John told a nun that men do not do these things but God, and he gave himself in obedience to God's will.
3. In divisive chapter meetings John tried to protect everyone's confidentiality, asking for secret ballots, which those in control did not want.
4. While Fr. Doria acted unfairly towards John, he still needed him; first because of his spirituality and vision of the reform, and secondly because of John's excellent business and administrative skills—both needed for construction work in Segovia.

CHALLENGES FOR TODAY
- What sacrifices have you endured in your service of the Lord?
- How do you handle others' misunderstanding?
- Is someone treating you unjustly at present and what is your response?

DAY 26 *FACING SICKNESS AND DEATH*

While in La Peñuela, John started feeling sick, experiencing high fever and painful swelling in his right leg. He needed to go to a larger monastery and chose to go to Ubeda where he was little known rather than other places where he was well-known and much loved. In Ubeda he was mistreated and humiliated by a vengeful friar, now superior, whom John had corrected years earlier. John's sickness worsened with abscesses and fever. So-called cures were brutal in those days, but John's patience under suffering was extraordinary. His health deteriorated, and John of the Cross died at midnight on Saturday, December 14th 1591. He was forty-nine years old and had given himself to the reform for twenty-three years.

1. Do the ordinary pressures of daily life, illness, weariness, quantity of work, travel, and so on, wear us down? John was able to maintain his spiritual dedication amidst all the real events of a busy life.
2. Death is the last stage and opportunity to manifest the values of our lives. John was a remarkable example of this.
3. Some people always seem to lose integrity under pressure, as did some in John's community. Can we maintain integrity under pressure?
4. In death, John was surrounded by a supportive community. For most of us we will be surrounded by hospital machines. How would you like your death to be?

CHALLENGES FOR TODAY
- How do you handle sickness?
- What values would you leave for others to consider and build their lives on?
- Who do you want to be with you when you die?

DAY 27 JOHN, AN INSPIRATION FOR US

From his earliest years, John, following the guidance of his mother, developed values that were to make up the general direction of his future. Poverty, charity, piety, study, authenticity, and deep love formed permanent parts of John's life. John was a person of destiny and had a clear picture of what he wanted from life and what he wanted to give during his life. Some people accumulate many small manifestations of love for God, whereas John always had a single-minded and single-hearted choice for God and saw everything else as secondary to the quest for God's love. Reading his life is exciting, for his goal is clear, never neglected, and never watered down. He also shows us how to live within a struggle-filled Church and an oppressive society. Through all his trials he maintained his priorities and proved to us all that contemplative union is possible in any situation.

1. Accumulated manifestations of love can be shown by a person who refuses to face the need for a total conversion and transformation. John, however, made a singular choice for love and never changed it.
2. Each stage in John's life is successful and brings satisfaction, but he renounces it and moves on to the one great goal of union with God in love.
3. John's life was one long dark night, but he always lived peacefully in the world of tensions.
4. John's teachings guide us, but his life is a wonderful example of these very teachings.

CHALLENGES FOR TODAY
- What is your destiny in life?
- Do you maintain your priorities amidst all the tensions and struggles you must face?
- What do you want from life?

DAY 28 *THE SECRET OF JOHN'S LIFE*

If we look at the interior world of John's personality, we find that he spontaneously gives the impression of being a person with a unified personality. People value John of the Cross for many different reasons—as a writer, a poet, a philosopher, a theologian, a mystic. Others appreciate him for his business and organizational skills, as an artist and sculptor, as a contractor who can design and build a monastery, and as a sensitive care-giver of the sick. What is the unifying point of all this? We find that the center of unity on a personality level is the same as the center of unity in his teachings and spiritual system. Perhaps a short formula that expresses dynamically his vision could be: Always seek God, through the nights, to union and renewal. At every stage of life John seeks God and when circumstances do not contribute to this he moves on. All his decisions imply renunciation of previous interests in life, but the capacity for renunciation is a distinctive part of authentic love. He never pursues personal growth or renewal but he seeks God alone and finds that in union with God all else is re-found, transformed and renewed.

1. We can try to frame John's life and system in a scheme, but we must remember that life is complex and beyond schemes.
2. Renunciation never means despising what we leave behind but it is a choice for what is better, the pursuit of love of God.
3. John is certainly concerned about the union of men and women with God, and his own life is a clear example of love poured out.
4. Compassionate love and concern for others is the great characteristic of John's life even when immersed in suffering.

CHALLENGES FOR TODAY
- What is the unifying principle of your life?
- For what do people appreciate you?
- Give examples of renunciation in your life.

DAY 29 *JOHN—A MULTI-GIFTED PERSON*

If you read John of the Cross be ready to encounter the exceptional. He is an exceptional person; humane, gentle, and serene, but challenging and rigorous in commitment. He is frugal, but extravagant to the sick and the poor. He is patient and long suffering in his trials, but strong-minded in business matters, in tolerating the brutal treatment in prison, in dealing with conflicting ecclesiastical power structures. John speaks of the dark night, but his own life also included the lighter side in music, art, sculpture, dance, and friendship. He speaks of darkness but has a taste and love for beauty and light. He is reserved, but can dance and sing in community. He is a lover of solitude who can foster easy companionship. He delights in seclusion but dedicates himself to pastoral ministry and outreach.

1. Some people used to think of John as hard, cold, rigorous, and inhuman. Nothing could be further from the truth.
2. John's is a rich and enriching personality. The sacrifices of his journey did not make him harder and more distant, but gentle, kind, more understanding, and more compassionate.
3. Do people who know us think we are better human beings because of our commitment to spiritual growth?
4. Contemporaries said that, although clearly ascetical, John had a pleasing appearance and was interesting to talk to. He was always in control of himself; peaceful, calm, and quietly joyful.

CHALLENGES FOR TODAY
- Do you use your gifts for the benefit of others?
- How would people describe you?
- What are you learning from studying John's life?

DAY 30 JOHN AND TERESA OF AVILA

John of the Cross met Teresa of Avila for the first time in 1567 when she met with John in Medina del Campo to interview him regarding a possible role in the reform of the men's branch of the order. Teresa concluded that John was the person she sought. Teresa was very concerned about the spiritual formation of the first friars and took John with her on her travels so she could have plenty of opportunity to teach him about her vision of the reform. John became intensely committed to the reform, so much so that Teresa, on a visit to Duruelo in 1569, advised him against any excesses in penance. John became Teresa's trusted novice master in the early communities of the reform. In 1571, Teresa was appointed prioress of the convent of the Incarnation in Avila. One of her first decisions was to appoint John of the Cross as confessor of the community. In 1580 John met Teresa for the first time since his sufferings in the Toledo prison; it was also the last time he saw her before her death the following year.

1. Teresa and John are together seen as the two founders of the Carmelite reform.
2. While Teresa remains the great Mother Foundress and John a disciple, John becomes a trusted co-worker.
3. Regarding John's readiness for the reform, Teresa said, "As for Father Fray John of the Cross, no trial was necessary. . . . he always lived a life of great perfection and religious observance" (*Foundations*, 13. 1).
4. While Teresa was concerned about John's formation in the spirit of the reform, maybe unexpectedly, Teresa found she was also learning from her new disciple, even sharing with him some of the confidences of her own inner spirit.

CHALLENGES FOR TODAY

- Read chapters 11-22 of Teresa's autobiography—a wonderful section on prayer.
- What qualities do you think Teresa saw in John to give her so much confidence?
- What have you learned from Teresa of Avila?

DAY 31 JOHN'S FULL LIFE

John of the Cross was a great theologian, poet, writer, administrator, and builder. He was also a reformer, contemplative, and mystic. He was a painter and sculptor; he liked to dance and sing. He is appreciated by theologians, philosophers, psychologists, and spiritual writers of every generation. He seemed to combine so many gifts in one person—he evidences an extraordinarily full life. The one integrating thing about his life, that which brought it all together, was his inner experience of the living God that gave meaning to everything else. "These main events in the short life of St. John of the Cross do not leave us with the full picture of his character and personal spirituality. His early first-hand acquaintance with deprivation, the later misunderstandings and imprisonment, the final persecution that he suffered, all might more easily have brought forth a bitter cynic; instead, the result was a man purified and enlightened. Events outwardly sad, but inwardly transforming, bore fruits in charity towards others and deep compassion for the sufferer" (See Kavanaugh, *Collected Works*, p. 15).

1. John shows that one can be a contemplative while immersed in a busy life with many responsibilities.
2. How well rounded is your life and your interests?
3. Let us think about what made John a great saint.
4. What are the greatest trials that believers face today?

CHALLENGES FOR TODAY
- Is your spirituality based on solid theology?
- What do you consider are the purifying trials of your life?
- What has spiritually enriched your life?

DAY 32 *JOHN—CALM AND PLEASANT*

Friars who have left us descriptions of John tell us he was a man of peace and love and that those qualities overflowed in an attractive personality and appearance. They say he was always in control of himself and never angry or impatient. He was a person of high moral qualities and integrity, but always joyful and serene. "He was the enemy of spiritual melancholy, and when he saw one of his subjects sad he would take him by the hand and carry him off for a walk with him in the huerta or out in the country and would not leave him until he was cheerful and optimistic again. Even when talking of the things of God, he liked to make his friars laugh, sprinkling his spiritual conversations with amusing stories" (See Crisógono de Jesús, p. 309).

1. John was fond of simplicity and straightforwardness and shunned all ostentation of authority.
2. He was kind towards everyone and never gave orders imperiously nor showed any sign of aggression.
3. He showed special affection and solicitousness for those who were sick, always taking care of them personally.
4. John valued friendships and truly missed his friends when he couldn't see them for a while.

CHALLENGES FOR TODAY
- What are your best qualities in dealing with other people?
- How do you exercise whatever authority you have?
- Do people leave your presence cheerful and optimistic?

A reconstruction of John's room.

2
John's Ministry

Although John of the Cross loved solitude and definitely preferred it to involvement in the many responsibilities of his life and daily work, he consistently gave himself to the service of others. Thus, his total pursuit of love overflowed in the concern and service of others. He was always available to anyone in need. He gave himself generously to the formation of the nuns and friars of the reform. He reached out to many laity who identified completely with his vision of spiritual life. His self-gift in spiritual direction extended itself in his writings, and this ministry involves us today. John often said that his ministry was restricted to the members of the Carmelite Reform, but he now ministers to us and he also teaches us what our ministry can be.

DAY 33 CONCERN FOR ANYONE IN NEED

John's central focus of life was the pursuit of the love of God, but this love overflowed in concern for the needy. Once John told a brother that it was a great sacrifice to leave his peaceful solitude to deal with people. However, nobody would ever have thought that, for he always made himself available with great generosity. He cherished opportunities to serve the sick, and he was likewise generous in providing help and nourishment to those who were poor, needy, and spiritually sick. He administered the sacraments and gave religious instruction to those in the region around the monasteries who needed spiritual strengthening. What is clear is that John of the Cross loved people and had a natural gift, enhanced by grace, of treating everyone with benevolence and goodness. He was always concerned about people, perennially compassionate to all, and always sought their greater good.

1. John was a person of single-minded dedication to the ministry of leading others to a deeper relationship with God.
2. John may have preferred the silence of the cave in Segovia, but his life evidences extraordinary concern to meet the needs of people in various situations.
3. John always took people as they were and presumed their basic yearning for goodness. He was certainly not a judgmental religious leader.
4. What are the greatest contemporary needs to which we as Christians ought to be responding?

CHALLENGES FOR TODAY
- How much of your time is given to serving others' needs?
- Would people who know you say that you really love others? What evidence would they give?
- Are your co-workers better people because they work with you?

DAY 34 *JOHN'S MINISTRY OF THE WORD*

John's primary ministry was sharing his knowledge of the spiritual journey through spiritual direction. He did not seem to have much inclination to write, but he eventually did so in response to others' spiritual needs or requests. In fact, his writing becomes a continuation of his spiritual direction. At first, John spontaneously wrote poetry for his own support and consolation and to express his inner mystical experiences. In prison he wrote most of the *Spiritual Canticle*, the "Romances," and two beautiful love poems. Later, he wrote to help solve real needs he perceived among the friars and nuns. As people benefitted from his writing they asked him for more teachings or to explain his poetry to them. In recent decades people from all walks of life have come to value the challenges of his writings and become his followers and directees.

1. John wrote the *Spiritual Canticle* for Mother Ann of Jesus, and the *Living Flame* for Doña Ana de Peñalosa. The *Ascent* and *Dark Night* he wrote to respond to specific needs he saw.
2. The *Sayings*, *Precautions*, *Counsels*, and letters all continue John's ministry of spiritual direction through the written word.
3. Even in his own day, John found that many laity responded to his teachings.
4. So many people during his life and now appreciate John's purity of intention, his single-minded dedication, and his rootedness in the essentials of Christian life.

CHALLENGES FOR TODAY
- Do you see yourself as a directee of John of the Cross?
- Spend some time this week reading some of John's poetry.
- Why do you look to John to guide you in your spiritual journey?

DAY 35 *JOHN'S MINISTRY TO US TODAY*

John tells us explicitly that he wrote to support and to challenge the nuns and friars of the reform. However, what we know from today's literary critics is that an author's intentions are not determinative of the outcome and impact of a work, but rather the response of readers. So, the fact that John wanted to write primarily for members of the reform is not a limiting factor at all. More people turn to John of the Cross today than ever in history. What John thought was a restricted ministry now appeals to others in an extraordinary way that he could never have anticipated. Even people who are afraid of John's rigorous presentation and profound challenges still have the nagging feeling he is probably right in the vision he lays before us. So many contemporary spiritualities are superficial, and people spend years immersed in spiritual trivia without ever progressing. John claims that the starting point for our journey leaves little doubt regarding humanity's sinfulness, the journey is much longer than many optimistic spiritualities of today, and the arrival point is richer and more profound.

1. John of the Cross continues his work of spiritual direction among us today through his writings.
2. Pope Pius XI declared John of the Cross a doctor of the Church on August 24 1926. All John's writings together amount to about one thousand pages—less than any other doctor of the Church. The quality is so exceptional, the teaching so profound, John is also referred to as the Mystical Doctor.
3. John spent so much time in spiritual direction that when we read his works we always tend to think he has someone in mind when he gives examples and explains his teachings.
4. John's is not an elitist spirituality; it is a universal call to holiness.

CHALLENGES FOR TODAY
- Are you willing to let John of the Cross guide you in your spiritual life?
- Thank God for John of the Cross as a gift to the universal Church.
- Are you working with someone who knows John of the Cross well enough to help you in your spiritual journey?

DAY 36 *A DIALOGUE WITH JOHN*

We do not read St. John so much as listen to him, trying to follow the central argument in his presentation, that clear line of the vital process he wishes to share with us. Let us keep focused on the major issues he is addressing and not be distracted by the many digressions. If we imagine that he is talking to us, we must listen to him, aware that it is a privilege to hear what he has to say. We approach him with a sense of need, emptiness, and longing to know how to journey through life. He can help us as he did so many people from all walks of life in his own time. What we need above all is to accept the invitation for a dialogue with him, attentive to him speaking to us through his life and in his various writings. John will disrupt our way of thinking and valuing, our view of religion, and our understanding of our destiny.

1. We must avoid entering John's works with any prejudice from past impressions or culturally different ways of expression.
2. We should read John's works directly, often, and reflectively, remembering that the poems are the most faithful living expression of John's mystical experiences.
3. We cannot leave John's message in the sixteenth century, but we must always make it relevant for today; we must interpret his language, concepts, dynamic development, and insights to our own situations.
4. Let us appreciate the unique focus and message of each of John's works, never taking the view and approach of one into another.

CHALLENGES FOR TODAY
- Take a couple of John's letters and try to listen to him talking directly to you.
- Do you dabble in the writings of various saints, or do you have a favorite?
- Which teachings of John are most relevant for you today?

DAY 37 JOHN TELLS IT LIKE IT IS

We all know lots of people who want to dedicate themselves to God but they never get beyond their initial commitment. John did because he was always open to growth and willing to take the whole costly journey to God. He sets a clear direction for us to follow and challenges us to do what needs to be done to get there. John of the Cross evidences a spiritual independence that makes him so attractive to people who seek a way to God. He tells it like it is and urges us to have the courage to respond. He is single-minded but avoids dogmatizing his own views. His teachings are very demanding but they present us with the demands of love. Many people can give us easier ways to God but are they efficacious? John's way is demanding, but a reader quickly arrives at the conviction that John knows the way to God, and if we follow him he guarantees we will arrive at union with God.

1. John is a person of integrity and wholeness; single-minded and single-hearted in his pursuit of God.

2. If you read John's works be ready to encounter the exceptional.

3. John decided early in life that if you want to climb Mount Carmel you must be willing to make hard decisions and journey to the top along the narrow path.

4. Let us spend a little time this week reflecting on St. John of the Cross' diagram of Mount Carmel. (The diagram is available in the *Collected Works of John of the Cross*).

CHALLENGES FOR TODAY

- Take it or leave it! No half measures.
- Do you prefer more comfortable and comforting ways to God? Or do you wish to gain a great deal in a short time?
- How do you understand John's advice, "endeavor to choose that which is most difficult"?

DAY 38 *THE TIMES OF JOHN OF THE CROSS*

Soon after John's birth the Catholic Church held the Council of Trent (1545-63) as a response to the reformation and the challenges of Martin Luther. The council's teaching would be of particular interest throughout the lives of Teresa and John, as the post-conciliar renewal paralleled their spiritual lives and the Carmelite reform. During most of John's adult life, Philip II was king of Spain. Philip was involved in many religious wars, heavily taxing his subjects to maintain them. He gave himself wholeheartedly to the reform of the Church in Spain, seeking a more austere reform of religious life even than that recommended by the Council of Trent. To aid the reforms of Philip and the Council of Trent, the Spanish Inquisition would play a major role as it had in the past. In its pursuit of its own view of orthodoxy, the Spanish Inquisition watched Christians everywhere, spying on bishops, theologians, scholars, and movements and individuals seeking spiritual renewal. John lived most of his life immersed in these efforts at renewal, the pressures of conflicting authorities, and the oppression of the Inquisition.

1. Every generation has people who present themselves as champions of the Church, persuading themselves that whatever they are doing is God's will. Often it is not!
2. Some people are always afraid of genuine reform. It is frightening that some people fear conversion and religious renewal unless they can control it.
3. Like John, we must all seek to live our values and faith in spite of the controlling influences of the inquisitions of the day.
4. There are always people, generally uninformed, uneducated, and spiritually immature, who want to tell everyone else how to live, what to believe, and how to think.

CHALLENGES FOR TODAY
- What are the inquisitions of today?
- Is John an example for you in post-conciliar renewal?
- Do you have to deal with various authorities who compete for your "obedience"?

DAY 39 *JOHN AND THE CARMELITE REFORM*

The fifteenth and sixteenth centuries were times of religious reform in Spain. Several religious communities undertook a return to the more primitive observance of their rules. Mother Teresa began her reform around 1562 when she founded the first house for her community in Avila. In the case of the Carmelites, first nuns and then friars, reform meant going back to the original, more rigorous observance of the Order's rule. When Teresa invited John and his first companion, Antonio de Heredia, to join the reform, it essentially meant a return to simplicity, authenticity of Religious Life, austerity, poverty, and contemplation. Teresa started the reform of the friars with two outstanding individuals, competent, educated, and committed to contemplation. Teresa had suffered for many years in her own mediocre religious life and need of conversion and spiritual renewal, and from incompetent spiritual directors. She insisted that both her nuns and friars be knowledgeable of religious issues. Leaders of the reform gave a good theological foundation to the spiritual renewal of their communities, and both Teresa and John wrote extensively, primarily for the formation of the nuns and friars. Teresa was not a trained theologian, but her works were reviewed by outstanding scholars. John was a trained philosopher and theologian. He knew spiritual theology and Scripture very well. So, the renewal was part of the enthusiasm of the times, but well grounded theologically, biblically, and spiritually. Above all, for John, reform was a daily necessity, as it is in the life of reflective people who long to give their hearts to God in love.

1. Some people are always afraid of genuine reform.
2. Dedicated Christians find that renewal needs solid foundations in the authentic sources of faith.
3. Let us think about some religious movements today and see whether they are solidly grounded in Scripture, theology, and spirituality.
4. Are our spiritualities grounded and up-to-date?

CHALLENGES FOR TODAY
- Do aspects of your life need reform?
- Could people describe your spirituality as pre-packaged or re-cycled?
- What would you like to reform in your local Church?

DAY 40 JOHN IS A PROPHET OF GOD

We often mistakenly think a prophet speaks about the future, but this function is minor and accidental to the prophet's main task. A prophet challenges people to live in the present according to the values of God, and surely there are few people to whom this applies more than John of the Cross. At times his is a voice in the wilderness proclaiming the wonders of God and calling us all to faithfully pursue transformative union even through the nights of life. As a prophet of God, John above all told us how to see God's love everywhere, in nature, in people, and even in oppressors. John appreciated his own enduring purpose in life, his own destiny. He yearned for transformation in loving union with God. He was not a lonely mystic in selfish pursuit of perfection. He was a man for others; enjoying others' company, facilitating their growth, and seeking whatever was best for them. More than anything, this prophet lived his life aware of a realm of life beyond this one that gives meaning to our present existence.

1. The word "prophet" comes from Greek and means to speak on behalf of God.
2. John speaks of God and reminds us the nights might be dark, but they can be guiding, transforming, and beautiful.
3. John, like Scripture's prophets, challenges injustice, consoles in oppression, and calls for hope and reconstruction.
4. Prophets bring the values of a realm of life beyond this one to influence what we do in this one.

CHALLENGES FOR TODAY
- John is a prophet, speaking to you on behalf of God.
- When you read John of the Cross' works do they challenge your life in the present?
- Are you a prophet? Does your life challenge others to justice, console those who are oppressed, and bring hope to those without it?

DAY 41 JOHN INCLUDES EVERYONE IN HIS TEACHINGS

John addresses his works to "the soul," which many commentators feel refers to the reader as one who yearns for the spiritual growth of which John speaks. In other words "the soul" is every disciple within the hopes of the Church. "[T]his is striking testimony to the abiding power of the Catholic sense of the community of faith expressed in a living tradition. *El alma* (the soul) of the *Ascent/Dark Night*, of the *Spiritual Canticle* and the *Living Flame* is *anima ecclesiastica* (the soul of the Church)" (See Collings, p. 16). In this sense no one is excluded from the world of grace that John describes. He has taken on himself the sense of the Church and presents a spirituality that is genuinely ecclesial. He is not writing for some elite group of mystics but for every Christian, indeed every human person who longs for love and spiritual union.

1. Perhaps the simplest way to understand "soul" is that it is John's term for the dedicated reader of his books.
2. Many books present an elitist approach to John's teaching and audience, but he gives us a universal call to holiness.
3. John is a Doctor of the Church and he calls all members of the Church to a shared reform and renewal.
4. John reminds us that we are an ecclesial community journeying together to union with God.

CHALLENGES FOR TODAY
- When you read John, remember he is talking to you. Do you listen attentively?
- What does it mean to be an everyday mystic?
- How does your personal spirituality relate to the Church?

DAY 42 JOHN'S CALL TO HOLINESS

Many laity were directees of John, and some of them were clearly well advanced in the spiritual life. Some were also married. John has no control over the ecclesial influence of his work. His writings may seem reserved for a spiritual elite, but "the soul" is easily understood as every human being who longs for deeper union with God. John does not consider that a person has two parts, natural and supernatural, material and spiritual, sense and spirit, lower and higher. John is encouraging people to give the whole of their lives to God. Any object—good as well as evil, can block one's progress. One can just as easily be attached to one's devotions or spiritual director as to money, or to seek self-satisfaction in prayer or in power. John wants us to integrate every aspect of life into our total gift to God. John dealt with people who were moving towards reform, change of lifestyle, even transformation; good, dedicated individuals who were making a fundamental option for a God-directed life. Many laity, including married, find themselves in such circumstances today. In fact, celibacy can become a spiritual good to which individuals and organizations become attached—an attachment that needs the purification of the passive night of spirit.

1. More people read John's works than ever and find their adult spirituality and strong love to be challenging.
2. There is nothing in John that requires celibacy for progress in the spiritual life.
3. John's teaching is readily available for all people who long to journey to union with God with the whole of their lives.
4. Today the Church sees John as a guide in its own dark nights.

CHALLENGES FOR TODAY
- Do you see John's writings as offered especially for you?
- Are you giving every aspect of your life to God?
- Is spirituality only a part of your life?

DAY 43 JOHN'S MINISTRY TO LAITY

Lay people played a major role in John's life, as friends, spiritual directees, advisors, and partners in ministry. In the earliest days of the reform John ministered and gave spiritual direction to merchants, prominent benefactors, married people. Some laity were recipients of his writings and collaborators in his work; Doña Ana de Mercado y Peñalosa played a crucial role in John's life, and in the spread of the Carmelite reform in Andalusia. In fact, as John moved to various cities he always attracted the friendship and spiritual commitment of laity; a farm laborer's wife and mystic, wealthy people, both men and women, a sculptor and painter, and doctors. John expresses genuine friendship and his delight in receiving letters from laity such as Juana de Pedraza, also speaks of love of God and obedience to the divine will in ways that presume these laity's spiritual maturity. John also attracted many young people to his spiritual guidance, and while some of them may have later become priests or religious, it was as laity that the initial commitment was made. Laity could identify with his view of family life, his spirituality of work, his ability to integrate community recreation into his life, his capacity for friendship, his ability to survive amidst both the strengths and weaknesses of the Church's life, his purity of intention and rootedness in the uncluttered core of Christian spiritual life

1. John's letters indicate his profound appreciation for the "noble and devout lady," Doña Ana de Mercado y Peñalosa, to whom he dedicated the *Living Flame*.
2. Laity could readily identify with John, even though he was wholeheartedly committed to the austerities of the reform.
3. John struck a cord and continues to do so in the lives of laity.
4. We see large numbers of laity today seeking guidance from John.

CHALLENGES FOR TODAY
- Which aspects of John's life do you identify with most?
- What are the principle components of lay spirituality?
- Why do you think John liked laity so much?

DAY 44 MINISTRY AND "HOLY-IDLENESS"

When we look at John's life of dedication to others, we find there is no doubt that he values the service of others in various ministries to the sick, the needy, those who are searching for spiritual growth, and those who long for peace, forgiveness, enlightenment, and answers to their restless search for God. However, John insists that we keep our values in appropriate perspective. Ministry is very important, but the pursuit of union with God takes precedence over everything. So, he speaks about the priority of "holy idleness" over ministry. "Let those, then, who are singularly active, who think they can win the world with their preaching and exterior works, observe here that they would profit the Church and please God more. . . . were they to spend half of this time with God in prayer" (C. 29. 3).

1. Ministry is a means but it is not an end of our journey.

2. "Doing" in ministry is never as important in our spiritual journey as is "being in love" with the God we serve.

3. Passivity, receptivity, and the appreciation of grace are the key qualities in our endeavor to be in union with God.

4. All that we are is gift; we do not earn anything.

CHALLENGES FOR TODAY

- Do not abandon your dedication in ministry, but keep it in perspective.
- Be empty, idle, and unproductive—at least now and again.
- In times of spiritual idleness, God transforms the soul in contemplation.

DAY 45 JESUS, A MODEL OF MINISTRY

Jesus was open and welcoming to everyone. He showed no discrimination to anyone who encountered him with good will. In fact, Jesus readily broke down barriers towards social and religious outcasts. This is the plan of action for all disciples—a radical response to the troubles of a divided, polarized, and embittered world. Universality is not a response to a problem or crisis. Rather, it is an awareness of a mystery of union, mutual inter-dependence, and reciprocal enrichment that is part of God's plan for the world. Universal love is the characteristic of followers of Jesus, and its absence is the single greatest indicator that someone belongs to the "world." Jesus makes it clear that all ethics and daily life are based on the command "love one another," and the theological and Christological reason is "because I have loved you." This leads us to live a theology of union with all, or what we might call a mysticism of universality. It is part of a new approach to life that illumines a world that otherwise lives in darkness. Universality means that the Father's love is given to all, that Jesus' mission is to bring a new vision of life to everyone, that discipleship calls for universal love and understanding. This commitment becomes our spirituality.

1. Disciples manifest their convictions and values in interaction with people who do not share them.
2. We must model our lives on the Father's universal love, "for he makes his sun rise on the evil and on the good, and sends rain on the righteous and on the unrighteous" (Matthew 5:45).
3. This approach is not just a practical outlook on life or a vision of social interaction. It is a mystical-religious vision and challenge regarding what is God's plan for the world.
4. We need to transcend particularity where groups or individuals act or even think of themselves as better, purer, more informed or enlightened, closer to God, than others.

CHALLENGES FOR TODAY
- Remember you are very blessed, but so too is everyone else.
- What does mutual mercy and mutual compassion mean to you?
- Do you ever approach others with preconceived ideas about them? Why?

DAY 46 MINISTERING IN JESUS' NAME

All followers of Jesus have a mission and a ministry as part of their solidarity with Christ. The Christian vocation by its very nature is a vocation to serve others—thus, disciples, as chosen partners, prolong and extend the work of Jesus. Mission and ministry are closely connected. Mission refers to the reason why people exist or are "sent." Ministry refers to services accomplished because of one's sense of mission. Mission is visionary, ministry is functional. Disciples, through their variety of ministries, manifest their sense of mission. These ministries are always centered on Christ and his values and vision. They are filled with compassion, as they free people from all kinds of ills of body, mind, heart, and soul. Disciples carry out this healing ministry aware of Jesus' compassionate, active presence to them. Ministries lead to the integral, holistic well-being of others through the creative development of new ministries to respond to new needs. The disciples' ministry is also a reflection of their community, justified by community, and a manifestation of its common values.

1. Ministering in Jesus' name leads us away from the acquisition of power to selfless service modeled on Jesus' own ministry—he came to give his life in the service of others.
2. Nothing about us as followers of Jesus should reflect wealth or status or selfishness, but only poverty, simplicity, and concern for others.
3. As disciples we need to be aware of our obligation to take care of others, to collaborate without vying for power, and to share ministry with each other.
4. Our ministry requires an enthusiastic acceptance of the cross, an imitation of selfless service, prayer, and confidence that Jesus is working through us.

CHALLENGES FOR TODAY
- Are you ready to accept persecution, and persevere with the fortitude of the prophets?
- What is your mission and ministry? Does it reflect Jesus'?
- How do you live out your sense of mission?

A statue of John in Avila, close to the home where Teresa was born.

3
The Importance of Spiritual Direction

John of the Cross spent much of his ministry sharing with others experiences he personally had and experiences that he learned from his spiritual direction of others. Spiritual direction was his primary ministry from the early formation work in Mancera de Abajo and Pastrana and later in the monastery of the Incarnation in Avila. After his imprisonment, his spiritual direction of nuns and friars increased, and he then began to extend his direction of others through his wonderful writings. No matter his responsibilities, the guidance of others on their journey to God was always of paramount importance to John. Let us spend a little time in the next week or so reflecting on John's insights and how he can become a spiritual guide for us too.

DAY 47 *JOHN, AN EXTRAORDINARY DIRECTOR*

John of the Cross was an experienced spiritual director involved in the formation and personal guidance of friars and nuns. At times he was asked to look into special cases, such as that of the Augustinian nun, Maria de Olivares, or the investigation of the prayer life of a Carmelite nun—a copy of which we have in the minor works of John. Throughout his life, the ministry of spiritual direction was of paramount importance to John. While John focused his attention especially on the nuns and friars of the reform, he also reached out to many clergy, religious, and laity, for so many sought his guidance. Of course John's writings became sources of guidance for many of his directees. John of the Cross' spiritual direction continues today to the innumerable followers who find guidance in his extraordinary writings.

1. John was spiritual director from the earliest time of the reform, and then as chaplain and confessor to the nuns of the monastery of the Incarnation in Avila.
2. John prepared himself well for spiritual direction and criticizes others who did not. He grounded himself in Scripture, theology, and spirituality.
3. In spite of his many responsibilities, he would prolong his guidance of others through his letters and through the *Maxims of Light and Love.*
4. When John writes his major works, they seem so down to earth in their advice and give the impression John has someone in mind—a former directee—when he gives an example.

CHALLENGES FOR TODAY
- John can be your spiritual director, too, through his writings.
- If you want a local director, choose him or her very carefully.
- Pray you may have a well-prepared spiritual director.

DAY 48 *IMPORTANCE OF GUIDANCE*

John stresses the importance of spiritual direction. At the outset of the *Ascent* he points out that some people do not enter the dark night because they are "without suitable and alert directors who will show them the way to the summit" (A. Prologue. 3). His worry is that these people then stay in their lowly methods of communion with God "because they receive no direction on breaking away from the methods of beginners" (A. Prologue. 3). In one of his letters to Juana de Pedraza, John stresses the importance of a spiritual director. "A soul should find its support wholly and entirely in its director, for not to do so would amount to no longer wanting a director. And when one director is sufficient and suitable, all the others are useless or a hindrance" (L. 10). John felt strongly that each one should have a spiritual director; otherwise a person wanders around in the dark. "The blind man who falls will not get up alone in his blindness, and if he does, he will take the wrong road" (S. 11).

1. John was convinced that lots of people make no progress in the spiritual life because they do not have a qualified spiritual director.
2. "The virtuous soul that is alone and without a master is like a lone burning coal; it will grow colder rather than hotter" (S. 7).
3. In another saying John affirmed, "Consider how much more can be accomplished by two together than by one alone" (S. 9).
4. Having a spiritual director is not the same as having a spiritual companion. Which do you want and why?

CHALLENGES FOR TODAY
- Are you making progress with the spiritual director you have?
- Some directors are general practitioners and others specialists. Have you chosen wisely?
- If you are a spiritual director, have you prepared well for this important ministry?

DAY 49 *CHOOSE A DIRECTOR CAREFULLY*

John of the Cross was very concerned about the quality and preparation of spiritual directors, and several times he suggests it is difficult to find an accomplished spiritual director. Moreover, he has more negative comments than positive ones about the directors he has seen. In the *Living Flame*, where John expresses his concerns about blind spiritual guides, he tells his readers that they must be very careful in the selection of a spiritual director. Moreover, some who can be helpful in earlier phases of the spiritual life are unqualified to guide others in the later stages. John tells his readers that they need to find someone who is learned and discreet, and experienced in the spiritual life. He states that the foundation for guiding a soul to life in the spirit is knowledge and discretion, but the director must also have experience of what a true and pure spirit is (F. 3. 30). These qualities are essential even before one undertakes spiritual direction, however, throughout the guidance of others the director must be a person given to holiness of life. In this context John constantly addresses the director's need of faith, hope, love, self-control, and commitment to prayer.

1. So, knowledge, discretion, experience, and holiness are the four key qualities for a spiritual director.
2. Spiritual directors must take their responsibilities seriously for they are intermediaries between God and the directee.
3. A director does not need to have made the whole journey to help you to get to your goal, but it helps.
4. For both Teresa and John knowledge was the most important quality in a spiritual guide.

CHALLENGES FOR TODAY
• What qualities do you seek in a spiritual director?
• Do you have the four key requirements for direction?
• Have you ever been blocked in spiritual growth by a director?

DAY 50 GOD IS THE PRIMARY GUIDE

A spiritual director's contributions begin with an awareness that God is the primary guide. "The soul, then, should avert that God is the principal agent in this matter, and that He acts as the blind man's guide who must lead it by the hand to the place it does not know how to reach" (F. 3.29). The work of the spiritual director is simply to facilitate this and not to get in the way of God's interventions in the life of the directee. This does not exclude the fact that sometimes a director will need to resist the pressures from followers who seek guidance to their own liking. So the director must be able to challenge the directee who wants to focus on his or her own will and resist the director's challenge. On a practical level the director should be able to maintain some distance between himself or herself and the directee.

1. If we long for spiritual growth, let us remember that God wants it more than we do.
2. The only thing that concerns us is bringing our will and desires in union with God's will.
3. We must be careful in selecting a guide for John calls many of them "blind guides."
4. Some directors have more personal need to be a spiritual director than followers have need of their guidance.

CHALLENGES FOR TODAY
- If you are a director for others, pray that you may never get in God's way.
- Who among your friends is an ideal spiritual director, and why do you think so?
- Pray for all spiritual directors.

DAY 51 *STAGES IN THE JOURNEY*

John always wanted a spiritual director who understood the stages of the spiritual journey. The spiritual director's task is to be a spiritual judge who gives pertinent instruction for each stage and requires full disclosure of the spiritual life of his or her directee. In the early stages of the spiritual life the director should be able to recognize the signs of the purification of the soul in the dark night. Problems can arise if the director does not, for sometimes the opposite happens and directors think someone is in the dark night when he or she is not. The important thing is to help the directee ready himself or herself for the challenges of God. Throughout the journey the director will need humility for in the dark night the directee finds no consolation in any teaching of the spiritual director, and the director must understand why. Moreover, he or she needs to realize that some souls cannot adequately explain to their director their experience of contemplation.

1. "[T]he chief concern of spiritual directors with their penitents is the immediate mortification of every appetite" (A. 1. 12.6).
2. Moral theology or other theological disciplines deal with prayer, virtues, asceticism, and so on. The difference with spirituality is that it deals with progress, movement, evolution, and growth of prayer, virtues, and so on in the journey. Hence, knowing the stages is critical.
3. Being a spiritual director requires a lot of study. No one should put his or her life in the hands of an amateur.
4. Spiritual direction needs humility in director and directee.

CHALLENGES FOR TODAY
- Where are you in the spiritual journey?
- A key question in spiritual direction is "what is your image of God and has it changed over time"?
- If John was your guide now, what would he say to you?

DAY 52 *INCOMPETENT SPIRITUAL DIRECTORS*

John sees the potential for spiritual growth in many people, and tells us that God wants to draw as many as possible to undertake the spiritual journey to union in love. However, they are often hindered by the absence or incompetence of spiritual directors. In his prologue to the *Ascent* he states, "For some spiritual directors are likely to be a hindrance and harm rather than a help to these souls that journey on this road. Such directors have neither the enlightenment nor experience of these ways" (A. Prologue. 4). John particularly stresses the lack of judgment in spiritual directors. The problem of poor judgment seems to arise particularly at the transition to contemplation. John also addresses failures of directors in dealing with the spiritual visions of directees, even saying that directors are often deluded in giving inappropriate importance to these visions. Some incompetent directors burden their directees with their neatly packaged methods. They fail to guide along the way of humility. Some do not understand the stages of the spiritual life and some especially do not appreciate the later stages.

1. Included in a spiritual director's wrong judgments would be that when someone is in darkness the director can suggest it is depression, or think that a person is falling back when he or she is without consolations!
2. Often the spiritual director insists on active prayer when passivity and receptivity are needed.
3. Directors need to be aware of their gifts and their own limitations; some are specialists and others are general practitioners.
4. The directee may not be able to make the whole journey with the same director. So, the directee needs to be free to change when he or she feels things are not right and the director no longer helpful.

CHALLENGES FOR TODAY
- Have you chosen the right spiritual director?
- If you could not find a spiritual director locally, what would you do?
- If you currently have a spiritual director what do you think are his or her qualifications?

DAY 53 *BLIND GUIDES LEAD ASTRAY*

John speaks at length about spiritual directors and says that a person should avoid placing any obstacle in the way of the work of the Lord. Because of his concern, John points out "it is very important that a person, desiring to advance in recollection and perfection, take care into whose hands he entrusts himself, for the disciple will become like the master" (F. 3.30). The problem for followers is that it is very hard to find an accomplished guide for the more advanced parts of the journey. If the director lacks the appropriate qualities he or she can cause great harm, especially by leading a person back to earlier stages in the spiritual life when such a decision is totally inappropriate. John says such directors do not understand anything more than pertains to beginners and do not want the directee to pass beyond what the spiritual director can manage.

1. Many good well-wishing people want to be spiritual directors and it is difficult to persuade them that they are not qualified.
2. It is critically important that directors know when they can lead and when they should refer a directee to someone more specialized.
3. What are the advantages and disadvantages of spiritual direction by phone or e-mail?
4. "God alone is the agent and one Who speaks secretly to the solitary and silent soul" (F. 3.44). The director's interference is not only useless it is harmful.

CHALLENGES FOR TODAY
- Do you want to become like your spiritual director?
- Who are the best qualified directors in the area where you live?
- Has your spiritual director been able to lead you forward in your spiritual journey?

DAY 54 DIRECTORS FACILITATE GOD'S INTERVENTIONS

John insists, "These directors should reflect that they themselves are not the chief agent, guide, and mover of souls in this matter, but that the principal guide is the Holy Spirit" (F. 3.46). The director is an instrument, facilitating God's guidance in directees. So, he or she should not impose his own methods on directees but lead them along the road God has chosen into solitude and freedom of spirit. John ends forcefully, "if he does not recognize it, he should leave them alone and not bother them" (F. 3.46). In the seeming emptiness at this time God is purifying the person. The trouble is that some directors do not understand contemplation because they have not reached it themselves, and so they hinder its development in others, turning them back to earlier practices in the spiritual life.

1. Both director and directee need humility and openness to the call of God.
2. John comments on directors who do not know their role. "These directors do not know what spirit is. They do a great injury to God and show disrespect toward Him by intruding with a rough hand where He is working" (F. 3.54).
3. We are not moving forward in spiritual direction. It is God who is drawing us forward and that changes the approach of both director and directee.
4. It is always important to be aware that God does not act in the ways we expect God to act.

CHALLENGES FOR TODAY
- Ask God to guide you, directly or through someone else.
- Are you humble enough for spiritual direction?
- What are you seeking in your spiritual journey?

DAY 55 *WHEN IT IS TIME TO CHANGE DIRECTORS*

There are few spiritual directors who are good for the whole journey to God. Some are excellent for the early stages but not knowledgeable enough for the later ones. Others are excellent for consultation on key experiences or problems but do not have the patience for the slow uneventful periods. Taking a spiritual director is a major decision but not a lifetime commitment. Of course, we should be careful not to choose someone we like who will not challenge us sufficiently. Nor do we want someone who will be hurt if we leave, and so we stay. There often comes a time when it is good for a change, especially when we realize we are at a standstill. Having a companion in the spiritual journey is not enough—there must be development. Some do not change when they should. They continue to follow blindly with misguided hope in their hearts.

1. What do you think are signs that it is time to change?
2. John says there comes a time when it seems it is as if one blind man is guiding another blind man. "[T]hese directors together with their penitents have gone astray and become bewildered" (A.2. 18.2).
3. Do you ever get the impression your director has a package deal in mind and is trying to fit you in it?
4. If your director is good he or she will be the first person to suggest you change and go to someone more qualified for the next part of the journey.

CHALLENGES FOR TODAY

- Are you satisfied with your director's guidance?
- Where are you going in the spiritual journey and is your current director able to get you there?
- Pray often for your spiritual director.

DAY 56 *TERESA'S APPRECIATION OF JOHN*

"I beg of you to have a talk with this Father and help him in his undertaking for, though he is small of stature, I believe he is great in the eyes of God. We are certainly going to miss him greatly for he is sensible and well fitted for our way of life so that I believe our Lord has called him for this work. There is not a friar but speaks well of him for he leads a life of great penitence, though he entered upon it so recently. But the Lord seems to be leading him by the hand for, although we had a few disagreements here over business matters, of which I have been the cause, and I have sometimes been vexed with him, we have never seen the least imperfection in him. He has courage: but, as he is quite alone, he needs all that the Lord gives him" (See Letter of Teresa of Avila to Francis of Salcedo, 1568).

1. Teresa appreciated John's many gifts, but they also disagreed over business matters as well as approaches to asceticism and contemplation.
2. With tongue in cheek, Teresa playfully criticized John's approach to spirituality; "It would be a bad business for us if we could not seek God till we were dead to the world."
3. Elsewhere Teresa wrote, "God deliver us from people who are so spiritual that they want to turn everything into perfect contemplation."
4. In letters we find that Teresa appreciated John for his own commitment, for his knowledge of the stages in the spiritual journey, and for his spiritual direction. She also chose him as her confessor.

CHALLEGES FOR TODAY
- Do people speak well of you and your spiritual life?
- Can you live in appreciation of others even though you may have different views on important aspects of life?
- What qualities do you need to be a good directee?

DAY 57 JOHN'S MESSAGE OF SALVATION

There are many who struggle for meaning in life who cannot come to grips with the doctrinal challenges of John of the Cross. Yet he has a message that goes to the heart of both the needs and the yearnings of modern men and women. If people would give him a chance he would penetrate their darkness. Those who feel wretched and long for healing will find that John gives light and guidance to find a way out of the false values and vision of contemporary life. "[I]f there are Christians over whom their God has not sufficiently triumphed, who cannot understand St. John of the Cross, who are frightened at his doctrine . . . or who grow deluded by not reading him aright, and manufacture a counterfeit mysticism for themselves, there are other souls, separated from God, and tortured by those evil powers that are overwhelming modern life, who find in him the instrument of their salvation" (See Maritain, p. xxv).

1. John and his doctrine can transform our burdened lives.
2. Jacques Maritain was the one who first called John of the Cross, "the mystical doctor" because of his supremacy in teachings on the spiritual life.
3. Everything in John is for the sake of love; our end is transformation in God by love.
4. John has a message that brings salvation; it is a universal call to holiness.

CHALLENGES FOR TODAY
- Think of John as the one who can save you from the evil that overwhelms modern life.
- Are you ever frightened by John's teachings?
- Remind yourself why you were created.

DAY 58 *THE DIRECTEE'S RESPONSIBILITY*

Growth in the spiritual life is primarily God's work within us. We do not earn advancement by our efforts. Rather, we are being drawn to union in love by God who is the primary Lover. However, John insists that we can contribute to preparing ourselves for the spiritual journey, and in his writings he makes several suggestions as to what we can do. We must have a determined desire to succeed in this journey. The first thing we can do is to want to progress to union with God in love. For some it is something in the back of their minds that they would like to accomplish but it is not the overriding desire of their lives, and for each of us it must be. Besides having this determined desire to progress we must do whatever we can to get rid of any obstacle that hinders progress in the journey. This is a period of self-discipline, correction of faults, establishing our priorities in life, and the removal of gratification in those things that seem they could lead to God, but actually lead away.

1. Many say they want progress in the spiritual life, but commitment to the journey is clearly not a priority for them.
2. We journey inward into the depths of our own souls to discover purpose in life and destiny in this world.
3. The most important step we can take as beginners is to participate wholeheartedly in the active night of sense.
4. We must acknowledge that destiny in this life is a preparation for our destiny in the next life—to live in union with God in love.

CHALLENGES FOR TODAY
- What can you contribute to your spiritual growth?
- What is your greatest desire in the spiritual life?
- What obstacles to growth remain?

DAY 59 *THE DIRECTEE'S PREPARATIONS*

As spiritual directees we should realize that our role is primarily to receive. One of the first great decisions we must make in the journey is to change attitudes to life and to affirm a new awareness—namely that we are empty and poor, and that each of us grows by receiving not by doing. The call to progress in the spiritual life is God's gift, and so essentially it emphasizes acceptance and receptivity. In journeying along the spiritual path it is important that we have a healthy image of God. It is easy enough to think that we are burdened in journeying to God by pleasures and satisfactions of sense that attract us and divert our attention from God. However, we are also burdened by what we know, what we remember and imagine, and what we desire and love, and also by how we know, remember, and love. In the spiritual journey God teaches us new ways to know, to possess all things, and to love God, and thus develop a new image of God. This is all part of God's gradual self-revelation, and it takes place in contemplation.

1. We are often burdened by an old image of God.
2. We must prepare ourselves to know, possess, and love God in new ways.
3. We will need to let go of old ways of knowing, remembering, and loving.
4. Let us think about what diverts our attention away from God.

CHALLENGES FOR TODAY
- Think about how you are empty and poor.
- Do you do too much instead of being receptive?
- Can you remember when God first called you to progress in the spiritual life?

DAY 60 PREPARE FOR CONTEMPLATION

Contemplation is God's gift to us, but there are some simple practices that can create a healthy environment in which prayer can develop. Besides cultivating a love for Christ and a desire to be the person God destines each of us to be, we need to become comfortable in solitude and meditation, seek genuine freedom of spirit, appreciate beauty, joy, and enthusiasm. If we can control body, mind, and emotions through fasting, temperance, attention to desires, thoughts, attitudes and feelings, we can contribute to the preparation necessary to receive a transformed image of God in contemplation. This will include simple practices of finding a sacred space and time for prayer, along with the creation of an environment that is uplifting with good posture, music, nourishing spiritual reading, and inspiring art.

1. The ancient writers tell us not to forget "the prayer of the body"—all we do to ready our bodies for prayer.
2. We cannot appreciate God unless we train ourselves to appreciate beauty, joy, and enthusiasm around us.
3. Can we create a suitable environment for prayer?
4. If we wish to pray we must love solitude.

CHALLENGES FOR TODAY
- Identify your own sacred space and sacred time.
- Are you enthusiastic about life and God?
- How do you nourish your spiritual life?

DAY 61 *TWO VALUABLE CHALLENGES*

There are so many suggestions that can be helpful in our spiritual journey—some more important than others. A key challenge is to look at the world through the lens of love. Once a person understands the major steps in the spiritual journey, it becomes easier seeing how each part fits in with the whole. One will find that one or two issues can hold together the whole of spiritual life. This current suggestion is so important that by itself it can give focus to the whole of life. If as spiritual directees, we center life on love, all else will fall into place. Then we must shift to life in the Spirit. When as spiritual directees we dedicate ourselves to pursue union with God, we must shift the focus of life from a life of sense (a self-centered, self-directed life) to a focus on the life of the Spirit (a God directed life). This journey to God, with its purification of sense and its purification and redirection of the intellect, memory, and will (in faith, hope, and love, respectively) is a preparation for union, and is at the same time a discovery of our true and authentic selves. This shift to life in the spirit not only leads to deeper union with God, but leads us to uncover or rediscover our true selves at every level of life: sense, spirit, and religious.

1. Our spiritual journey is above all a transformation through faith, hope, and love.
2. How do we shift from a life of sense to a life of spirit?
3. As Christians we must see everything through the lens of love.
4. Can we say that key aspects of our lives are falling into place?

CHALLENGES FOR TODAY
- Try this week to see everything through the lens of love.
- Which one single quality holds your life together?
- Has your spiritual commitment helped you discover your authentic self?

DAY 62 *TWO IMPORTANT ATTITUDES*

In journeying to God we should accept the pain that comes with this journey and also celebrate the achievements too. The journey is one of transformation but it brings pain. The spiritual journey is very challenging but it is not a destructive undertaking, in which we scramble to take a few steps forward. In this journey we are being drawn by the love of God who is always the "primary Lover." So, we must try to match God's gift of selfless love with our own choice to focus exclusively on a life of love. Transformation will take place in contemplation when a person becomes receptive to God's activity within, as God purifies all false desires and false gods and fills a person with an inflow of divine love. Although we need to bear the pain, we should also celebrate each stage on the journey. Each step we make, or God gives, is worth celebrating, from the first step to control disordered, voluntary behaviors and desires and imperfections that can lead away from God, to a prayer of loving presence to God, and to the development which God fosters when a person is willing to let go of previous forms of communication with God.

1. Let us think about the pains that come in this spiritual journey.
2. Do we focus exclusively on love in our spiritual growth?
3. We must constantly celebrate in gratitude how God has guided us.
4. We need to let go of false securities and let God take over our lives.

CHALLENGES FOR TODAY
- What do you have to celebrate?
- How do you communicate with God?
- How does God communicate with you?

The chapel and tomb of St. John of the Cross in Segovia.

4

The Nature of Spirituality

Spirituality is the life that results from faith. It refers to the interaction of God's gift of transforming life with the efforts of the believer in the concrete circumstances of history. Spirituality never refers to static concepts but only to dynamic ones; it deals only with the stages of growth in a God-directed life and the maturing of values proposed by God in Christ. In spiritual life there are some values that are perennial, others that change as situations and circumstances change, and there are ways and methods that also vary to preserve the unchanging values and to live them in relevant ways for changing times. In this section we look at some of the insights of contemporary spirituality and also some of the extraordinary insights of St. John of the Cross in his approach to spirituality.

DAY 63 *JOHN OF THE CROSS AND SPIRITUALITY*

St. John of the Cross is a figure of prime importance in the history of spirituality. Interest in his teachings and appreciation of his extraordinary insights into Christian spirituality are higher than ever and still growing. For John, the spiritual life is an unwavering search for a union in which seekers not only find God but also their true selves. John rarely talks about mystical experiences since such experiences can be quite subjective. Rather, wishing to emphasize that the encounter with God is real and not merely subjective, John prefers to speak about union. So, John sees spiritual life as a universal call to search constantly for union with God. This is a continual process of growth or regression, but never stationary. He does not speak of static states in life but of appetites and desires—aspects of a person that are always in movement.

1. "Everyone knows that not to go forward on this road is to go back" (A.1 11.5).
2. The spiritual journey is a major undertaking of love, and we must never relent but constantly strive to develop our positive capacities and energies and rectify maladjusted ones.
3. We have been overwhelmed over the centuries into thinking that John of the Cross presents an elitist spirituality. This is far from the truth.
4. John's spirituality is a personal exodus from our own captivity to the promised land of love and union with God.

CHALLENGES FOR TODAY
- Remember that John of the Cross can be your guide in the spiritual journey.
- Ask yourself do you really want to make this journey?
- Do you believe with John that the encounter with God is real?

DAY 64 CHRISTIAN SPIRITUALITY

Spirituality never refers to static concepts but only to dynamic ones. It is not interested in prayer but growth in prayer, not charity but growth in charity, not social justice but growth in our commitment to social justice. Faithful following of a call from God in Christ leads us to find fulfillment, and to a dedication that makes a qualitative difference in the way we behave in our daily lives, giving us values, vision, purpose, and perspective on life. It opens the way to the fullest and deepest values of human growth, the profound and intimate values we cherish most: the yearning for self-fulfillment, for community, and for transcendence. Rooted in the message of Jesus, Christian spirituality studies the growth of the person from God's perspective. Spirituality is more than a segment of life, a Sunday addition, it is a way of viewing the whole of life.

1. Christian spirituality stresses the means and methods that facilitate development in life.
2. Spirituality can offer people a strategy for their own growth while appreciating that each individual's way to human-Christian maturity may vary.
3. Christian spirituality brings life and growth into authentic focus as it highlights the genuine concerns of life and human hope.
4. Christian spirituality aims to integrate the unique message of Jesus with the best of all human values.

CHALLENGES FOR TODAY
- Are the spiritual values of your life in constant growth or are they static?
- Do you think you are a better human being because you are Christian?
- Is every aspect of your life influenced by your Christian convictions?

DAY 65 *RECENT DEVELOPMENTS IN SPIRITUALITY*

Spirituality for us as people of faith is the interaction of God's gift of transforming life with our efforts in concrete circumstances of each day. Thus, it is always a transitory manifestation of perennial values. Rooted in the great tradition of Christ's message, we cannot allow it to degenerate into religious fads while neglecting essential values of faith. Each of us, faced with our own emptiness, needs to be open to grace and to develop the faith-filled skill of waiting for God's interventions, together with an attitude of readiness to receive God's gifts and use them creatively. Contemporary spirituality concerns itself with the concrete circumstances of our own age, and stresses spontaneity, personal authenticity, global vision, and vital needs. Recent spiritual renewal focuses on a rediscovery of the essential source values of faith and an opening to the autonomous values of the world.

1. Spirituality includes an awareness of personal responsibility for others, and a new community consciousness in believers.
2. Contemporary developments in spirituality have led us to new ways of thinking and living Christianity that imply a new value for human and earthly realities.
3. Spirituality refers to who we are and who we ought to be in Christ.
4. Our spirituality must speak to today rather than to what spirituality was over two thousand years ago.

CHALLENGES FOR TODAY
- What does spirituality mean to you?
- Look over your life to see whether your spirituality has matured as you have.
- Would you describe your spirituality as a very relevant approach to the modern world?

DAY 66 A CALL TO FULLNESS OF LIFE

Spirituality embraces all of our lives, making sure that every facet responds to the inner call to live fully at any given moment. This implies that our spirituality is all about relationships, with oneself, others, communities, the world around us, and God. It is the ordering of our lives so that the values of the inner self shine forth in all that we do. Jesus Christ said, "I have come that you may have life and have it to the full" (John 10:10); and an early Christian writer called Irenaeus said, "The glory of God is when a man or woman is fully alive"; that is spirituality! Spirituality is not some non-descript emotional feeling of piety and religious devotion, but it takes as its starting point the concrete circumstances of our daily lives; our lived experience in the world we know. It is a journey in which the best values of humanity, especially faith, hope, and love, help give direction to our lives and help us advance towards achieving the enrichment of an adult personality. It refers to our entire lives based upon decisions that show fidelity to the inner motivation of our lives.

1. Christian spirituality presumes a positive approach to creation, the world around us, and our human nature created and redeemed by God.
2. Spirituality now refers to making our faith real and effective on a day to day basis.
3. Spirituality is a journey of faith in oneself, in others, in the goodness of creation, in ultimate values, and in God.
4. Spirituality permeates every moment of every day.

CHALLENGES FOR TODAY
- Is spirituality the most important aspect of your life?
- Re-examine your relationships in light of faith.
- Do you dedicate your life to something or someone bigger than yourself?

DAY 67 A JOURNEY BASED ON FAITH

Spirituality is a journey of faith in ourselves, in others, in the goodness of creation, in ultimate values, and in God. However, it is at the same time a journey of authentic, unconditional love of oneself, of others in relationships, of the world in which we live, of ultimate goodness and of God. No journey is straight forward and smooth; there are always ups and downs and temporary setbacks; there are frequently delays, diversions, and longer sections of the journey than expected. Sometimes, when we think we have arrived, we find it is just a junction leading to another section of the highway. We cannot grow to our full potential unless we can also accept emptiness—emptiness that the Lord can then fill. Spirituality is our faith brought to birth in ever-changing circumstances of modern life. Faith allows God's power to be fruitful in us. Spirituality grows principally by purifying, directing, and enriching our lives and not by sacrificing or escaping from life. Spirituality is rooted in a faith experience, in our case in Christ and our common search to bring about the coming of the kingdom he announced.

1. Our spirituality demands deliberate action on our part based on decisions made in light of values.
2. There are lots of experiences of emptiness in our journey, such as lost careers, lost status, lost privileges, lost loves, lost friends, and so on.
3. Spirituality is not just what we do, but also what happens within us as a result of a faithful living of motivating values.
4. Spirituality is receptivity, openness to God's grace within us.

CHALLENGES FOR TODAY
- Do you give God chance to work within you?
- Are you constantly critical of your own life and values?
- Have you personally responded to God's call within you?

DAY 68 *SPIRITUALITY INCLUDES OTHERS*

Spiritual development only occurs with others. They who can not share life or the service of others, or who can not cooperate or collaborate, or who can not celebrate together or build community together, are at an enormous disadvantage from a Christian point of view. Rather, genuine growth includes a letting go of selfishness and self-pity, and it calls for confident and courageous growth with others. The interaction with others is a way of embodying spirituality, and at the same time the interaction with others in mutual service creates and constitutes the spirituality. Spirituality is a manifestation of reality and the way in which people can become their true selves in response to God's call. It must be lived by individuals responding to their lives and destiny with God. For each of us God's call in the Lord is to become who we are truly capable of being.

1. Our spirituality must imply constant creativity rather than any acceptance of pre-packaged and recycled spirituality, whether in the form of saints from the past or spiritual movements of more recent times.
2. Spirituality touches the masculine and feminine in each of us, never turning the values of either into an unacceptable enemy, as happened in some spiritual tendencies in the past.
3. We must learn to find and then leave aside the worst of ourselves.
4. Whatever convictions regarding the meaning of life lie at the core of our hearts, conversion implies basing our entire lives on those convictions.

CHALLENGES FOR TODAY
- What role do others play in your spirituality?
- Examine yourself for selfish tendencies.
- What are the major convictions of your life?

DAY 69 *INTEGRATION OF DAILY LIFE*

One of the major developments in the last couple of decades has been an extraordinary interest in integrating faith and daily life and activity. Spirituality permeates our commitment to every aspect of life. This results when we realize that all life including our family and working lives with their new focuses of call are always a re-living of the baptismal challenge to belong to Christ, to live and love for him. This leads us to relate differently to self, to others, and even to the cosmos because of a new way of living our relationship to Jesus. The service of others in daily life is a particularly splendid way of realizing this. This call will need to be renewed on a daily basis, as we face increasing demands that must never lead to a reduced ideal of our calling. Both feeling called by faith and yearning for personal integration, we as Christians strive to respond each day to the implications of that call we feel deep in our hearts.

1. Spirituality includes a sense of humility, as we struggle daily to become what we hear the Lord calling us to be.
2. For each of us, no period can pass without learning something new either in prayer, in sharing with peers, in ongoing study, in reflective application of the Word of God, in discussion with other believers.
3. We cannot drift in mediocrity, unfocused and uncaring, without purpose or mission, for this leads to a loss of dedication.
4. Let us reflect on the importance of baptism in every aspect of our spirituality.

CHALLENGES FOR TODAY
- Is your daily life integrated with your faith?
- Do you see religion as a Sunday activity?
- Describe how your family is a Christian family.

DAY 70 ROOT, INTERPRET, AND DISCOVER

Spirituality is a response to a fundamental demand in the depths of our hearts that urges us to take life seriously, giving primacy to God-directed values. We reverence these perennial values but interpret them in transitory forms. In fact the exploratory dimension of spirituality preserves its relevance. Christian spirituality must relate these values to present trends and developments. There are three essential components of the way we approach Christian spirituality. First, rootedness—the perennial values must always be the same. Second interpretation—the essential and unchanging core values need to be lived with the same spirit and life as they always were, which often requires that their articulation will change in order that the essence remain. Third, discovery—an attitude of constant openness to the Spirit's challenge in each generation, calling us to give new life to the rooted and interpreted call.

1. Our spirituality evolves and does so in varied ways as new generations find new ways of living out their call.
2. All interpretations, including the Bible's, are provisional.
3. We cannot live spiritualities as people in the past lived them.
4. Even our latest understandings and experiences of God can block our encounter with God.

CHALLENGES FOR TODAY

- Does your life tell people what spirituality is or what spirituality was?
- Which traditions of spirituality appeal to you?
- Who do you think embodies Jesus' challeges in a relevant way today?

DAY 71 A REVIEW OF SOME SIGNIFICANT ASPECTS OF SPIRITUALITY

Let us spend a little time today thinking about some key components of spirituality and use them as a check of our own approach to spiritual life. Which of these qualities are already an integral part of your spiritual commitment and to which do you need to give more attention?

- Spirituality is based on a motivating experience of faith and of God
- Spirituality is rooted in the best values of our lives
- Spirituality concentrates on what is essential to the spirit
- Spirituality emphasizes a sense of community
- Spirituality reaches out in service to others
- Spirituality includes a responsibility for justice
- Spirituality is always open to the search for truth

Spirituality includes:
- An emphasis on the simplicity and intensity of the present moment
- A focus on an experience that changes life
- A concentration on authentic, unconditional love of self, of others, of the world around us, and of God
- An acceptance of our mission and destiny in God's call
- A generous commitment to transcend ourselves and become other-centered
- A shared dedication to the common good for all people of the world

CHALLENGES FOR TODAY
- Use this short list as a way of revising your own spirituality.
- What key qualities would you add to this list?
- Describe the greatest spiritual experience of your life.

DAY 72 JOHN'S SYSTEMATIC APPROACH TO SPIRITUALITY

John is a witness to God, to God's ways, and to how we can encounter God. He is also a witness to the call of humanity, for he knows the misery into which we can fall, and the greatness to which we are called. When John writes his major works he has already completed the journey and arrived at the destination of union with God, and he can look back over the whole journey and appreciate the stages that led to the goal. He has thought through the whole develpopment of the spiritual life and observed many common traits in his spiritual direction, so that he can see Christian growth patterns in terms of an organic synthesis. The system presupposed in all John's works is itself simple, fruitful, relatively easy for directors to use, and available to almost everyone. The process of the spiritual life is not entirely predictable, nor identical for all, but if we know the key moments in the journey then we too can be guided towards our goal. So, John offers us a systematic approach to the whole journey to God; it is a total experience. We should give ourselves wholeheartedly to the entire journey and not pick and choose parts or dabble with some ideas but leave others aside.

1. When John directs others he can rejoice when they are sad for he knows that good things will happen in the purification. He can also be sad when people rejoice in what appeals to them but leads nowhere.
2. Often in his writings he makes parentheses, referring to the past or future, for he sees the whole journey.
3. John is an excellent systematic theologian as well as a mystic, and he can formulate and explain the system that underlies his thought.
4. Many spiritualities, old and new, do not offer a systematic approach to the spiritual life but deal with selected aspects only, and that is not enough.

CHALLENGES FOR TODAY
- Are you willing to commit yourself to a life-long journey to God?
- Entrust yourself to John's guidance willingly, for he has already completed the journey.
- Does your current spiritual director give the impression that he or she knows the whole journey, or is he or she responding to symptoms of the spiritual life from week to week?

DAY 73 WE START IN DISORDER

John's point of departure for the spiritual journey is awareness that we are born into a situation of disorder; our entire lives ought to be subordinated to the Spirit, but instead they go the other way, to sense. More men and women are guided by sense than by the Spirit. The result of this natural decline is that a person hides his or her own true image, dignity, and finality, tends to continually regress instead of making progress, and even blocks divine interventions in life. We are surrounded by disorders; but, let us be clear, we cause these disorders because we are disordered people—we lack order or direction in our spiritual lives. We want to progress but at times we are unable to do so, in fact we even seem to be paralyzed. So, if we wish to make the journey to God where alone we will find our authentic selves, then we must be willing to undertake the rigors of this journey. John's approach to men and women is always functional; he is seeking to change us, to transform us into who we are capable of being. This process begins by removing disorders.

1. Disorder is measured in relation to what ought to be, and our lives ought to be subordinated to the life of the Spirit.
2. Good intentions are not enough and we can only get out of our disorders through complete purification.
3. Seeing the harmful effects of disorders and our inability to change should convince us that the system of spirituality we are using does not work.
4. It is more difficult to discover disorders when they are the normal order of the day and everyone is involved in them

CHALLENGES FOR TODAY
- What are the disorders in your life?
- Identify the causes of the disorders that afflict you.
- Too much of the wrong kind of spirituality is also a disorder.

DAY 74 *THE QUEST FOR AUTHENTICITY*

John tells us that there are two qualities necessary for the spiritual journey, poverty and nakedness. Again, we must interpret these dynamically and not statically. The journey consists in us striving every day to become poor in spirit, and endeavoring each day to strip ourselves of any false values that lead us away from God. John considers that we are inauthentic when we accumulate goods—material or spiritual. Let us keep in mind that authenticity is not achieved by accumulation, by adding on more qualities—as if the symptom of our disorder is hunger. Rather, authenticity is found in the depth of each of us in that zone of divine life that God has placed in each of us. The problem is that our lives are cluttered with too many false values that block our progress. We are not primarily hungry for spiritual life; rather we have indigestion from too much artificiality, false values, and greed for a merely sensual life. We must attain poverty and nakedness on all levels, not only material, but moral, spiritual, and religious as well.

1. The quest for authenticity means we must totally empty ourselves and let go even of those religious experiences that have calmed, consoled, and comforted us.
2. A significant obstacle in the spiritual journey is spiritual avarice.
3. Poverty and nakedness helps us remove all that is not God and choose only God and the things of God.
4. The purpose of John's approach is not destruction but rather the acquisition of true values.

CHALLENGES FOR TODAY
- You can only find God when you are completely empty and aware of your own poverty and nakedness.
- Only in emptiness can you find freedom of heart.
- Abandon everything that does not strengthen true love.

DAY 75 SPIRITUALITY—A HARD CLIMB

We have already seen that John often used a diagram to explain the spiritual journey. It shows Mount Carmel and all around the peak are listed the fruits of the Holy Spirit, aspects of life that they who reach the summit enjoy. There are three paths that lead into the mountain. Two of them are wide, comfortable, and seem to give easy access to the mountain top; the valley of earthly goods, and the valley of heavenly goods, both of which we mistakenly think lead us to God. Some people falsely think that accumulating either material goods or spiritual goods that could lead to God is the way to growth in the spiritual life—more devotions, prayer structures, religious books, retreats, spiritual directors, and so on. This approach is an example of childish and distasteful spiritual gluttony. On the diagram, both of these valleys are dead ends. In the center is the narrow road that leads directly to the summit, and this straight and narrow path to the summit is a journey of denial. From the top of this mountain everything looks different—the valley below, the journey, the training, yourself, the world, and God.

1. In some versions of John's diagram later artists often show one or both of these paths eventually meandering to the top.
2. Only the narrow road in the middle of the diagram clearly reaches its goal and is the quick way or shortcut to the summit.
3. The center path has many ups and downs, arduous ascents and painful crises.
4. On the center path John of the Cross has written seven times "nothing," reminding us that this ascent requires denial of all that is not God.

CHALLENGES FOR TODAY
- Beware of comfort and easy success in the spiritual journey.
- Which path have you selected?
- Pray for fortitude to endure the climb.

DAY 76 THE CENTER PATH

Many writers before John described the center road as an arduous path in three stages, beginners, proficients, and perfect, corresponding to the three phases of the spiritual journey—purgative, illuminative, and unitive. John explicitly accepts this threefold division but he adds a new insight of his own, a careful analysis of the two crucial tansitions. The transition from beginners to proficients corresponds to the time of contemplation in the passive night of sense. The transition from proficients to perfect is the decisive experience of life and is the passive night of spirit. So, the center path has several ups and downs as a person moves from beginners and the active night of sense through the passive night of sense to a period of illumination and the active night of spirit and on to the passive night of spirit to the final phase of union. This journey is difficult, but we must remember one thing: we are not laboriously journeying forward through all these difficulties; rather God in love is drawing us forward towards the desired goal. The point of departure is not our love for God but God's love for us.

1. Our task is not to fill the journey with effort, but rather to let go of false values that keep us tied down to a disordered life.
2. For those who need it there is a plateau period of rest between the night of sense and the night of spirit.
3. This simple overview of the stages can be helpful provided we always remember that life is more complicated than a sketch.
4. The painful experiences of this journey are often the moments of greatest grace and progress.

CHALLENGES FOR TODAY

- Where do you think you are in this journey?
- Why does John call these transitions "nights"?
- Is your spiritual director knowledgeable about these stages?

DAY 77 THE JOURNEY OF FAITH

There are two emphases, aspects, or levels to this journey; at one time we may emphasize one of them and at other times the other. As long as it is clear that both must go together in an integrated spiritual commitment. First, we must center the journey on faith. This is a process of interiorization and purification of our concepts of God. It is important because the person who does not purify faith remains stunted, never touches the reality of God, drags along behind him or her an image of God from former times, and ends up seeing self when he or she looks at God. God is nothing like we think God is, and we must remove all the idols and false images of God. So, we must eliminate all false, sensible images and all intellectual information about God that we may have valued in the past, for God is not like creatures, and most images we have are just idols. However, in addition to experiencing that God is not like we think God is, we also find that God does not act towards us in the ways we thought God would; God does not correspond to ideas we have of divine life. So, we will find there are two rhythms to the journey of faith; a theoretical one challenging us to purify our image of God, and a vital one in which God in contemplation teaches us that God acts differently towards us than we expected.

1. We can never earn the right to make this journey; it is an invitation from a loving God.
2. Some people do not want to undergo this journey of faith and its purification, because their image of God is part of the comfort and consolation they find in religion.
3. Some people who would like to encounter God do not see God acting in their lives because their image acts like a cataract that hinders clear vision.
4. "However impressive may be one's knowledge or experience of God, that knowledge or experience will have no resemblance to God and amount to very little" (A.2 4.3).

CHALLENGES FOR TODAY
- Have you created your own image of God?
- What have you learned about God in recent years?
- What can you purify about your image of God?

DAY 78 *THE JOURNEY OF LOVE*

We must ask ourselves whether the journey of faith is enough. No! It is not. The journey of love includes an anxious search for the Beloved with all its painful longings, followed by the joy of encounter with its accompanying preoccupation at the possibility of future loss, then total union with the joy of benefits of this love, and finally further intense desire for union in glory. If the journey of faith is the purification of our knowledge of God and of our ways of knowing God, then the journey of love is the purification of our love of God and of our ways of loving God. During this journey of love we will have three different experiences, all contributions to our ways of loving God. First, there is the love of absence: when God seems absent from us, we can experience God's transcendence. Second, there is the love of union: in union we will feel God present in everything and find that true love is participation. This is a time to experience God's love and goodness. Third, there is the experience of absence even when we are in union. In loving union we realize our own insufficiencies and unworthiness, anxiety rises, and we feel absence at a deeper level even though we are in union, for the union is not permanent.

1. "[L]ove alone, which at this period burns by soliciting the heart for the Beloved, is what guides and moves it and makes it soar to God in an unknown way along the road of solitude" (N.2. 25.4).
2. The journey of faith includes a confident loving self-gift that substitutes for light lost in the darkness of the struggle.
3. In the journey of love we must purify our love by controlling desires and satisfaction in anything that is not God.
4. John presents the dynamism and stages of love in the *Spiritual Canticle* and the fullness and satisfaction of union in the *Living Flame*.

CHALLENGES FOR TODAY
- Have you purified the way you love God?
- Do not choose faith or love as your way to God. Rather integrate both.
- To make this journey you will need the beautiful Christian quality of fortitude.

DAY 79 JOURNEY PREPARATIONS

Growth in the spiritual life is primarily God's work within us, we do not earn advancement, but we are being drawn forward by God. For our part we must desire to succeed in this journey; we must really want it more than anything else. Many say they do, but their half-hearted commitment shows clearly it is not a priority for them. We can show our desire by getting rid of any obstacles that hinder progress in the journey. This will include self-discipline, correction of faults, establishing priorities, removal of gratification in anything that leads away from God. We must also cultivate a healthy image of God by finding new ways to know, remember, and love God. While contemplation is God's gift, we can create a suitable environment in which prayer can develop. We need to become comfortable in solitude and meditation, seek genuine freedom of spirit, and appreciate beauty, joy, and enthusiasm.

1. We are not only burdened by false desires and pleasures, but also by what we know, what we remember and imagine, and what we desire and love.
2. These preparations are not easy for they imply leaving something we knew well and moving to the unknown.
3. We should find sacred space and time for prayer, develop a suitable environment that is uplifting with good posture, music, nourishing spiritual reading, and inspiring art.
4. So, four preparations—intense desire, removal of obstacles, cultivation of a healthy image of God, practices to prepare for prayer.

CHALLENGES FOR TODAY
- Should God call you to deeper prayer, you need to be ready.
- Do you have a strong desire to progress in this spiritual journey?
- Do not rush anything; let God set the pace.

DAY 80 SOME DOUBLE QUALITIES

In spirituality there are several indispensable attitudes—double qualities—that at first seem opposed to one another but are not. At one time one quality is needed and, at a different time, another. Patience-urgency. We will need to be patient for maturing is slow, but it is also urgent that we do make progress. Perseverance-flexibility. We must, at all costs, persevere in our efforts, methods, and practices. However, we must also be ready to leave them aside and not become attached to them. Detachment-integration. We must detach ourselves from everything that is not God. However, all aspects of the world are God's gifts and we must not despise them but rather integrate everything in one great commitment to God. Fortitude-emptiness. Fortitude is a gift from God, but it results from our appreciation of our own emptiness that is not weakness but strength. Personal solitude-community. There are times when each is needed, they wax or wane together, and they mutually enrich each other. Live here-live elsewhere. We must unite the two horizons of life—the here and now and the there and then, so that the life beyond this one can give meaning to this one. All-nothing. In order to gain the "all" of God we must desire "nothing" else.

1. If we emphasize only one of each of these qualities to the neglect of the other then problems arise.
2. Spiritual direction or personal discernment can help decide when it is necessary to emphasize one or other of these qualities.
3. These double qualities are mentioned throughout John's writings and bring remarkable balance and maturity to our spiritual journey.
4. The spiritual journey is a cooperative venture; some of these qualities emphasize God's role and others emphasize ours.

CHALLENGES FOR TODAY
- Is yours an all-or-nothing kind of commitment; no half-hearted dedication.
- Never separate the challenges of this life from those of the next, but integrate them.
- In the spiritual journey, maintain balance and avoid extremes.

DAY 81 *THE GOAL OF SPIRITUALITY*

We should always keep our eyes focused on the goal of our spiritual journey. What do we really want out of life? Why are we making this spiritual journey? What are the goals of all our efforts and all our letting go of former things we cherished? What do we hope to be like at the end of this journey? Focusing our attention on the peak of the mountain that we seek to climb becomes a motivation in our struggles to respond to the call of God. The goal we seek is union with God through love. This union is a union of likeness, which means it is a union produced by God's love within us, making us like God in love, and enabling us to love God with the same love with which God loves us. This love purifies us, transforms us, and immerses us in God. While this is God's gift to us, we do have a role to play, especially in the continual phase of purification, as we learn how the darkness of faith leads us to our goal. There will be hard times as we journey to God, but the goal makes all worthwhile.

1. Let us celebrate each stage, realizing all growth is God's gift.
2. The purpose of this journey is to seek union with God in love, but a by-product is the total renewal of our lives.
3. To arrive at this goal we must seek God through the nights making sure every decision is one of love.
4. As we keep our eyes focused on the goal, let us be convinced that there is more to life than we ever thought,

CHALLENGES FOR TODAY
- Make purposeful choices in your spiritual journey.
- Move away from all forms of self-centeredness and move towards self transcendence.
- In your spirituality, maintain a clear focus on the destination; it is the only thing that gives meaning to the struggles of the journey.

DAY 82 *IMPORTANCE OF SPIRITUALITY*

There is nothing more important for each of us than spirituality—that focus on our fidelity to the inner values of our hearts and our response to God. These values come from peak experiences in our lives and motivate us to become our best selves. Some of us will live out our convictions within institutionalized religion, others in non-traditional community experiences, but the majority of us will take personal responsibility to find the means and supports of spiritual life wherever seems best to us. Among all the giants of the spiritual life there is none so clear in his challenges, so well-focused in his system, and so helpful in his suggestions, as St. John of the Cross. Spirituality will embrace, affect, and color every aspect of our lives. It is that constant call to be more authentic in how we live and respond to others and to our world. It is a genuine abandonment to life and to God. Our deepest human qualities and experiences open us to ever newer possibilities and challenge us to continual renewal of life.

1. Spirituality is letting our lives develop in the love-filled atmosphere of God's grace.
2. With God's help, we grow naturally and effortlessly, provided we remove all hindrances to growth.
3. Spirituality implies a concentration on authentic, unconditional love of self, of others, of the world around us, and of God.
4. Can we describe ourselves as people who yearn for union with God in love?

CHALLENGES FOR TODAY
- How would you describe the meaning of your life?
- What do you consider to be the strengths and weaknesses of your present journeying to God?
- Identify values that you wish were part of your life.

DAY 83 *SPIRITUALITY AND THE FUTURE*

Christian spirituality of the future will include perennial values and some new focuses. The great Jesuit theologian, Karl Rahner, suggested five characteristics of the spirituality of the future: 1. The new spirituality will remain the old spirituality of the Church, 2. It will concentrate on what is essential to piety, 3. It will live out of a solitary and immediate experience of God, 4. It will emphasize a sense of Christian community, 5. It will embody a new sense of community. The common components of a perennial Christian spirituality are a sense of baptismal vocation, an awareness that life is grace and gift of God, a commitment to evangelical life, and an openness to new priorities. Each generation strives faithfully to respond to the implications of the Sermon on the Mount for changed times. This renewed and renewing response is to God in worship, to Christ in his redeeming love, to oneself in openness to destiny, to others in their mutual growth, and to the world in its history.

1. Our faithful response to the heart of the great tradition of the Lord will lead to a personal experience of divine life, shared in community, and manifested to the world in the Church.
2. Many elements that make up the fabric of our spiritual lives will need to be developed to deal with contemporary changes.
3. Spirituality consists in men's and women's grace-filled efforts to become who they are capable of being.
4. Christian spirituality is also a faith- and love-filled response in hope to one's destiny under God.

CHALLENGES FOR TODAY
- As a dedicated Christian are you spiritually ready for the future?
- Reflect on the common components of Christian spirituality.
- How are you living the Sermon on the Mount?

DAY 84 *BE AN EVERYDAY MYSTIC*

As Christians who are ready for the future we must be mystics—people who have a genuine experience of God. People of interiority and faith, our Christian spiritual experience will flow from personal experiences of God's mercy, forgiveness, compassion, and love. This experience of faith leads us to live with a sense of wonder, appreciating that the whole of life is aflame with the presence of God. However, life in the Spirit is nurtured in solitude, where we reaffirm faith and re-experience what we believe in. As believers, our experience of God produces the life of faith and hope that results from and causes love. After all, mysticism means not knowing, but experiencing that God is love. It gives rise to a passionate love for life, beauty, and wisdom, a thirsting for life itself—a power that drives us to union. Thus, spirituality, the mystical experience of the living God, is the level of our faith, hope, and love that as Christians we live and foster in others. The call to become a mystic, an ordinary mystic, is the most important challenge of our lives.

1. As Christians we do not share the life of a particular religion with others but the fruit of our own life with God.
2. The love we seek is an integration of eros, philia, and agape; passionate love, friendship love, and the faith- and hope-filled love of Christian community.
3. Having experienced God's love, we then find that this love demands action on behalf of others everywhere.
4. Our spirituality is a daily pilgrimage that requires courage and determination.

CHALLENGES FOR TODAY
- Are you an ordinary, everyday mystic?
- Do you spend enough time in prayer?
- Think about your most profound experience of God?

DAY 85 *SPIRITUALITY AND EMPOWERMENT*

Many know John of the Cross for his rigorous program of denial, and unfortunately they seem unaware that John is above all a master of empowerment. John tells us that God is not seeking negation but offering fullness of life. John himself achieved a wonderful synthesis of experience, thought, and poetical expression. It seems his mystical encounter energized and brought him fulfillment. "God is the 'deepest center' of the life and personality of St. John of the Cross. He is the fount and root of all that John is, does, says, and writes. This is true on the human level of his life as well as on the level of his deep religiosity. . . . John enjoys an exceptional, harmonious unity (of his many qualities). He is in all and above all a man of God" (See Ruiz, p. x).

1. John is one of the most integrated personalities of the history of spirituality.
2. In the center of each of us there is a zone which is naturally divine.
3. Beware of the word detachment in John; he generally seeks integration.
4. Some spiritualities are supremely ineffective. Let us choose ours carefully.

CHALLENGES FOR TODAY
- Would people call you a person of God?
- Pray that God will empower you.
- Is everything you do done for God?

DAY 86 *JOHN KNOWS WHAT HE IS TALKING ABOUT*

John was a very experienced spiritual director as well as a fine theologian and teacher. He had studied key spiritual writers and learned from his extensive spiritual guidance of people from all walks of life. In spiritual matters, he knew what he was talking about. "He was a man of the most enkindled spirituality and of great insight into all that concerns mystical theology and matters of prayer; I consider it impossible that he could have spoken so well about all the virtues if he had not been most proficient in the spiritual life, and I really think he knew the whole Bible by heart, so far as one could judge from the various Biblical passages which he could quote at chapters and in the refectory, without any great effort, but as one who goes where the Spirit leads him" (See Fray Pablo de Santa Maria).

1. John has immersed himself in the Bible and challenges us to do the same.
2. There is so much trivia in religion today, but John is rooted in the perennial solid values of Scripture and theology.
3. Like John we can find daily inspiration for our spiritual journey in Scripture, theology, and the writings of mystics.
4. John shares with others the fruits of his personal experience of the living God. We too should realize that our effectiveness in service of others depends on our experience of God.

CHALLENGES FOR TODAY
- Pope Francis has asked that we read a passage of Scripture every day and even carry a pocket edition of the Bible with us.
- What is your favorite passage of Scripture and why?
- If you have not been readings Scripture daily, begin today!

DAY 87 THE IMPORTANCE OF PRAYER

"To St. Teresa prayer is the greatest of all blessings in this life, the channel through which all the favors of God pass to the soul, the beginning of every virtue and the plainly marked highroad which leads to the summit of Mount Carmel. She can hardly conceive of a person in full spiritual health whose life is not one of prayer" (See Allison Peers, *Ascent*, pp. 83-84). For John of the Cross, as it was for Teresa, prayer is not a practice or exercise but a way of living one's spiritual life. Moreover, both Teresa and John are concerned with growth in prayer and so they give us stages that lead to deeper union with God. Everything else, such as virtues, gifts, and personal talents and potentialities all lead to or support the life of prayer.

1. In his teachings on prayer John presumes that readers know, understand, and practice the rudiments of the spiritual life.
2. To journey through the stages of prayer one must pass through the dark night and learn the importance of emptiness and self-sacrifice.
3. Prayer is life; it must grow and mature, and must never be stunted in primitive forms.
4. Prayer grows in two ways: by our own efforts assisted by God's grace, and by God's action within us.

CHALLENGES FOR TODAY
- Is prayer the most important aspect of your spiritual life?
- Describe how your prayer has matured in recent years.
- Spend time this week praying that God will lead you in prayer.

DAY 88 *JOHN—AN AUTHORITY IN SPIRITUALITY*

John of the Cross is considered by theologians of all generations as one of the greatest of all spiritual and mystical theologians. He has not only received praise for his literary and poetical genius, but also for the depth and perception of spiritual wisdom. In 1926 Pope Pius XI declared John a doctor of the universal Church. His magisterium, found primarily in the four great works, *Ascent of Mount Carmel, Dark Night of the Soul, Spiritual Canticle*, and *Living Flame of Love*, is viewed by many as canonical expressions of the stages in the spiritual life.

"Saint John of the Cross' contributions to mystical theology have been equated with the magnificent contribution made by Saint Thomas Aquinas to dogmatic theology. Through Saint Thomas we have received the ecclesiastical tradition of the Church on questions of religious belief; through Saint John we have inherited an equally venerable tradition on questions of divine love. Both writers combined sainthood with genius—and in the case of Saint John, astonishing poetic fervor" (See Allison Peers, *Living Flame*, Preface).

1. When we follow St. John of the Cross, we put ourselves in reliable hands.
2. It is interesting how John is appreciated by people from so many varied states of life; he is a multi-gifted person who now seeks to guide us to God.
3. John presents us with the most challenging of human goals—transformation in union with God, and shows us how to get there.
4. John is not any spiritual guide. He has been designated by the Church as the Mystical Doctor.

CHALLENGES FOR TODAY
- Prepare yourself well to approach John's teaching.
- If you choose John as your spiritual guide you can have confidence that you will grow.
- You cannot dabble in the teachings of John; you must study him carefully, try to understand his teachings, and then live his challenges.

DAY 89 *THE ESSENTIAL UNITY OF HUMAN BEINGS*

John sees human beings in an essential unity. Every aspect of life must be united in total and complete self-gift to God. When life is not God-directed it moves to focus on the things of this world. Thus, one's capacity is given to God or taken away from God. So, John constantly urges followers to cut themselves away from all that is not God in order to give themselves totally to God. "Fundamental to the whole outlook of the two saints (Teresa and John) is their understanding that the human being is essentially a unity (*Night*, II.i.I), a single entity in whom body and soul are inextricably interdependent. . . . The body does indeed give rise to all kinds of conflicting and disturbing impulses, the 'natural passions' of scholastic psychology; and the inner peace and equilibrium without which one cannot respond freely to the love of God is to be found only by bringing these impulses under control. But the body is also an integral part of the human make-up by which God may be loved and served and glorified" (See Truman Dicken, 366).

1. Every aspect of our lives can be integrated into our total commitment to God. We seek detachment from what is not God.
2. We express the inner values of our hearts and minds through our bodies; they are integral parts of our God-directed lives.
3. John opposes making created things objects in themselves and so substitutes for God.
4. While Teresa and John want us to develop a life of prayer, they spend much time on the importance of growth in virtues as a preparation for prayer.

CHALLENGES FOR TODAY
- Are you free from detachments that hinder growth in prayer?
- You can only find security in continual detachment.
- Think about how you use your body to communicate your inner values.

DAY 90 NO STRAITJACKET FOR SPIRITUAL DEVELOPMENT

While it is true that John presents us with a systematic approach to the spiritual life, he does not want to impose it on anyone. He is not placing us in a straitjacket of absolutely essential stages in spiritual development. The basic stages of spiritual development—beginners, proficients, and perfect, corresponding to the purgative, illuminative, and unitive periods of spiritual growth—have been held by many spiritual leaders for centuries. These stages are not part of a preconceived ascetical program that everyone must follow. Rather, they simply describe what has been observed in the healthy spiritual development of untold numbers of faithful over the centuries. Having observed what has happened to many helps directors in the guidance of others too. However, no one, especially John, wants to suggest that everyone goes through these stages in the same way. Teresa and John have different approaches to these stages while respecting the common elements.

1. We can appreciate the stages in spiritual maturation in general terms without becoming slaves to them. They are very helpful to all of us and especially to spiritual directors.
2. Let us always remember that we are not laboriously achieving one stage after another, but God is drawing us towards divine life, and does so in various ways.
3. Purgation comes first and continues throughout the journey even into later stages; illumination generally comes after purgation and then it too continues; union only comes after purgation and illumination although it can be anticipated in smaller experiences.
4. Some system is necessary, even though we treat it with flexibility.

CHALLENGES FOR TODAY
- Do you have a clear sense of direction in the spiritual life, knowing where you have come from and where you are going?
- Entrust yourself to the Lord and let him guide you.
- Spiritual growth is a personal relationship and you know a lot about stages in interpersonal development from other aspects of life that you can apply to your spiritual growth.

DAY 91 *FAITH AND SPIRITUALITY*

Faith gives us insight into the meaning of life, a sense of community belonging, an understanding of right and wrong, and a sense of wonder and awe. In fact, with dedication we live at the level of mystery, and feel called to develop every facet of our lives in order to become our authentic selves. This is our spirituality, and it refers to becoming a person in the fullest sense, animated and motivated by the values of faith, and enriched by sharing within the faith community. This response includes all aspects of life in depth and in extent.

The life that results from a faith-filled dedication implies in each of us an awareness of a call to continual growth in life, both personally and as community. We feel we cannot stand still but need to be dedicated to something or someone bigger than ourselves, and this clarifies for us our own place in this world and our own destiny. It is the challenge to make every effort to be the best of which we are capable. At the same time, we seek to be critical of our own lives and values, having the humility to leave aside the worst of ourselves, and having the courage to develop our best selves. Fidelity to this response gives meaning to our lives.

1. Can we re-live the profound experiences of our faith?
2. How does our faith give us insight into the meaning of our lives?
3. Let us savor for a while an experience of our faith when we felt God's love touch us in a special way.
4. Let us ask ourselves four key questions: Who are we? Where are we going? How will we get there? When will we get there?

CHALLENGES FOR TODAY

- Think about what you learned from being close to God in your own experience of faith.
- Think about how you experience the fullness of life.
- Consider how you can become a more reflective person.

A contemporary portrayal of John of the Cross.

5

John of the Cross—A Friend and Guide

We have been reflecting on John of the Cross' life, ministry, spiritual direction, and spirituality to give us an idea of who he was and the values that motivated him. Before we turn to reflect on each of his writings, both short and long, let us spend a few days thinking about our own relationship with John. Who can he be for us? What challenges does he present us with?

DAY 92 JOHN CALLS US AWAY FROM INDIFFERENCE

In his Christmas message of 2014, Pope Francis spoke about the globalization of indifference. Certainly, we see indifference all around us; indifference to suffering, poverty, hatred, destruction of life, and fanaticism. We also experience a total loss of a sense of the divine and of the second horizon of life beyond this one. Our world does not seem to have much interest in God and God's values and priorities, and certainly does not think that God has much interest in us. The problem is that many seek God but the wrong God—one who is distant, powerful, and uncaring. How can we break away from this indifference and find God? Some try to find God in religion and in belief systems of those who do not know God and have never really tried to encounter God. But God is not an explanation or a solution, but a gift of love. Religious indifference is a curse to genuine spiritual growth. We have seen that John in his life, ministry, and loving service calls us away from this indifference. We must change ourselves and the situations we are in. If we fail to respond to this call in our hearts, it will rob us of our happiness.

1. What kind of world have we made for ourselves?
2. Confronting indifference is part of the personal and social purification of the dark night.
3. We often do not reject indifference because we are afraid of the consequences of new convictions.
4. We need to daily reject the social evils that impinge upon us.

CHALLENGES FOR TODAY
- Evaluate your own indifference.
- Think about the small God of contemporary religion.
- Meditate on Jesus' words, "Where your treasure is there your heart is also" (Matt. 6.21).

DAY 93 *JOHN CHALLENGES US TO GIVE FOCUS TO OUR SPIRITUAL LIVES*

Often our spirituality provides a framework for our religious hopes, but does no more than indicate just how much further we need to journey. We live within a spiritual framework for years and even become shackled to it, but often we never see the goals we thought were ahead. For the most part in our spiritual lives we wander around, disoriented, until we conclude that the spiritual lives we live are artificial. There is nothing wrong with them—they are just not a recipe for success! John of the Cross presents us with an entire redoing of the spiritual system. He is not interested in any upgrades or additional improvements to what we have. For him, all outer changes are very secondary and are at the most aids in the inner transformation he wants for us. Nothing from the outside works; we must listen to what is within. Most people, even spiritually dedicated, dabble in spirituality. John wants us to give a clear focus to our spiritual lives, and then pursue that vision and goal relentlessly.

1. Let us identify, for example, four of the major focuses of our present spiritual lives.
2. Can we clarify what is our sense of direction in our spiritual commitment?
3. God helps us in this dedication. Our prime role is to remove obstacles to God's involvement.
4. Spirituality can never be a segment of our lives; it is a way of living our entire personal and community reality.

CHALLENGES FOR TODAY
- Check your own life for signs of mediocrity.
- Have you ever pursued spirituality as if it was a flavor of the month?
- Think about the goals you have for your spiritual life. How will you achieve them?

DAY 94 JOHN URGES US TO BECOME CONTEMPLATIVES

If we wish to be prayerful people who can reflect with purpose on John's writings then we need to be people of deep reflection, and we call such people contemplatives. Contemplatives are persons who are comfortable with themselves, at ease with their own strengths and weaknesses, and yearn to identify who they are capable of being. Contemplatives are not afraid to be alone, isolated from others for a while in silence, emptiness, and stillness. Contemplatives are people with a sense of purpose, free from distracting and disintegrating secondary values. Their lives are unified in one great commitment to the vision they pursue. Contemplatives appreciate anything that is beautiful: people, senses, music, art, literature, or drama. Contemplatives are skillful in finding opportunities to reflect, either spontaneously while out in the country or in parks, or by deliberately preparing a part of their home to be conducive to a reflective experience. Contemplatives know the importance of the body for quality reflection and prayer. They take diet and exercise seriously and appreciate that the Christian tradition of fasting can have a healthy impact on a life that is reflective. Contemplation needs nourishing with ongoing education in values, complemented with good literature of all kinds and an awareness of contemporary world events.

1. Growth is a gift, and we do no more than prepare ourselves to receive the gift.
2. Time alone can also be an experience of self-emptying which precedes times of real fulfillment.
3. A contemplative experience cannot be fitted into a tight schedule but needs a prolonged, open-ended time.
4. Authenticity is found in the center of ourselves; not by having more or doing more but by being more.

CHALLENGES FOR TODAY
- Do you want to be a contemplative person?
- Which of the above components are your strengths?
- Which components are your weaknesses?

DAY 95 JOHN ASKS US NOT TO BE AFRAID OF THE UNKNOWN

As we make efforts each day to believe and accept what we do not understand, we should not be afraid of the unknown. The experience of this journey may well suck the life out of us, but it will also lead us to enlightenment. However, we must not make the journey one of spiritual endurance alone, but rather one motivated by love. In this spiritual journey, God's work is our transformation, our contribution is to consent to enter the unknown. We will need courage—the courage of a person fully aware of his or her longing for something or someone beyond the limited known elements of daily life, and aware of the poverty of all human resources and knowledge. We can be clear-eyed about our weaknesses and equally helpless to do anything about them. We can only enter the unknown and wait with watchfulness for God who alone gives growth. If we are fortunate enough to receive God's blessings we will discover openings into the inner world of divine love.

1. Our spiritual journey into the unknown is a long one in which love matures gradually.
2. In the unknown we may not be able to see, but we can still have a clear vision of our lives.
3. We must beware of those who think they know and insist we must know what they know!
4. John calls this journey into the unknown "this adventuring in God."

CHALLENGES FOR TODAY
- Are you convinced that what you know of God is not worth knowing?
- Are you afraid of the unknown?
- What have you learned in recent years about God and what have you unlearned?

DAY 96 *JOHN INSISTS THAT LIFE IS BETTER IN DARKNESS*

As we move ahead to immerse ourselves in John's writings, we will find that he is a master of emptiness and of darkness. He is not concerned about either. In fact, he assures us that life is better in darkness when we can appreciate our own emptiness. What we should be concerned about is the fullness and illumination we think we already have, for they do not lead us to God. We look but do not see. Sometimes it seems we will never get out of the darkness—as John said, we move from darkness to darkness guided by darkness. Everything changes when we encounter God in darkness. Alone we are helpless; with God as our light we can move through darkness. "The light is with you for a little longer. Walk while you have the light, lest the darkness overtake you; he who walks in the darkness does not know where he is going" (John 12:35-36). When we enter darkness in pursuit of God, life becomes better. We can look back and see that living in dark times was a wonderful experience, for the night can be dark, but it can also be guiding, more lovely than the dawn, a time to encounter one's lover. We should never be afraid of darkness and the emptiness it brings for they can help us to see and be filled by the reality of God. In our spiritual lives we must guard against ourselves and the light we think we have. In darkness God can break through our selfish defenses and bring us genuine illumination.

1. Darkness fosters the absolute conviction of divine transcendence.
2. Our spiritual lives can always be enriched by the dawn of darkness.
3. Some people live all day and every day in artificial light.
4. The darkness of which John speaks is the dark night of contemplation.

CHALLENGES FOR TODAY
- Pray that you may benefit from darkness.
- Think about when you last felt alone, empty, and in darkness.
- Prepare your mind and heart for reflecting on John's readings.

DAY 97 *JOHN PLEADS WITH US TO MATURE OUR SPIRITUAL LIVES*

Often in our spiritual lives we seem to drift into semi-consciousness without any spiritual depth or vision of spiritual development. We feel lonely and we long for meaning and fulfillment. John shares his conviction that we find meaning and fulfillment in love; it is the only way to alleviate the personal pain and longing to be who we are called to be. However, our capacity for love depends on the exclusive and integrated focus of every aspect of our lives. John tells us that our lives are longing for healing and health and can only be satisfied with the commitment to the mature development of our spiritual growth. John has no interest in religion's trivia, and he wants us to overcome childish approaches to religion and to spirituality, to help us mature as total human beings, and to guide us in striving for the goal of our destinies. One of John's greatest gifts to us is to introduce disruptions in our normal way of thinking about the spiritual life and thus insist on change and maturity. As we become conscious of our calling, a fresh kind of life emerges and matures. Love gives meaning to life.

1. Are we living without a future?
2. What kind of short or long-term future motivates us?
3. Can we live the fullness of the present moment in view of the goals of our spiritual lives?
4. How can our reflecting on John's readings help us mature in our spiritual lives?

CHALLENGES FOR TODAY
- Have you made great steps in the spiritual life?
- Do organizations you belong to help you mature in your spiritual commitment?
- Do others consider you spiritually mature?

DAY 98 *JOHN CALLS US TO EMBRACE SACRIFICE FOR LOVE*

I recently walked down a street in Tuscany and passed a cultural center that announced that evening an author would read from his recent book, "Il dolore pazzo dell' amore"—"The crazy pain of love." I thought the title was a wonderful interpretation of sacrifice in John. When our world seems to give signs every day of the destruction of love, John responds as a prophet of authentic love that always includes pain and sacrifice. As we turn to read John's writings we will find many examples of sacrifice that seem exaggerated or too focused on the pain of seeking one's lover. I have shared the title of this book with many people who have immediately responded with identification—there is a lot of crazy pain in love. Love has its own ways and they always include renunciation and sacrifice. Kahil Gibran stated: "And think not you can guide the course of Love, for Love, if it finds you worthy shall guide your course." There will be pain, but the pain is part of the harmonious response of love. The development of love is only possible in a heart that is free and has overcome and controlled all attachments of false loves that hurt true love. True lovers embrace the pain and suffering, for sacrifice is seen as a positive reality, part of the mystery of seeking life together.

1. Let us be aware of the signs of love all around us.
2. "Some love lasts a lifetime. True love lasts forever" (Unknown).
3. "Where true love is dwelling, God is dwelling there; Love's own loving presence love does ever share" (Office of readings, week 4, Thursday).
4. God's love is our future hope and it overwhelms and overcomes the depressing misery of our world.

CHALLENGES FOR TODAY
- Don't give up the pursuit of love because of sacrifice.
- What does "the crazy pain of love" mean to you?
- Evaluate whether you have a negative understanding of sacrifice.

DAY 99 *JOHN EXEMPLIFIES HOW FROM SOLITUDE WE BUILD COMMUNITY*

John is the "mystical doctor" who loves solitude and silence. In reading John's writings we will discover the importance he gives to silence, solitude, and passivity in his pursuit of union with God. He puts it simply when he points out that lovers like to be alone together away from everyone else. In fact, he acknowledges that he finds interaction with others a burden. However, when we reflect on his life and read his works we see clearly how his concern and love for others permeates every facet of his spiritual commitment. He might have preferred solitude, but he was a co-founder, reformer, spiritual director, community builder, educator, and a social and religious leader of significant stature. As we read his works we will become part of his community, and we will also discover his challenges to let inner solitude reach out to build community all around us. After all, it is one thing to make yourself better. It is something else to make everyone around you better.

1. What do we think solitude contributes to building community?
2. Let us think about John's contributions to community.
3. As we approach his writings, let us ask John to become our guide and friend.
4. As we prepare to reflect on John's writings let us make sure we free ourselves from all prejudice and preconceptions.

CHALLENGES FOR TODAY
- When you read John's works, do so in times of silence and solitude.
- What does your spiritual commitment contribute to community?
- What do you understand by solitude?

DAY 100 *JOHN OFFERS US HIS FRIENDSHIP AND GUIDANCE*

When we read John's works we should do so with simplicity of spirit, striving to participate in the circle of love he creates. We respect the love that inspires him and seek to share it. We should develop mutual friendship with him, as he endeavors to establish a communion between himself and us, his readers. At the same time we will need a willingness to be empty, receptive, and eager to learn. If we do, there is a chance he will carry us along in the direction he pursues. In his time, people loved John of the Cross and longed for his guidance. It is clear he is forceful and energetic, and longs for our growth. We remember that through all his hardships John maintained his values, strove after unchanging goals, and never became like his persecutors nor succumbed to bitterness. He came through it all an extraordinary human being, who achieved his goals without trampling on anyone, without abusing the power religion gives, and without reducing the ideals he had maintained from his youth.

1. We all need someone special in our lives as a guide whom we can rely on no matter the circumstances. John is such a person!
2. Let us ask ourselves what it is that we like most about St. John of the Cross and his teachings.
3. Let us read about John and get to know his life really well.
4. Once we know what kind of a person John was, we will be enthused by him and his challenges.

CHALLENGES FOR TODAY
- Have your ideas grown since your youth, or weakened?
- Do you think of St. John of the Cross as a friend?
- Do you maintain your values no matter the problems you encounter?

The monastery of the Incarnation where John wrote
many of his sayings.

6

Shorter Works of John of
the Cross—the Sayings

IN addition to letters that John wrote to directees he also
maintained his spiritual direction of followers by means of short
spiritual maxims which he placed in directees' places in the dining
room to help focus their commitment. He started this practice when
he was chaplain at the monastery of the Incarnation in Avila and
continued it later, for example, when he was provincial vicar of
Andalusia. The most important collection is the *Sayings of Light and
Love*, seventy short sayings of particular importance because we still
have the original handwritten copy, preserved in the parish church of
Andújar. In addition to the Andújar collection there are others:
Maxims on Love, Degrees of Perfection, and *Other Counsels*. There are
now a total of 175 sayings, and in some editions they are presented as a
single collection. The major themes of the sayings are the necessity of
spiritual direction, denial of one's appetites, the importance of being
guided by reason rather than feelings of taste, the nature of authentic
love, and intimacy with God. In the next few days we can reflect on the
wisdom contained in these sayings that often successfully condense

John's spiritual vision in a single short statement. Each of the readings in this section is a summary of a few of John's sayings that have a common theme and a clear and specific focus. They are short reminders of key ideas that form part of his total picture of the spiritual life.

DAY 101 *PURIFYING FALSE DESIRES*
(See *Sayings*, 22, 23, 40, 41, 43, 56, 98, 125)

In our spiritual journey we must purify ourselves from false desires that lead us away from God. We are only truly free when we control our pursuit of false desires and comforting spiritual consolations. This will demand of us self-sacrifice, abandonment, humility, and submission of heart. Keep in mind that when we focus on objects of worldly interest as ends in themselves they can never strengthen the spirit, but only the Spirit of God can. Let us shake off all the cares of false desires and quiet them. We must detach ourselves from addiction to things, whether exterior or interior that are not focused on God. What we need most in the spiritual life is to silence all our faculties and false desires before our God, for God listens to silent love.

1. Only when we empty our spirit from false attachments to creatures can we create space for God.
2. We are moving in the right direction when we take control over things and neither seek satisfaction in them nor are saddened when they fail to satisfy us.
3. If we purify our attachment to things we will understand them spiritually and enjoy their truth and reality.
4. God is inaccessible and so beyond all that our faculties of intellect, memory, and will can comprehend

CHALLENGES FOR TODAY
- Purify yourself of all false attachments and God will grant you God's own purity, satisfaction, and will.
- Don't destroy your desires; rather integrate and use them to propel you to total dedication to God.
- Your spiritual commitment is a journey away from self-centeredness to centering life on God.

DAY 102 DETERMINATION IN THE SPIRITUAL JOURNEY (See *Sayings*, 1, 3, 4, 42, 85, 95, 103, 168)

We undertake the spiritual journey surrounded by the evils of this world, but accompanied always by the wisdom and gifts of God. We will need tenacity of spirit in face of the many burdens and trials that we will encounter in our journey, and also courageous and persevering dedication as we journey on. Religion is not only a source of delights, but we should choose a robust spirit, detached from everything that is not God.

1. We must bear fortitude in our hearts in opposition to anything that is not God, living as a friend of the crucified Christ.
2. We are not the principal agents of growth in our journey; it is all gift from God. God does not look at the greatness of our achievements but the greatness of our humility.
3. Lukewarmness in our dedication is close to total failure.
4. Although we are being drawn by God through the various stages of our journey, we must still exercise determination in our grace-filled efforts and responses.

CHALLENGES FOR TODAY

- Look at your spiritual journey over this last year; how much determination have you shown?
- What needs does God answer in your life and what needs does God create in your life?
- Do you think you have made any progress in the spiritual life in the last few years? If yes, why? If no, why not?

DAY 103 *PRACTICAL ASCETICISM*

(See *Sayings*, 61, 62, 71, 72, 75, 79, 80, 81, 82, 90, 91, 92, 93, 94, 96, 109, 122, 159, 161, 170)

In daily life, we should control speech and thoughts, feed our spirit on God alone, and always be attentive to the love of God in all we do. Let us enter within ourselves and concentrate on the Lord within us, never allowing anything that lacks spiritual substance to distract us. We should endeavor to abide in recollection, forgetful of all created things. In fact, we should accept trials with love as a way of pleasing the Lord by accepting his will. Let us be interiorly detached from making temporal things ends in themselves, and rather concentrate on God alone. A critical part of our practical asceticism is our attitude to others. We should never listen to others' faults or peoples' complaints about others. Let us strive never to offend anyone by speech, don't contradict them, don't bother whether others support us or are against us.

1. Let Christ crucified be enough for us as we imitate his sufferings and self-sacrifice.
2. Wisdom comes through love, silence, and sacrifice, and knows nothing is gained from concern about others' comments, actions, achievements, and lives.
3. Voluntary imperfections, including unconquered attachments, hinder divine union.
4. If we endeavor to withdraw from earthly things we will approach closer to God.

CHALLENGES FOR TODAY

- A simple agenda in your asceticism is to reject evil, always do good, and constantly seek peace.
- In cultivating recollection, practice stillness of body, inspiration by the Spirit, concentration with Christ, and silence in God.
- Review your attitudes and responses to others.

DAY 104 MODELING OUR LIVES ON THE
LORD'S (See Sayings, 44, 50, 87, 100, 127, 169)

God will always grant us what we need. In fact, God longs to grant us divine union, participation in God's own life. Even now, any goodness we possess is lent to us by God. However, we should seek God, especially God's infinite knowledge and hidden secrets, rather than the comforting blessings of God. Above all we must endeavor to model our lives on the Lord's. We must forgive others as the Lord lovingly lifts up anyone who offends him. He never distances himself from those who offend him but remains close at hand. For our part we live inwardly and outwardly crucified with Christ and thus attain fullness of life with him. So, let us desire all that is rugged and toilsome. Modeling our lives on the Lord's we must seek inner recollection and contemplation. Never abandon prayer; it is one of the most important things we do.

1. The Father spoke one Word, the Son, in the silence of our hearts, and we base our lives on this Word.
2. The purest suffering in love, modeled on Christ's, leads to purest understanding.
3. God is essentially generosity towards us, and we should strive to bring this generosity to birth in our own lives and in relation to others.
4. We should concentrate on important things, seek silence and solitude, responsiveness to the Holy Spirit, and the will of God.

CHALLENGES FOR TODAY
- Read as an aid to meditation; pray as a step to contemplation.
- Do you think people who see you are convinced you model your life on Christ's?
- Which key qualities of the Lord do you lack?

DAY 105 SETTING A DIRECTION
(See *Sayings*, 2, 12, 13, 32, 44, 45, 46, 48, 123, 125, 135, 136, 137, 146)

We seek God with simple and pure love, knowing God is also seeking us. Our approach includes purity of conscience, obedience, and submissiveness. We must utilize every opportunity offered to us to grow in the Lord; if we lose an opportunity we may never recover it. Our reason will tell us what is conducive to the ways of God, so let us leave aside what is simply to our liking and do things according to reason and justice.

A key element in setting a direction for ourselves is a spirit of poverty. We must strive to be content with nothing and be satisfied with our own emptiness. This alone will bring tranquility and peace of soul. We should maintain an honest sense of self-concept with humility, not displaying our own gifts and blessings, but recognizing they all come from God. It means recognizing our own creatureliness and emptiness, and appreciating our need of God. Let's be unselfish and always give praise to others.

1. Let us identify what are the overriding convictions of our lives.
2. As Christians we have a destiny in this world and with God's help must achieve it.
3. What role do our closest friends and family play in setting our direction in life?
4. Let us describe ourselves to God.

CHALLENGES FOR TODAY
• Do you plan and strategize for growth in your spiritual life?
• Who among your friends and acquaintances do you admire and desire to imitate?
• Explain what you understand by poverty.

DAY 106 JOURNEYING WITH THE LORD
(See *Sayings*, 30, 33, 34, 36, 39, 53, 54, 68, 81, 88, 102, 124, 126, 128, 134, 142, 144)

We often do not know the Lord because we focus more on things than on God. If we are rooted in God, everything around us can change, but our unchanging center is God. All our thoughts should be concentrated on the spirit of God, never forgetting we need nourishing by the Lord. When we remain peaceful and disinterested in all else, God dwells in us. Let us remember more is gained from God's good gifts than from all our efforts. We must journey always in the presence of God. So, as we journey through life, let us draw near in silence to the Supreme Good, resting in his arms. We must surrender ourselves to God if we seek God's surrender to us. We should strive to keep God ever present to us and strive to preserve the complete single-minded commitment God teaches. In our spiritual journey we need the support of a master and guide. No matter how virtuous, each of us needs a guide to draw the best out of us and to be there to challenge us when we fail.

1. "Going everywhere, my God, with you, everywhere things will happen as I desire for you" (S. 53).
2. We don't need to be afraid of falling as we journey, especially when someone is there to help us rise, for two working together can achieve more than each one separately.
3. In our journey we maintain a loving attentiveness to God without seeking spiritual consolations.
4. John suggests that in one sense we should live in this world as if only we and God lived here. Although in another sense he was always attentive to the needs of others.

CHALLENGES FOR TODAY
- Rejoice in the Lord who is your salvation; accept all suffering for love of him.
- Make your journey one of daily surrender.
- Who is your guide or companion on your spiritual journey?

DAY 107 PURITY OF INTENTION
(See *Sayings*, 20, 21, 73, 74, 75, 76, 83, 105, 116)

Good works should be done in secret without showiness, but rather in pure love of God. We should give to God what God asks of us rather than anything to which we are inclined. One of our tasks is to constantly examine our thoughts, words, and deeds, making sure all are centered on God. Let us remember that we must all appear before God in judgment. We know we must walk the narrow path, take care of idle use of our tongue, with knowledge that although many are called few respond. We must use our time well so we don't look back with sorrow. We should cleanse ourselves of all false desires, attachments, and ambitions. In light of judgment we should preserve a habitual remembrance of eternal life.

1. When Scripture lists purity of heart among the beatitudes, it refers to the single-minded and single-hearted pursuit of God.
2. We must live here amidst all the challenges of contemporary life while also living elsewhere—motivated by the life beyond this one.
3. Let us reflect on the short reading, asking what we can add to it to guarantee purity of intention.
4. We should ask ourselves if our daily decisions reflect a God-directed life.

CHALLENGES FOR TODAY
- Is your life contaminated by interests that weaken the purity of your intention and commitment?
- What would you like to be doing now in view of the final judgment?
- Are you satisfied with the use of your time?

DAY 108 *IN THE SERVICE OF THE LORD*

(See *Sayings*, 37, 59, 70, 72, 79, 104)

We should never wait until we feel like doing something in the service of the Lord; we should respond whenever the opportunity presents itself. So let us respond, whether we feel like it or not. Let us make ourselves available to the Lord, aware that doing more and more is less important than serving with good will without any concern for possessiveness and human respect. To serve God truly we must leave aside everything and seek solitude, prayer, spiritual reading, and forgetfulness of all else. In this way we bear authentic witness in our concern for others. After all we are beneficiaries of God's loving self-gift and we should do the same for others.

1. Serve God according to the divine will and take nothing else into account, abide in peace and banish cares.
2. In performing your service deny yourself, submit to God, and then you will make progress.
3. We should try to make sure that a spirit of service of the Lord permeates everything we do.
4. Why should we think that John prefers "holy idleness" to ministerial involvement?

CHALLENGES FOR TODAY

- In what ways do you serve the Lord?
- How does God want you to serve?
- Does the Lord need your service?

DAY 109 *FACING TRIALS*

(See *Sayings*, 57, 58, 64, 66, 69, 164, 171)

We should not be disturbed by the trials and adversities of this world, but should rejoice in whatever the Lord sends us. We need not become saddened by the adversities of our times, for we do not know their true role in the plan of God. Among the important and difficult trials we must face is aridity in our spiritual life, that total lack of satisfaction in our religious dedication. God values our acceptance of dryness in our spiritual lives and suffering for love more than all spiritual consolations. We must deny all minor desires and seek never to do our own will but always do everything in conformity with the will of God

1. Our spiritual life demands control of the will more than knowledge, self-sacrifice more than pleasure and satisfactions.
2. In tribulation we should draw near to God with confidence. In joys and pleasure we should ask that we not be deceived.
3. In aridity and trial let us submit ourselves to God's will.
4. Suffering for love is greater than many activities.

CHALLENGES FOR TODAY
- Try to be patient with yourself as well as with your neighbor.
- Identify the present trials that cause you pain.
- Examine yourself to see if your will is in union with God's will for you.

DAY 110 LOVE
(See *Sayings*, 29, 30, 54, 60, 97, 115, 118, 129, 130, 167)

If we become hardhearted because of self-love we start a process of self-degradation and become ever more coldhearted and cannot get out of it without God's help. However, the evil intolerance and lack of respect for humanity should be addressed by us, individually and as community. If we are aflame with love we become soft and gentle, meek, humble, and patient. In the evening of life we will be judged on our love, and so we should learn to love as God desires, for one who loves never grows tired in his or her dedication. Love leads to detachment and imitation of the Lord's suffering and self-sacrifice, and then such love protects us from sin.

1. "The love of God in the pure and simple soul is almost continually in act" (S. 54).
2. Let us become old friends of God, friends who never fail God.
3. When we reach and practice the love of God it helps us control the movements of sin.
4. John says that the love of God is so little known but whoever finds it has discovered a treasure.

CHALLENGES FOR TODAY
- Does your love of God overflow in love of neighbor.
- Remember there is no love without detachment and suffering.
- Preserve a loving attentiveness to God throughout each day.

DAY 111 *SEEKING DEEPER LOVE*
(See "Prayer of a soul taken with love")

We pray for God's help in the pursuit of love, knowing God will always be with us when we seek deeper love. We can do everything for the love of God, and dedicate ourselves totally to the discovery of the God of love. Sometimes we think our sins hold us back, or that God is reluctant to grant us this gift of love. We might even think God is waiting for our good works or desires to see greater commitment to the sufferings that lead to love. Then again we remember that there is no reason for God to wait, we are not earning anything, everything is gift anyway. We cannot free ourselves from lowly ways of loving unless God achieve this for us. In this great gift of love God gives us everything else. So, John can proclaim, "all things are mine; and God Himself is mine and for me, because Christ is mine and all for me." We must never accept anything less that this total gift of God's love and be always ready to receive it.

1. This beautiful saying develops in a continuing crescendo from the misery of sin, to humble abandonment, to confidence in Jesus, and finally to the enthusiastic possession of everything in the Lord.
2. This extraordinary saying sounds like an autobiographical summary of John's life.
3. There is no reason to wait for God's great love, we have it already.
4. We must continue to remind ourselves that we do not earn this love; it is a gift.

CHALLENGES FOR TODAY
- Do you insistently seek deeper love of the Lord?
- Do you live aware that you are immersed in God's love?
- If you reject everything but God, you will possess everything in God.

DAY 112 *STRIVING FOR PERFECTION*
(See in some editions of John's works, *Degrees of Perfection*, 1-17)

In striving for perfection we must make some firm decisions. First, we need to avoid all sin, serious and lesser, as well as all imperfections. This must include avoiding all distractions, especially those coming from involvement in other peoples' affairs. Also we should avoid interference in what doesn't concern us, obstinately involving ourselves as if we have responsibility when we do not. Let us remember, never give up prayer, in spite of difficulty and dryness.

Second, persevere in mental prayer at all costs; likewise constantly practice examination of conscience. Use time well, always centering on the love of God. Let us keep things in perspective, with great humility, aware of our own place in life, our sinfulness, then faithfully carry out our duties.

Third, let us live in the presence of God, giving honor to God in all we do. Let God be the only final goal of our lives, for this is our purpose and destiny—the only reason we came into this world. As we journey, let us remember that everything that happens is part of God plan for us. In daily life we should give precedence to others without any concern or interest in ourselves.

1. If we desire perfection, we must abandon our own wills, take up poverty of spirit, follow Christ in meekness and humility, and carry our own cross (*Counsels*, 7).
2. We do not earn perfection. In fact, our contribution is to seek emptiness.
3. We must never cling to old ways and methods of seeking perfection, but be ever open to God's new challenges.
4. Making decisions in light of death aids our concentration on perfection.

CHALLENGES FOR TODAY
- Can you hide in your own nothingness (*Counsels*, 5)?
- What would make your life more spiritually perfect?
- What disrupts your efforts to strive for more perfect dedication to the Lord?

A view of the castle of Segovia from the Carmelite monastery.

7
Shorter Works—Poetry

We turn our attention to some of John of the Cross' minor poetical works. Brevity is a poor criterion for any approach to his works, but it helps us to bring together some of the works seldom considered and often overshadowed by his great classical masterpieces. In this section we will reflect on his poetry. The three most important poems that John wrote are those that precede his major works. He also wrote nine "Romances" or ballads on the Trinity and Incarnation, together with a tenth on the psalm 137, "By the waters of Babylon." John also wrote five poetic glosses, that is, a series of stanzas that comment on a basic theme, repeating it in the last line of each stanza. Two of these glosses contain "a lo divino" in the title, indicating that they are secular poems transposed to a spiritual level. Then there are two poems of exceptional beauty that are generally considered apart; "For I know well the spring," and "A lone young shepherd."

DAY 113 *THE TRINITY'S LIFE OF ETERNAL LOVE* (See "Romances," 1)

In the first "Romance" John presents the vision of the eternal life of God and the shared love in the intercommunication of the Trinity, and the three Persons' eternal mutual loving. The Three are bound together in eternal love. The eternal begetting of the Word is an act of love by the Father, and their sharing of love is the Holy Spirit, so that there is "one beloved among all three." The Trinity's life of love is the example on which we base our personal lives and our life in community. One author calls this vision of love, "the Gospel of John of the Cross." It presents us with the only way of life suitable for John's vision and for our own ultimate journey.

1. These poems were written before the major works and are the theological foundation for all else.
2. These poems focus on God's plan for the world, and they complement the disciple's return journey to God which John describes in his four major works.
3. Everything John presents in his other works that describe our return journey to God is modelled on God's journey to us described in these poems.
4. A boundless love unites the Trinity; love is the essence of the Trinity

CHALLENGES FOR TODAY
- Is love the essence of who you are?
- Is your relationship with others based on love?
- Reflect on the Trinity as the model for your own life.

DAY 114 *THE TRINITY COMMUNICATES WITH EACH OTHER IN LOVE* (See "Romances," 2)

In the second "Romance," John describes how the communication between the Three Persons is expressed in love. It describes the dynamism of love internal to the Trinity that then extends itself to the world. The Father's love for the Son sets the scene for all future spirituality: "My Son, I will give myself to him who loves you, and I will love him with the same love I have for you, because he has loved you whom I love so." So, the Father loves the Son's disciples for one reason only—because they love the Son. This is Christianity's agenda. It is the core of the Gospel teaching on which we must focus our spiritual commitment. It distinguishes the Christians' approach to the Church and to the world.

1. Love always wants to extend itself, and the Trinity extends its love to the world.
2. We are called to find satisfaction in the love of the Son.
3. The Father shares his love with those who are like the Son.
4. In a world full of hatred, Christianity's message is that love is the basis for human interaction.

CHALLENGES FOR TODAY
- The Father loves in you what he has always loved in the Son. In what ways are you like the Son?
- Do you always communicate with others in love?
- Think about your contribution to community, local, parish, and beyond.

DAY 115 *CREATION AS A PROJECT OF LOVE*
(See "Romances," 3)

The third step in the Father's strategy of love is the plan to extend the love between Father and Son to the whole creation. The third "Romance" is a dialogue between Father and Son. The former wanting a bride for the Son, and the latter wanting a bride who glorifies the Father. The bride that the Father gives the Son is the created world. This reminds us of the words of the evangelist John, "For God so loved the world that he gave his only Son, so that everyone who believes in him may not perish but may have eternal life" (John 3.16). So, the love we find in the world is an epiphany of God's love for us all. This world must be loved, nurtured, tenderly cared for in all its dimensions. As Christians we can and should re-create the world.

1. The purpose of creation is to extend the love between the Father and the Son.
2. This is the first reference in John to what he calls "spiritual marriage," a profound union of believers with God and a reflection of the life of love in the Trinity.
3. We deserve to share the company of the Father if we love the Son.
4. The Son pledges to show the world how great the Father's love is.

CHALLENGES FOR TODAY
- Reflect on why the Father loves you.
- Can you set the world on fire with love for God?
- What part do you play in God's strategy of love?

DAY 116 FURTHER THOUGHTS ON CREATION
(See "Romances," 4)

The decision between Father and Son to extend their love to the whole world seems so right to them that the Father declares, "Let it be done." The world is created because the Son's love deserves it. This world is called to love. It is divided into two realms, a higher one of spiritual beings, and a lower one where humanity dwells. But the Son's love binds everything together. The higher level already possesses the Son's love in joy and gratitude, while those of the lower level strive and yearn for the same love because of their faith. The Son helps them by becoming one of them, abiding in them, and guiding them to the love he teaches. Thus, he lives and loves in them, bringing them together as one community of love.

1. Love is the reason for the world and its destiny.
2. Christian faith centers on love; we believe in love.
3. John tells us that God finds joy in a world in which people love each other.
4. Jesus did everything he could to identify with each of us, including the Incarnation. Do we seek to identify and discover common ground with others or do we compare and discriminate?

CHALLENGES FOR TODAY
- Live in love and strive for greater love.
- Are you ever caught up in this world's competitiveness, indifference, loveless, and hate-filled approach to life?
- See if you can strategize to extend love, as the Father and Son did.

DAY 117 *THE WORLD'S HOPE FOR THE COMING OF LOVE* (See "Romances," 5-6)

Creation is a loving gift from Father to Son, a way in which the Father extends his love to the world. The promise of stanza four, a promise of love, becomes the hope of this fifth stanza. This hope is portrayed in the longings of humanity throughout salvation history, as people sought a savior who would transform the world. This hope is expressed by the prophet Simeon in the Gospel of Luke, and when he encounters Jesus he rejoices in the salvation he brings. These longings continue today when people everywhere yearn for a transforming vision that can lead them to healing, transformation, and love.

1. While humanity yearns for transformation, God takes a gamble with us, hoping we will respond in love.
2. Simeon who longed for transformation for most of his life recognized it when he saw Jesus. Let us hope that we do too.
3. Our world cries out for the healing presence of love. It is an indication of how much the world needs God.
4. Love is God's strategy for dealing with the world. What is ours?

CHALLENGES FOR TODAY
- The answer to your yearnings has come. Receive it and live accordingly.
- Imitate Jesus and show others how to love.
- Set up a plan for extending love to those around you.

DAY 118 *THE INCARNATION OF LOVE*

(See "Romances," 7)

The seventh "Romance" describes the Incarnation, in which the lover becomes like the one he loves. The Father urges the Son to become like his bride, and the Son responds in love to the Father by willing the Incarnation; and so the Son takes on the full mantle of humanity. The Father stresses the need for likeness between the lover and the beloved to create perfect love between lovers, "that the lover becomes like the one he loves." John will continue this theme in the *Spiritual Canticle*. In this new life the Son affirms his love is so strong "I will die for her" and "I will restore her to you." So the cycle of love returns to the Trinity from which it started.

1. John sees the Incarnation as the Son's design to establish a likeness of love.
2. In the *Living Flame*, John tells us that we understand creation through God and not God through creation.
3. Christianity is the only religion that bases its entire teachings on God's love for the world and all humanity.
4. Jesus says he will die to prove love. What are the limits of our love?

CHALLENGES FOR TODAY

- Examine the quality of your love for family, friends, co-workers, and others throughout the world.
- Do others think of you as a loving person?
- Work in your local church to give priority to Jesus' vision of love.

DAY 119 *THE BIRTH OF LOVE* (See "Romances," 8-9)

The eighth and ninth "Romances" bring the hope, the plan, and the promise into history through the revelation of Jesus' conception and birth through the mother, Mary. This is the moment of the spiritual marriage of the Son with the world. John presents it as the extraordinary betrothal of the baby by his mother to humanity; "Men sang songs and angels melodies celebrating the marriage of two such as these." Thus, the Son comes to his bride and the world is turned upside down because of the love of the Father and the Son; "such an exchange; things usually so strange." Certainly, this is the strangest conviction in the history of humanity, that God so loves the world that he sends the Son to show us love, call us to love, and teach us to love. God's love manifested in Christ draws us to divine love.

1. This vision of God as essentially love that reaches out in love to us all is the point of departure for understanding John's works.
2. This divine love transforms our human love into an extension, and then a participation, in God's own life of love.
3. The whole world around us constantly gives us reminders of God's love.
4. Why is it that so few leaders live out of a vision of love?

CHALLENGES FOR TODAY
- Give some time this week to celebrating God's love for you.
- Reprioritize your values to make sure that love is the first.
- Mary gave birth to love, how can you do that in daily life?

DAY 120 LONGING FOR GOD'S DELIVERANCE
(See "By the waters of Babylon" Psalm 137)

This commentary on Psalm 137 seems like a tenth "Romance." It is not directly linked to the other nine, but it portrays the psalmist's pain, hope, and longing for God's deliverance and for salvation in Jesus. John writes this in the first person, and it becomes an appropriate expression of his own love and longing for deliverance from his prison. John says, "And there love wounded me and took away my heart." Then he goes on, "I begged love to kill me since it had so wounded me." "I threw myself in its fire. . . . I died within myself for you." He longs for the deliverance that only love can bring.

1. This is a beautiful poem that describes love's painful longing for union.
2. Richard Rolle, in *The Fire of Love*, wrote, "All or nothing he accepts . . . . God does not bother with half-hearted love."
3. These "Romances" set the scene for everything else that John writes. Spiritual life does not begin with our journey to God but with God's journey to us.
4. Let us review with friends what are the deepest longings of our lives.

CHALLENGES FOR TODAY
- Do you ever think of throwing yourself into the fire of God's love?
- Is love the central experience of your life?
- Describe the most intense experience of love you have ever had. What can you learn from it?

DAY 121 UNKNOWING
(See "I entered into unknowing")

The journey through the nights includes the purification of our knowledge of God. Our part in the journey is to "unknow" what we previously thought, relied on, and cherished as insights into God. We lay aside the security we formerly had and enter into darkness, as our intellect abandons all that generally formed its normal object. We discover that we do not know God by the accumulation of information but by a total commitment in faith. This unknowing transcends all knowledge. John wrote about this experience in the *Ascent* and *Dark Night*, but also gave us a glimpse into this experience in this poem "I entered into unknowing." In the poem he explains the concept of unknowing. This contemplative experience brings an understanding of great things, and in this profound solitude one enjoys peace and holiness. It is an overwhelming experience, beyond the senses; a new understanding which the person does not understand. It implies leaving aside all previous knowledge, and soaring to a new unknowing that transcends all knowledge.

1. This new knowledge is received passively; we do not earn it.
2. In contemplation we cut ourselves free from all that we formerly knew.
3. This contemplative experience is a work of God's mercy.
4. Only when we are empty of former ways of knowing can we encounter God in a way that transcends all knowledge.

CHALLENGES FOR TODAY
- Let this poem remind you that the greatest knowledge you have of God is nothing compared to who God is.
- Reflect on your image of God, picking out aspects that may be false.
- Is your image of God dependent on someone else's image of God?

DAY 122 *LONGING TO SEE GOD*
(See "I live, but not in myself")

This poem describes how a person suffers with longing to see God, exclaiming in the last line of each stanza, "I am dying because I do not die." Knowing that total union is not possible in this life, the soul's longing is so intense that he or she wants to die in order to be with his or her lover. "I cannot live without God." This present life is an imprisonment, "no life at all"; in fact, "I pity myself for I go on and on living"; "I am dying because I do not die." Partial experiences of God's presence always help but also remind one of the pain of God's absence, "since I do not see you as I desire." So, the person in the poem is longing for his or her true life, and tells God "I do not desire this life . . . this life that I live is no life at all." The intensity of desire to be with God shows that even if it means death to this life, it is exactly what the person in the poem wants—to be with God in eternity, where he or she can say, "Now I live because I do not die."

1. St. Teresa of Avila wrote a poem with the same first line and similar themes. If we were to write a poem on this topic what would we say?
2. The person in this poem speaks like the bride in the *Spiritual Canticle* and reading her comments could be complementary to this poem.
3. This poem is an expression of one's desire to see God; it is a poem about hope.
4. This is a love poem that presents us with the pain of love.

CHALLENGES FOR TODAY
- Think about the greatest longings of your life.
- Reflect on the pain of love in your own life.
- What kind of love do you hope for?

DAY 123 *SEEKING LOVE* (See "I went out seeking love")

This poem substitutes the image of hunting for prey instead of longing for love. The motivation for this hunt, "this adventuring in God," is love alone. It still presents the pain and darkness of this pursuit; "since I was seeking love the leap I made was blind and dark." In spite of the difficulties, one must seek love with unfaltering hope, for "this seeking is my only hope." In the spiritual hunt one focuses living on Christ and thus purify our hope in him. John points out that seeking temporal love never satisfies and only leads to frustration, whereas, "the hope of heaven attains as much as it hopes for."

1. This is a secular poem to which John gives a religious interpretation, reminding us how human love stories have much to offer us in our journey to God.
2. Each stanza ends with the conviction of achieving the goal of the hunt, "That I took the prey."
3. We must dedicate ourselves to the pursuit of love. "This seeking is my only hope."
4. This poem links together with care and vision the three theological virtues of faith, hope, and love.

CHALLENGES FOR TODAY
- Reflect on John's thought that this conquest is achieved in darkness.
- Plan carefully for this hunt and you will not be disappointed.
- What are your greatest hopes?

DAY 124 *A KEY ATTITUDE DURING THE SPIRITUAL JOURNEY*
(See "Without support yet with support")

This poem describes a key attitude that one must maintain during the spiritual journey. When one journeys "without support" of any created things, one will then discover that he or she is "with support" of God. This is the journey of strong love, for it implies "living without light, in darkness." It is similar to the idea of experiencing God's presence even though God seems absent in our prayer life. This poem is divided into three stanzas successively focusing on faith, hope, and charity. One's faith leads a person to radical trust in God, and to abandon everything except the pursuit of God. One's hope for heaven gives meaning to this life. One's love turns everything to goodness, a delightful flame that transforms the whole of life.

1. The disciple is dissatisfied with everything else except the pursuit of the love of God.
2. This is a secular poem that John of the Cross interprets to focus on religious values.
3. It does not matter whether things go well or badly, love can turn all to God.
4. This is one of the occasions when John mentions the living flame of love.

CHALLENGES FOR TODAY
- Disentangle yourself from created things that distract you from God.
- Does hope throw light on your journey? How?
- What are your supports in life?

DAY 125 *RESTLESS IN THE PURSUIT OF GOD*
(See "Not for all beauty")

Once a disciple has experienced the beauty of God nothing else will ever bring satisfaction. The main metaphor of this poem is food and eating, and John compared all the delights of this world to those of the next life, which he calls the "I don't know what." The former bring no satisfaction, "they tire the appetite and spoil the palate." This is because "He who is sick with love . . . finds his tastes so changed." Such a person becomes sick of all creatures and cannot find contentment except in God. This poem describes "a person so in love, who takes no delight in all creation," but longs for a loving union beyond this world's limitations, "for I-don't-know-what which is so gladly found."

1. This is a secular poem transposed to a religious level. It takes on extraordinary meaning for John who identifies beauty as the essence of God.
2. This journey requires a generous heart that never delays in advancing.
3. We must always keep in the forefront of our minds and hearts the end of the journey so that it can motivate us.
4. Appreciation of God's beauty is only open to those of faith.

CHALLENGES FOR TODAY
- Think about what really satisfies you in life.
- Are you restless to find God or is your commitment to the journey haphazard?
- Do you ever have indigestion from religious devotions that lead you nowhere?

DAY 126 *SAVED FROM A LOVELESS LIFE*
(See "A lone young shepherd")

In this poem, one of the most beautiful of all John of the Cross' poems, the shepherd is Christ and the shepherd-girl is humanity. Thus, the poem is an expression of the foundational story of Christianity: the good shepherd who gives his life for those he loves. His love is so strong he willingly lives in pain, "his heart an open wound with love." What brings pain to the shepherd is that in spite of his love for humanity, men and women frequently forget him, they ignore or draw away from his love, and they do not seek the joy of his presence. Nevertheless, his love continues, "he bows to brutal handling in a foreign land," and even goes to death on the cross to show his love. The poem describes the selfless love of the shepherd and gives no sign of the shepherd-girl's love. It is a reminder of how the redemptive love of the good shepherd redeems the shepherd-girl—humanity from a loveless life.

1. "A lone young shepherd" is a beautiful secular love poem that John transposes to a religious level (a lo divino).
2. Let us remember that the shepherd "weeps in knowing he's been forgotten."
3. This is wonderful synthesis of Christ's love for each of his disciples.
4. Strong love always includes pain.

CHALLENGES FOR TODAY
- Do you ever ignore or draw away from the Lord's love?
- Reflect on how much God has loved you in Christ.
- Re-examine your own love for others alongside Christ's for you.

DAY 127 *THE WATERS OF LIFE*
(See "For I know well the spring that flows and runs")

This is a particularly beautiful poem that describes the soul who rejoices in knowing God through faith. When John wrote this poem, he had been deprived of the Eucharist for six months, living in his dark cell, with little light and overwhelmed by darkness. He can hear the rhythmic flowing of the river Tagus outside his cell. In this poem he professes his experience of God through faith in the Trinity; the Father—the eternal spring, without origin, whose bottomless love nurtures the world; the Son, "the stream that flows from this spring" and the Holy Spirit, "the stream proceeding from these two." Then John affirms that his entire faith in God is now expressed in the Eucharist, "this living bread for our life's sake," that satisfies us totally. He concludes "This living spring that I long for, I see in this bread of life." This is an expression of John's faith totally permeated by love. He weaves biblical themes of living water and bread of life throughout this beautiful doctrinal presentation. He ends each stanza with the insistent refrain "although it is night." He can satisfy his thirst for God "although living in darkness, because it is night." Night for John is guiding, transforming, tranquil, and leads to the union of the dawn.

1. John wrote this poem while in prison in Toledo, probably around the octave of the feast of Corpus Christi.
2. The two experiences of the darkness of his prison cell and the rhythmic sound of the flowing river Tagus echo throughout this poem.
3. In this poem John presents an exceptional doctrinal development from the eternal uncreated divinity, to belief in the Trinity, Incarnation, and the presence of the Lord in the Eucharist.
4. This is the result of John's extraordinary experience in the Toledo prison with its painful darkness and loving illumination.

CHALLENGES FOR TODAY
- Meditate on this poem, giving it plenty of time.
- How do you integrate your belief in the Eucharist into your spiritual journey?
- Is your life permeated with conviction of the importance of the night?

DAY 128 SPAIN'S GREAT POET

Menéndez Pelayo and Dámaso Alonso, respectively, claimed that John was the greatest poet of Spain and one of its greatest writers. The brilliance of his poetry continues in the beautiful lyrical features of his commentaries, and both become sources of inspiration for readers. It is not an exaggeration to say that he conveys a sense of wonder and awe in the presentation of his works even before we consider the content. In fact, he "seems to be writing twentieth-century poetry 400 years before its time" (Thompson, p. 14). However, John does not just write such beautiful poetry because he is skillful and artistic. The beauty does not come from poetical insight but from mystical experience. He is writing about the most wonderful and beautiful experience of his life.

1. John writes beautifully, not because he is a great poet but because he is sharing with us a wonderful mystical experience.
2. John is ahead of his time, not only in poetical expression but also in his teachings on spirituality.
3. It is interesting how one who has suffered so much is known for such beauty in his poetry and prose.
4. Mystical experiences are ineffable and best expressed in poetry or art, music and dance.

CHALLENGES FOR TODAY
- Read John's poetry and enjoy it.
- John wrote his poems as a support for himself in times of trial, and they can help us in the same way.
- Write a few lines of poetry to express an unusual experience in your spiritual life.

DAY 129 *POET OF LOVE*

John is the poet of divine and human love. His final work, The *Living Flame* of love describes the experience of spiritual marriage, but this same theme was already present in some of his earliest writings, the "Romances." These poems form the point of departure for John's vision of life with God and they describe God's strategy of love that culminates in spiritual marriage between the Son and the world. "The ballads on the Trinity . . . link the passionate and sensuous encounter of the two lovers in the *liras* with the divine Trinity's embrace of all humanity through use of the same fundamental image, the marriage" (See Thompson, p. 55).

1. John's "Romances" present the descending aspect of our spirituality, namely God's journey to us, and God's motivation in coming to us as love.
2. The Son takes the world as his bride and marries her to the glory of the Father.
3. Our return journey to God, seen in John's major works, is modeled on God's love, seen in the "Romances."
4. The relationship between lovers becomes the basis for the presentation of God's relationship to the world.

CHALLENGES FOR TODAY
- Think about your own love relationship and what it can tell you about your search for God.
- Why is love the most important aspect of spirituality?
- Who is the greatest model of love for you and why?

DAY 130 JOHN'S POETRY

John of the Cross is well known for the rigors of the spiritual journey and for the demands he makes on himself and on others in the pursuit of life with God. It is interesting that one who is so demanding also writes with such beauty and passion. "San Juan de la Cruz has always been considered the straightest of arrows in the passage from earth to sky. His writings and his direction of souls have always emphasized a journey with no baggage. . . And yet, it is this same San Juan de la Cruz who left us a poetry permeated with feeling. In human terms we may say that this poetry is so fully sensuous, so affective, so filled with the desire of the whole world, that one has to wonder if in reality San Juan de la Cruz was as detached from human sensations as he claimed" (See de Nicolás, pp. 60-61).

1. John always has a positive approach to this world, and thus can speak of it with beauty. He only criticizes approaches that make creatures ends in themselves.
2. Perhaps John would like the practice of modern airlines of charging excessively for every piece of baggage you take on your journey!
3. John is a wonderful example of single-mindedness in the pursuit of God.
4. "Nothing" for John is always a means to the "all."

CHALLENGES FOR TODAY
- Are you relentless in your pursuit of spiritual growth?
- Do you really know what you want in life?
- Do others see you as a model of total commitment?

The monastery in Segovia where John lived and is buried..

8
Shorter Works—Prose

In the next few days we will be looking at the challenges in some of St. John of the Cross's letters. We have thirty five of John's letters, thirteen in John's original handwriting. They all belong to the last ten years of John's life, 1581-1591. Three of the letters deal with official matters, such as foundations and permissions, and many deal with spiritual direction. Unfortunately, many of John's letters were destroyed during the final years of persecution. We have none to members of his family, nor to Mother Teresa of Avila, but we do have a series that offer autobiographical information regarding John's role in foundations, his feelings and interests, and his own state of mind and heart during his final persecution. Let us reflect on these letters as if John is writing them to each of us. John also wrote a series of warnings, *Precautions*, probably for the nuns in Beas, during 1578-79 while he was their confessor. They form a group of nine norms to keep in mind in order to avoid the typical dangers of spiritual life. Similar in both style and content to the *Precautions* are the *Counsels to a Religious on How to Reach Perfection*. The four counsels are resignation, mortification, practice of virtue, and solitude.

DAY 131 *ACCEPT THE TRIALS OF LIFE*
(See Letters 1, 2, 26, 27, 32)

John shares how he feels abandoned and alone. He reminds us of his sufferings in prison and his assignment to work in the south when he would prefer to be in Castile near Mother Teresa. He tells us that abandonment in darkness can lead to illumination and great light. He tells one directee not to allow what is happening to him to cause any grief, and insists that it is not causing him any. Then he adds that people do not cause these unpleasant situations. Rather, God allows them to happen for our good. John asked his directees not to grieve over the trials imposed on him.

1. John's concern for his directees is evident in these short extracts when he goes out of his way to contact someone who feels abandoned.
2. When unpleasant things happen to us, we should make sure we do not put the blame on someone else. All are part of God's will for us.
3. God ordains all and where there is no love we should put love and then we will draw out love.
4. Often God ordains things differently from what we want and we must conform ourselves to the divine will.

CHALLENGES FOR TODAY
- When unpleasant things arise don't let them cause a disruption in your commitment.
- Try to show love to those who fail to love you.
- What are the present trials in your life?

DAY 132 DO NOT LET FEAR AND ANXIETY CONTROL YOU (See Letters 3, 4, 5, 30)

We should never walk in fear that can threaten our peace of soul. We should rather live simply, remembering to thank God for the many gifts we have received. When we are filled with fear we create an image of God in our own likeness, rather than appreciating God's extraordinary generosity. We must journey with maturity, never dependent on others, always ready to endure the purifications of life. When we are filled with fear and hesitations we simply lose precious time in our journey to God. These anxieties can be related to a lack of trust or courage and to not living in the moment of grace.

1. John takes time to write to a disciple precisely when he is immersed in business matters, reminding us that spiritual life develops amidst all the normal activities of daily life.
2. In his correspondence John says that we cannot surmount one ruse without using another one—an unusual but telling comment on the reality of the lives of the saints.
3. In a later letter John shares with one of his directees the trials saintly people must suffer.
4. Our lives are always in God's hands, and God is the one who protects us and makes us holy.

CHALLENGES FOR TODAY
- Can you endure trials in silence and hope?
- What do you worry about and why?
- Rather than worry, be excited about the opportunities God gives you.

DAY 133 LET US FOCUS ON GOD'S WILL FOR US
(See Letters 6, 9, 20)

We remain always aware that God allows trials to those God loves, often allowing them to pass through dryness and emptiness. In times of distraction we should always keep our thoughts centered on the liturgical feasts of the year, thus leaving aside all other disturbing thoughts, whether personal or from others. Let us not worry about thoughts or images that come to us when we do not deliberately accept them. We should forget about them and not let them bother us. Let us always watch what we say so as not to do harm by our speech and conversations. In everything we do we must keep our motives focused on God's will. We should remember to live in faith and hope even though in darkness, knowing God is protecting us and will never leave us.

1. John is so down to earth in his spiritual advice.
2. Passing through darkness is integral to John's vision of spiritual growth.
3. Times of dryness and emptiness are always part of our spiritual journey.
4. God draws us to divine life in whatever circumstances we find ourselves.

CHALLENGES FOR TODAY
- Is God the fulfillment of all your hopes and desires?
- Reflect on God's call to you in solitude and love.
- What is your purpose in this life?

DAY 134 *LET US ENGAGE IN A SINGLEMINDED PURSUIT OF GOD* (See Letters 7 and 8)

The seeking of spiritual growth is a special gift of God, a gift from on high that must not be contaminated by the corruptions of this world's systems and values. This must be our overwhelming desire and focus, filling our hearts and leaving no room for anything else. Always we need to remain empty of all other desires so as to be filled with God alone. Our journey needs to be in sacrifice, patience, silence, and self-denial, so as to enjoy the inner resurrection of the Spirit. In silence, prayer, service, and work we will find strength of spirit, and in solitude and forgetfulness of all that does not lead us to God, we can pursue the deepening of our commitment.

1. John challenges his directees but at the same time is affirming of everyone's efforts in the spiritual journey.
2. John feels he has shared enough, now it is our responsibility to carry out his teachings.
3. If we allow other lesser desires to fill our hearts we can never be filled by God alone.
4. When we see our role in the spiritual journey we must seek no further answers but dedicate ourselves in patience, silence, humility, charity, and self-sacrifice.

CHALLENGES FOR TODAY

- Keep your heart in peace and love so as to face anything that comes along whether adversity or prosperity.
- Practice periods of silence for it is in such quiet times you can converse with God.
- Is your commitment contaminated by the distractions, lures, and corruptions of this world?

DAY 135 *LIVING IN THE LOVE AND SERVICE OF GOD* (See Letter 12)

We must employ ourselves in all that leads to the love and service of God. This is our destiny—the reason God created and redeemed us. Thus, we must avoid all sin. This might well imply avoiding interaction and conversation with people who do not lead us to God. Furthermore, we must give ourselves to seek the will of God in all we do, imitating the Lord in his passion. It is important that we keep everything in perspective with no exaggerations. Everything this world has to offer is of little value in comparison to living in the grace of God.

1. Let us always think of everything we deal with in its relationship to the will of God.
2. When we give importance to things that do not lead us to God, they lead us away from God.
3. We should entrust all our daily concerns to the Lord.
4. We should review what are our dearest values and whether they lead us to God or away from God.

CHALLENGES FOR TODAY

- Do you give yourself entirely to the love and service of God?
- Keep the passion of our Lord before your eyes in every decision you make.
- Think of the image you have of yourself; is it permeated with true humility that appreciates your strengths and your weaknesses.

DAY 136 SURRENDERING OUR WILLS TO GOD
(See Letter 13)

It is important that we maintain a great desire to seek the will of God and to love God alone above all else. Desires of course are not enough; we must also carry them out. Problems arise because the will desires what appears good and satisfying and often is not. This results in disturbance and restlessness, as one seeks satisfaction in objects that do not lead us to God. We must purify these false desires, keeping in mind that the will cannot find in God the kind of satisfaction it finds in creatures. Since God transcends all natural objects of the will, we must purify these limited desires in order to seek and love God in a new way.

1. God is incomprehensible and cannot be the object of our human powers of knowing, hoping, and loving that have not been transformed.
2. With God's help we must empty the will of all disordered desires so that we can occupy ourselves in discovering and loving God in a new way.
3. The only way we can gain understanding of God and be in union with God is through love and never through gratification of the addictions of our appetites.
4. We seek God and the divine will for us when we are grounded in emptiness of faith and in charity.

CHALLENGES FOR TODAY
- Do you seek your own pleasure rather than the will of God?
- Surrender your entire will to God.
- Do not make anything in this world an end or goal in itself; God is the only acceptable goal of life.

DAY 137 POVERTY OF SPIRIT (See Letters 16, 21)

We can love God and give witness to God's generosity towards us by living faithfully what we profess. We should surround ourselves with people of similar interests and commitment—those who have the spirit of poverty, detachment from anything that hinders the pursuit of God, and who have the desire to seek God alone. Being poor in spirit makes us happier and more constant in the midst of want because this basic spiritual attitude of poverty gives us freedom of heart and disinterest in all that does not lead to love. We should desire and seek poverty of spirit, recognize our true lacks and wants. Our main attitude should be forgetfulness of all that is not God and an ardent desire for union with God who alone satisfies us.

1. Our commitment to spiritual development is not something childish but requires a robust will and strong love.
2. The spiritual journey does not always include comfort and consolation but suffering, silence, penance, solitude, hope, and love.
3. The only objects that control us are those to which we submit our hearts.
4. Poverty of spirit is the foundational quality that imbues our spiritual life and growth.

CHALLENGES FOR TODAY

- Consider your initial enthusiasm for the spiritual journey. Is it still strong?
- Remember anxiety creates needs and worries that distract you from your commitment.
- Let others know what you profess.

DAY 138 COMPANIONSHIP WITH GOD
(See Letters 15, 22)

God places us in specific situations and circumstances where we can do the good God wants from us, and through which we can grow spiritually. God is so generous to us in every aspect of life, it seems God is constantly seeking to fill us with divine blessings. Of course, God truly loves us and desires to be our special companion and the prime source of all our happiness. For our part we must long for this union and distance ourselves from anything that blocks this relationship.

1. We must beware of any affliction that can cause bitterness and harm our spiritual commitment.
2. Let us avoid giving importance to temptations that distract us from our pursuit of union with God.
3. We must learn to forget about this thing and that and maintain our focus on God's love for us.
4. Many things that bother and distract the central commitment of our lives have no importance at all.

CHALLENGES FOR TODAY
- Be courageous in your life and prayer.
- In every situation in life be responsive to the call of the Holy Spirit.
- Be thankful for the circumstances and situations in which God places you.

DAY 139 ACCEPTING GOD'S WILL AND PLAN FOR US (See Letter 25)

Sometimes things do not turn out as we want, but in these times, too, we should thank God, since everything forms part of God's plan to refashion us. We should willingly accept all that God has arranged for us or allowed to happen to us, and do so not only in thought but also in actions. When something happens that does not please us it doesn't mean it is harmful for us. Rather, in the long run it can lead to other opportunities, both for ourselves and for others. We see this in relationships, work opportunities, and personal challenges.

1. In this letter, John shares his own response to having been stripped of responsibility in the community.
2. John points out that all deprivations can lead to peace, solitude, and forgetfulness of self, if viewed through the lens of a loving God.
3. When faced with trials let's remember to imitate the suffering Lord who was humbled and crucified.
4. Sometimes we worry about what lies ahead and how it may affect us. Rather, we should leave all in the hands of God.

CHALLENGES FOR TODAY
- May the Lord preserve you and increase his love in you.
- Do you see each stage in your life as part of God's plan for you?
- Reflect on your patient or resentful attitudes in dealing with unpleasant circumstances.

DAY 140 FIRM RESOLUTIONS
(See Letters 17, 27, 29)

One of the challenges we all face is the importance of firm resolutions in our spiritual commitment. There are times and situations we deal with when we must remind ourselves that God does not want sluggish or cowardly souls, still less those who love only themselves. With courageous determination and God's help we can advance. We will always face sacrifice. To possess God in all, we must leave aside a desire to possess anything else so that our hearts belong to God alone. We must be careful that our own possessiveness not become the great thief who steals our peace of soul. May God deliver us from ourselves. Rather, let us accept whatever God pleases, aware that God is our greatest treasure.

1. Possessions can trouble and disturb us.
2. Our true joy comes from pleasing God and giving no undue attention to the self-centered values and corrupt systems of this world.
3. Our responsibility is not to consent knowingly to sin but to retain right intentions in everything we do.
4. Let us remember Mother Teresa' advice about the need of "a determined determination" as a required attitude in our spiritual journey.

CHALLENGES FOR TODAY
- Think about the strength of your resolution.
- Are you possessive of something or someone?
- From what aspects of yourself do you want God to free you?

DAY 141 *LIFE IN THE DESERT* (See Letters 28, 31)

John expresses his joy in his experience of life in the desert—a place that gives glory to God. He also insists that the vastness of the desert is a great help to the soul and body. At the same time there are wonderful benefits to the spiritual desert, and John says that life in the desert is admirable as he finds joy in holy solitude. The desert was also the place of prayer for Jesus and many spiritual figures.

1. John expresses his happiness in the simple joys of life.
2. The desert provides its own beauty and food to nourish us.
3. Times of withdrawal can provide strength for times of involvement.
4. In these two letters to the "noble and devout lady," John moves from spiritual vision to the practicalities of daily life and business decisions.

CHALLENGES FOR TODAY

- Create a spiritual desert for yourself where you can enjoy periods of solitude.
- Let others see and benefit from the joy in your heart.
- Take care of your soul, look after your health, never cease to pray.

DAY 142 *THE LONELINESS OF THE NIGHT*
(See Letters 11 and 19)

One of John's directees in Granada, with whom he also maintained contact in correspondence, was Doña Juana de Pedraza. In these letters she seems to be experiencing some of the pain, afflictions, and loneliness that so frequently come with the experience of the dark night. She becomes a model for us, and John's advice is helpful to us as we face similar experiences. In such times John urges us to be calm and peaceful in these struggles, for they are like knockings at the door of our hearts and challenges from God to love more. We must persevere in this pain for we must accept the cross with love as Jesus did. John reminds us that when we walk in darkness and spiritual poverty, this experience is a great sign we are on the right road. In fact at this time we should not worry but be happy, for these pains are part of God's favors to those who are willing to enter the dark night. John tells Juana de Pedraza and us too, that "God is leading you by a road most suitable for you." "Desire no other path than this." This darkness is a test of love which we must undergo in confidence, patience, and ever deeper faith.

1. The experiences of the dark night are proof of God's loving interventions in our lives.
2. The night is essential to growth, for growth takes place in transitions and crises.
3. When John's directees rejoice in their satisfying experiences of spiritual life, John worries. When they are immersed in darkness, he rejoices, knowing good things are happening in them.
4. It is a time of renunciation and sacrifice, but these are never negative. Rather, they are always choices made in love for a better, risen life of love and union.

CHALLENGES FOR TODAY
- Remember the dark night is our truest, safest, and only light and guide.
- If you find yourself in the dark night it is a sure sign of God's presence to you.
- When these things happen be calm, do not worry, but be at peace.

DAY 143 DETACHMENT
(See *Precautions*, "Against the world")

In order not to be hindered or contaminated by the false values of the world around us we ought to keep our love centered on God, making sure that no other loves are detrimental to this. Any relationship, whether towards family, friends, or acquaintances, must be part of our total self-gift in love to God. We treat all with equal respect, never letting any relationship become an end in itself. Likewise, no possession should ever take such importance that we become possessive of it, that it becomes the center of our hearts' desires. Finally, no community must become the center of our lives. Everyone and everything can become part of our total self-gift to God, but no one or nothing must ever replace God as the center of our love and commitment.

1. John was very attentive and loving towards his own family, friends, and members in community. This first warning, like so much of John's teaching, is against possessiveness that results in someone or something other than God taking God's place in the center of our hearts.
2. We do so much harm to our spiritual growth in the ways we think about others, compare ourselves to them, and allow them and their petty concerns to disrupt our spiritual journey and transformation.
3. These warnings do not refer to the special ways or vocations through which we go to God, for example in conjugal, family, or religious community life. John is not criticizing the beauty of God's gifts, but rather, possessiveness and misdirected loves.
4. Christians in the contemporary world are and must be involved in all kinds of societal and political issues and must deal with all these while respecting John's challenges for detachment and the need for integration.

CHALLENGES FOR TODAY
- Is there someone or something that takes more of your heart's attention than appropriate, or leads you away from God?
- How do you understand the difference between detachment and integration?
- Do your various modern communities aid or hinder spiritual development? How?

DAY 144 *ACCEPTING THE WILL OF GOD* (See *Precautions*, "Against the devil")

We are surrounded by the forces of evil, always in the appearance of good. So, it is common to be deceived by such evil in our world. One way to avoid such deception is through constant obedience to the will of God, seen in a religious superior or a spiritual director or through the careful practice of prayerful discernment. We should not take upon ourselves responsibilities that are not clearly discerned to be part of God's will for us. In all we do we should seek conformity of our will with God's.

1. If we lack harmony of our will with God's we run the risk of arrogance in what we do and of seeking our own desires instead of God's.
2. Our present world is full of individuals, including religiously motivated ones, who do enormous harm claiming something is God's will for them or for others.
3. We need humility to protect ourselves against the threats and deception of evil in our world.
4. We must guard against blasphemy which is more common than ever, as people all around us, including political and religious leaders, constantly insist that what they do is in God's name, when clearly it is not.

CHALLENGES FOR TODAY
- How do you decide what is God's will for you?
- Who helps you in discernment and decision-making?
- Do you falsely claim God's will for what you want to do?

DAY 145 GIVING IN TO HUMAN WEAKNESSES
(See *Precautions*, "Against the flesh")

Life is hard and living with others in family, friendship, and community brings us up against their different approaches that at times wear on us, knock off the hard corners, and help us become more human in relationship to others. People around us, whether they intend it or not, or whether we want it or not, all help to mold us into who we are to become. Not only people but also circumstances help form us; our ancestry, our place of birth, our work, and so on. We can carry out our responsibilities whether they give us pleasure or not, for we do all for the service of God. We should also avoid any superficial satisfactions in spiritual exercises. In all it is better to be inclined towards that which is more difficult and thus contribute to the maturity of life and the removal of human weaknesses.

1. We can apply the practical wisdom of the precautions to whatever walk of life in which we find ourselves.
2. We should embrace the many ways in which people and situations around us help form us and mature us.
3. Many people spend their spiritual lives enthusiastically pursuing trivia. John wants us to take a short cut and always choose to make the difficult decisions that can change our lives. Thus, we get to our goals more speedily.
4. This acceptance of the purifying aspects of the world around us is not passivity but the enthusiastic embracing of all possibilities of growth.

CHALLENGES FOR TODAY
- Don't run away from the problems people present. Use them.
- Spiritual challenges should help you become more human. Does it?
- Be more sensitive towards others than you think they are to you.

DAY 146 *RESIGNATION*
(See *Counsels to a Religious*, 1)

While living surrounded by others we should maintain a spirit of resignation and patient submission, living our lives with intensity, as though no one else was around. In practice this means maintaining distance from all the pressures that come from people around us. We should not be disturbed, nor meddle in word or thought in what is taking place around us. Rather, we should not be disturbed by individuals or communities with their concerns and anxieties. Nor should we concern ourselves with others' conduct or their good or bad qualities. Let us live simply in peace and tranquility, undisturbed by anything around us, maintaining always tranquility in our solitude.

1. These four counsels are necessary for anyone who wishes to advance in virtue and enjoy the blessings of the Holy Spirit.
2. Let us practice this resignation with fortitude.
3. When we lack this peaceful resignation amidst the world's turmoil, we easily get distracted and even weaken our spiritual commitment.
4. Resignation is a wonderful quality that enriches our entire spiritual journey.

CHALLENGES FOR TODAY
- Can you maintain peace of soul amidst all the activities around you?
- Who are the people who you know disturb your peace of soul?
- In what situations do you lack resignation? When is activism required?

DAY 147 SELF-DENIAL IN OUR INTERACTIONS WITH DIFFICULT PEOPLE AND SITUATIONS
(See Counsels to a Religious, 2)

Spiritual development implies formation during which period we are molded and crafted into people ready for union with God. This is a process of putting to death what hinders this development and re-educating and redirecting aspects of our lives to focus on God alone. This is primarily God's work, sometimes with the help of a spiritual director. However, this formation also takes place through the interactions of people around us. Some will challenge us in words, telling us things about ourselves we would rather not hear. Others will do things to us that we would rather prefer not to deal with. Still others with a clash of temperaments become bothersome, annoying, and unloving. We must react with patience, silence, and acceptance.

1. This spirit of self-control and self-denial leads us to humility, quietude, joy in the Holy Spirit, and peace of soul.
2. We gain much from the knocks and challenges received from others and must not think less of them because of their role in our lives.
3. "Mortification" literally means putting to death, but it is more appropriately described as a process of re-education and redirection of aspects of our lives.
4. It is important that we bear patiently the trials that come to us through others.

CHALLENGES FOR TODAY
- Reflect on the irritating people around you—do they help you in any way?
- How does God purify you through others?
- Which aspect of your life would you like to see "put to death"?

DAY 148 *THE PRACTICE OF VIRTUE*
(See *Counsels for a Religious*, 3)

The ongoing practice of virtues begins with religious observance, obedience to the will of God, and disinterest and detachment from this world's false values. We must fulfill all our duties to please God, whether we like them or not. Approaching our daily lives with responsibility, fortitude, and constancy, strengthens our practice of virtues. This will include accepting what is difficult rather than what is easy, what is rugged than what is soft, what is hard and distasteful than what is delightful and pleasant. In these ways we can follow the Lord and carry his cross.

1. John presents his view of these issues when he describes the center, narrow road on his diagram of Mount Carmel. Let us reread his comments.
2. Constancy in these simple virtues paves the way for what lies ahead.
3. Carrying lighter burdens achieves very little on the journey to the cross.
4. This active contribution to spiritual development is a responsibility we need to diligently pursue each day.

CHALLENGES FOR TODAY
- Can you choose that which is most difficult?
- Are you constant in your daily duties?
- Which virtues are you lacking?

DAY 149 SOLITUDE (See *Counsels to a Religious*, 4)

The pursuit of transformation and union with God implies seeking life beyond this one that gives meaning to our existence. Hence, we should have solitude in our lives aware that this world and its values are passing away. Thus, we pay no heed to this world unless it prepares us for the next. Moreover, there are advantages to be gained from withdrawal from idle gossip, useless encounters, unnecessary business interactions, frivolous entertainment, and so on. We must create space in which prayer and union with God take precedence. We must also allow ourselves to be drawn to God in solitude on a daily basis.

1. Solitude does not mean we are unfaithful to the duties of daily life. Rather, we must fulfil them responsibly.
2. In all our daily activities we should maintain recollection and focused attention, do all in the presence of God, and keep our hearts focused on God in all we do.
3. Everything we do can be integrated into our commitment to God— we can do all in God's presence.
4. These four counsels are interdependent, and they all wax or wane together.

CHALLENGES FOR TODAY
* Can you live in the "here and now" while thinking always of the "there and then"?
* Where and when do you have quiet times?
* Do you like to be alone with God?

DAY 150 *SEEKING DEEP SILENCE*

Our lives and culture are filled with noise and distractions of all kinds. It seems no one values silence. Yet all spiritual traditions speak of the importance of silence and of the temptations to be found in incessant noise and distractions. We learn nothing from constant noise, but silence presents us with opportunities for reflection, self-discovery, and openness to the call of God. Silence is one of those basic qualities that nurture other important aspects of our lives. Without silence we can neither foster contemplation nor a reflective approach to activity. The desert tradition pointed out that silence leads to three basic virtues. "The first is discretion or the ability to judge between what is good and evil, wise and shallow, prudent and foolish.. . . The second is moderation or finding the happy mean between excesses . . . The third disposition is diligence" (See Muto, pp. 43-44). These three qualities that result from the practice of deep silence add integrity to our lives of dedication.

1. Those who love silence respond with gentleness.
2. We must treasure silence, find a quite place both materially and in our own hearts.
3. We need quiet time and a special place to listen to the whispers of the Holy Spirit.
4. Let us examine ourselves on the three qualities—discretion, moderation, and diligence.

CHALLENGES FOR TODAY
- Where do you go for times of deep silence?
- Do you have the gift of patience to wait and listen?
- What have you learned in silence?

DAY 151 *IT IS EASY TO MISREPRESENT ST. JOHN OF THE CROSS*

John of the Cross has suffered from all kinds of misrepresentation. A few quotes here and there taken out of context can easily make John seem obsessed by dangers to the spiritual life, fanatical about abnegation and purification, and opposed to every aspect of the world, as if temptation were everywhere. However, a careful reading of John's three great poems should be enough to correct any misunderstanding. They are filled with beautiful imagery, passion, and even sensual love. We have already seen how denials in John are always made for the sake of a greater affirmation. Negation is never an end in itself, but always a means towards a more positive end.

1. One of the ways of misrepresenting John is to over categorize the stages of the spiritual life.

2. Another way of misrepresenting John is to interpret detachment in old ways instead of appreciating that for John it means integration—he wants detachment only from objects that are ends in themselves and replace God.

3. John has a system it is true, but he never absolutizes it and always appreciates exceptions.

4. John is very modern insofar as his works are to be interpreted dynamically and not statically. Each of his great poems begins with a dynamic action word in the first line.

CHALLENGES FOR TODAY

- Do not take prejudice from former times into your reading of John of the Cross.
- Try to appreciate the general flow of his presentation without digressing on distracting language or ideas from history.
- Reread his poems and let them speak to you today.

DAY 152 JOHN OF THE CROSS AND THE BIBLE

"With his purified soul, John reached a point in which he could feel with the Bible, feel the Bible as though it were a song springing spontaneously from his own soul. . . . He saw the Bible as a unique and inexhaustible source of our knowledge of God. In the Bible he uncovered the principles of God's activity and was able to apply them to the divine action in the spiritual lives of individuals" (See Kavanaugh, *Selected Writings,* pp. 28-29).

John sees Scripture as an unerring guide, and in using Scripture says he does not wish "to deviate from the true meaning of Sacred Scripture" (A. Prologue.2). The Bible is John's main source for his teachings. He uses stories and images from Scripture throughout his writings. Each of his great poems contains an action word in the first verse—like an exodus theme. John uses stories from Scripture that are archetypes of our own stories, symbolic expressions of common human experiences. So, John's use of Scripture is more as revealed symbols of our own life and calling.

1. John knows Scripture very well; he quotes the Old Testament 684 times, and the New Testament 376 times.
2. John also uses stories and images from Scripture throughout his writings as archetypes of our own lives.
3. John uses Scripture as revealed symbols of our own life and calling.
4. Scripture is the revelation of a person, Jesus Christ.

CHALLENGES FOR TODAY
- Is Scripture central to your own life?
- How often do you read Scripture?
- What does Scripture do for you?

The High altar in the church in Segovia, representing John's four major works..

9
The Ascent of Mount Carmel

We turn our attention and our daily reflections to St. John of the Cross' major works, beginning with the masterpiece, *The Ascent of Mount Carmel*. John wrote this treatise between 1581 and 1585, beginning it while he was in the Andalusian monastery of El Calvario, continuing it while he was rector in Baeza, and completing it while he was prior in Granada. This is generally placed first among John's major works because it is the most detailed regarding the earlier stages of the spiritual life. Each of John's major works is preceded by a poem and is presented as a commentary on the poem. However, the pedagogical aid that John used for the *Ascent* is not so much the poem as the diagram or sketch of Mount Carmel. John considered this diagram an important visual synthesis of his doctrine in the treatise, and he made many copies for the nuns in Beas and the friars in Baeza and Granada. The diagram shows Mount Carmel and on the summit are all the gifts and fruits of the Holy Spirit. Those who seek to arrive at the top of the mountain can choose one of three ways. Two of them are broad roads, to the left and right: "ways of the imperfect spirit," consisting in the pursuit of the "goods of heaven" or "the goods of earth." Seekers who follow these broad roads can become attached to the heavenly or earthly goods that are merely means to God. In the center of the diagram is the narrow "path of the perfect spirit" that leads to divine union. The radical attitude necessary in ascending this path is "all-nothing" –pursue everything that leads to God and accept nothing that leads away from God.

The *Ascent* is the fruit of long experience and personal observation. It is a serious treatise with a logical structure, mental rigor, and solid biblical foundations. The principal divisions of the work are: Book I, a general introduction to the active night of sense and the control of the appetites; Book II, an introduction to the active night of spirit and a detailed consideration of the active night of the intellect in faith; and Book III, a discussion of the active night of the spirit as it purifies the memory in hope and the will in charity. This is a beautiful book, full of insight and challenge, and it should be a great source of spiritual guidance for us as we spend the next days reflecting on it.

For further reading to accompany the reflections in this section, see Leonard Doohan, *The Contemporary Challenge of John of the Cross*, 1995; see also Leonard Doohan, *John of the Cross: Your Spiritual Guide*, 2013.

DAY 153 *THE ASCENT OF MOUNT CARMEL*
(See *Ascent*, **Prologue**)

If we choose to journey to the top of Mount Carmel we must pass through a dark night on the way to union with God in love. The trials we must face on this climb are numerous and intense and even beyond our understanding. However, we must acknowledge that many who begin this journey do not complete it because they do not want to face the pain and darkness, or because they just do not understand what is happening to them, or because they have no suitable guide to help them. God calls many to make this journey and gives them the grace for advancing. If we desire to make this climb and are ready to make the effort, then God will help us.

1. Many people make little progress because they never break away from the methods of beginners.
2. Some people, instead of abandoning themselves to God and cooperating with divine grace, block such help by inappropriate action or by resistance to grace.
3. We will need to leave aside the satisfaction that comes with primitive devotions and accept the aridity of this transition.
4. God works in us, purifying our former ways of spiritual life.

CHALLENGES FOR TODAY
- Do you resist God's call to make this journey?
- Are you moving forward or going back in your spiritual life?
- Are you ready to ask God to place you in the dark night?

DAY 154 *THE NIGHTS OF LIFE*
(See *Ascent*, 1. 1)

In our spiritual journey we must pass through two dark experiences or nights—one is the purgation of sense—an experience of beginners, and the other of spirit—an experience of proficients. We can only undertake this exodus when motivated by love of God. The first part of this night is the loss or denial and purification of all sensible appetites for external things that we think lead us to God. These must be controlled before moving on.

1. John of the Cross considers these nights in so far as they are active in the *Ascent*, leaving the passive experience to his book on the *Dark Night* of the soul.
2. One cannot enter this night of one's own initiative. It is a grace when God places one in this night.
3. This first night is the lot of beginners as God introduces them into the state of contemplation.
4. Journeying through the nights is a shortcut to growth in the spiritual life.

CHALLENGES FOR TODAY
- Are you willing to accept the hardships of this journey?
- Try letting go of attachments you have to objects of sense.
- Remember darkness will be painful but it leads to light.

DAY 155 THE NIGHT OF SENSE
(See *Ascent*, 1. 2)

Our journey is a night because it involves painful deprivation which is like a night to our senses. It is a night for our intellect which will need to leave aside knowledge to emphasize faith. It is a night because the end of our journey is God who is clouded in darkness for us while we remain in this life. These are three parts of one developing night that moves from early evening when things fade out of sight (deprivation), to the total darkness of midnight (faith), then on to the early dawn and a new rising (encountering God).

1. We must purify our hearts from all false affections and attachments.
2. We learn to know God in faith and not through intellectual information.
3. God communicates to us in the night of contemplation.
4. We cannot make this journey unless we are fired by love's urgent longings.

CHALLENGES FOR TODAY
- Pray for the determination and fortitude to make this journey.
- Remember God is drawing you forward; you are not on your own.
- Find someone you trust who has made this part of the journey and can help you.

DAY 156 THE CONTROL OF APPETITES
(See Ascent, 1. 3)

The spiritual journey to union in love leads us to the best situation possible for us in life. We become our best and true selves. However, it begins with the challenge to purify all experiences that come through our senses. The gratifications that come through senses hinder us from getting to know God, and we must deny our appetites for these false values and goals. When John uses the term "appetites" he means self-indulgent, voluntary attachments, affections, or desires for creatures as habitual ends in themselves. John points out, "[T]he appetites are not all equally detrimental, nor are all equally a hindrance to the soul . . . to mortify them entirely is impossible in this life . . . they are not such a hindrance as to prevent one from attaining divine union" (A.1 11.2). So, we do not seek to destroy our senses and faculties, but to re-direct, re-educate, and refocus them on God and divine values. However, when we deny our appetites their normal objects, there remains a void within us which is a darkness in our lives.

1. The controlling of appetites is like a night, for they feel in darkness without being able to see the objects they normally desire.
2. Without the knowledge that comes through our senses we remain ignorant because no knowledge is communicated to us from any other source.
3. Until God purifies our senses we are as if helpless in a prison unable to see anything.
4. This process of deprivation is an experience of poverty and nakedness; we become poor without the values of former gratifications and we strip ourselves of all false attachments.

CHALLENGES FOR TODAY
* This week, be careful to deny yourself in the use of senses.
* Does anything you receive through senses help in your journey to God?
* Are you afraid of letting go of the satisfactions you experience?

DAY 157 *THE IMPORTANCE OF JOURNEYING THROUGH THE NIGHT* (See *Ascent*, 1. 4-5)

If we wish to journey to union with God we must pass through this dark night of sense. We remain incapable of enlightenment until all appetites and false desires are purified. Attachment to creatures as ends in themselves cannot coexist with the illumination that comes from God alone. No one can serve two masters. This extends to all human knowledge which is ignorance in comparison to the wisdom of God. To journey towards God we must walk away from all that is not God. We must learn not to make a big deal of ourselves or of things.

1. If we identify with creatures we becomes like them. If we identify with God we draw near to union.
2. Transformation in God is impossible when we are excessively attached to creatures.
3. Only those who leave aside their own imperfect knowledge and walk in God's service receive the enlightenment that leads to God.
4. The spiritual journey is a journey away from slavery to false values that control our liberty of spirit.

CHALLENGES FOR TODAY
- Where does your heart find its values and satisfaction?
- Remember you need to be empty of false values before God can fill you with new life.
- Act as if you are poor, empty, and naked in God's sight.

DAY 158 HARM CAUSED BY APPETITES
(See *Ascent*, 1. 6)

We find in spiritual life that giving free rein to appetites – deliberate attachment to creatures—causes harm to a person in two ways; it deprives a person of the ability to recognize God's spirit and it wearies, weakens, and torments a person in his or her life and the pursuit of God. Love of God and attachments to creatures cannot coexist. This night of sense consists in the purification of all disordered, habitual, voluntary appetites that crave inappropriate sensory satisfaction. We seek self-control of those habitual voluntary appetites that impede union with God.

1. Attachment to anything finite never satisfies our infinite longings in life, whereas the Spirit of God brings fullness.
2. When we give free rein to appetites we are always dissatisfied and bitter, and hungry for more.
3. If we do not refrain from disordered appetites they end up controlling and tormenting us.
4. "Appetite" comes from the word "to desire" and refers to all the false desires that lead us away from God.

CHALLENGES FOR TODAY
* Identify in your life the impediments to the pursuit of God.
* Are you burdened and oppressed by endless wants?
* Do you make gratification the motivation for your life and choices?

DAY 159 *FURTHER HARM FROM APPETITIES*
(See *Ascent*, 1. 7-10)

Uncontrolled appetites torment us, and instead of us controlling them we are controlled by them. These attachments, affections, or desires also blind us and leave us in darkness and block the light of God's illumination. Sometimes we think these yearnings will not do us much harm and we can manage them. Not so! These false desires also drag us down with their worthlessness and degrade us in the heat of powerful emotions. One uncontrolled inclination or desire hinders our conformity to God's will, for they sap our strength needed for perseverance in our dedication and weaken our pursuit of God.

1. Attachments left to themselves take possession of us.
2. If we let our desires capture us we are never free.
3. False desires can overwhelm us and the intellect so that we cannot think or see clearly.
4. Attachments can just as easily be for religious devotions as for merely sense objects.

CHALLENGES FOR TODAY
- Free yourself from the weight of cares and useless desires.
- This week concentrate your attention on renunciation of something you already know leads you away from God.
- Examine to what extent your efforts are all integrated in the single-minded pursuit of God.

DAY 160 IMPORTANCE OF CONTROLLING APPETITES (See *Ascent*, 1. 11-12)

Let us be clear—we cannot control some appetites and leave others unchecked. It is not possible to gain total control in this life, and some desires do not hinder union provided they are spontaneous, not deliberate with forethought. But in general all voluntary appetites that involve sin must be controlled. Any one of the voluntary appetites, even if trifling, is sufficient to impede union if not controlled. We must seek liberation to arrive at union, for we cannot seek God's will while also seeking other objects apart from God. Union means our will and God's become one. "Deny your desires and you will find what your heart longs for" (S. 15).

1. One cannot attain union with God's will without first being freed from evil, enslaving appetites.
2. People can fall into imperfections, minor sins, and natural appetites without yielding complete control to them, since these are not determined habits.
3. Some people can break attachments to major issues and remain bound by minor ones.
4. Some people not only fail to advance but they turn back because of some small attachment.

CHALLENGES FOR TODAY
- You probably know what your habitual imperfections are. What are you doing about them?
- Realize you must cut out attachments in the bud before they grow.
- Pray for totality of commitment.

DAY 161 METHODS FOR ENTERING THE NIGHT

(See *Ascent*, 1. 13).

We enter the active night of sense in two ways. First, with God's grace we actively contribute with our own efforts. Second, God accomplishes the work in us, and we are passive recipients. (John deals with this second in the book of the *Dark Night*). Regarding our active involvement we should do the following.

1. Have a habitual desire to get to know Christ and to imitate him in all we do.
2. Renounce all sensory satisfactions, develop indifference to gratification, and stress only the will of God.
3. Control and purify the four passions—joy, hope, fear, and sorrow, by always being ready to make the difficult life-changing decisions.
4. Intensify self-knowledge with awareness of our emptiness before God; have a habit of mind to question and be suspicious of our motives, biases, and needs.

1. John of the Cross is convinced that if we embrace these commitments earnestly and put them into practice they will lead to significant benefits.

2. These four counsels prepare us for entry into the night of sense. John gives a fuller explanation in the *Dark Night* (N.1. 13.3).

3. We focus on John's call for "todo-nada," "all-nothing." If we choose nothing we are on the road to all.

4. We make hard decisions for love without desire to wallow in negativity.

CHALLENGES FOR TODAY

- Reflect again on John of the Cross' diagram of Mount Carmel and its wonderful advice.
- How can you train yourself for this journey?
- Choose one of John's four recommendations as a focal point for the coming week.

DAY 162 *A JOURNEY MOTIVATED BY LOVE*
(See *Ascent*, 1. 14-15)

To journey through the nights we need courage and constancy and these qualities will be supported by intense love. The longing of love for union with the Lord enables us to confront the appetites and control and deny any satisfaction that does not lead to God. Our desire for union is what motivates us. We must have a greater love for Christ than for anything else. Love will be the motivation for all further stages in this exciting journey. "O great God of love, and Lord. How many riches do you place in the soul that neither loves nor is satisfied except in you alone, for you give yourself to it and become one with it through love" (L. 11).

1. There begins a sense of joy in being liberated from captivity to senses, passions, and appetites.
2. The first part of the journey involves denial and purification.
3. Only when the appetites no longer war against the spirit can we experience the peace of early encounters with the Lord.
4. The journey through the nights is full of darkness and suffering but once made a person looks back with joy.

CHALLENGES FOR TODAY
- Express gratitude to God for any and all achievements in these early stages.
- Examine yourself to see what there is in your life that is not conducive to union with God.
- Pray for courage and constancy.

DAY 163 THE ACTIVE NIGHT OF SPIRIT
(See Ascent, 2. 1)

Book two of the *Ascent* describes the active night of spirit which consists in the purification or divesting the spirit of all its imperfections and appetites for spiritual possessions. This is a more intense and painful experience than the night of sense. We are dealing with the purification of the intellect in faith. When the intellect no longer focuses on its own natural objects of knowledge and information it finds itself in painful darkness until illumined by faith.

1. When freed from evil and temporal and rational objects, we are able to walk unharmed in faith.
2. This night implies the complete purification of all spiritual faculties, gratifications, and appetites.
3. A person who lives in this darkness without the light of the intellect can climb the ladder of faith that alone leads to the true communications of God.
4. A person who strives to progress through this night is concealed and protected by God. He or she travels like a blind person with God as guide.

CHALLENGES FOR TODAY
- While God draws you to deeper faith, this is an active night and demands your contribution.
- Ask God to strengthen you for the total darkness of this night.
- Remind yourself that the less you work with your own abilities the more progress you can make. Place yourself in God's hands.

DAY 164 *FAITH IS THE CAUSE OF THIS DARK NIGHT* (See *Ascent*, 2. 2-3)

We speak of night for three reasons. The beginning of the journey is a night, the means to advance, faith, is a night, and our goal, God, is a dark night experience to us all in this life. John describes these three experiences as twilight, midnight, and dawn. Faith is the darkest part of this experience. It is darker and more interior because it deprives the rational, superior part of light and understanding. Our knowledge is generally acquired through the intellect, but not the knowledge that faith gives. However, faith brings darkness not because of the absence of light but because of the overwhelming brightness and illumination of a new knowledge of God.

1. Faith is obscure for us because it deals with divinely revealed truths which transcend human understanding. The brightness of revealed truths overwhelms and blinds us.
2. Faith informs us of matters we have never seen or known. It is beyond all natural knowledge.
3. The night of faith becomes our guide. The dark night is our only light.
4. Faith blinds a person to all false knowledge of God as it leads him or her to illumination.

CHALLENGES FOR TODAY
- What do you know about God and how do you know it?
- How do you understand faith? A list of truths? A life of an organization? How else?
- Have you ever stood in the headlights of a car? Did the brightness blind you and leave you in darkness?

DAY 165 *THE NEED OF DARKNESS FOR GUIDANCE THROUGH FAITH* (See *Ascent*, 2. 4)

We need to be in darkness in order to be guided by faith. This darkness not only regards the sense part of a person but also that part which relates to God and to spiritual things, so the rational and higher part of human nature. After all, we seek a supernatural encounter—so beyond the natural. This means voluntarily emptying ourselves of any affection or desire for earthly or heavenly goods. Moreover, this night of spirit refers to what we can achieve through our own efforts. We must stop relying on anything that we can understand, taste, feel, or imagine. Faith is beyond all this understanding, tasting, feeling, and imagining.

1. Only when we are blind and empty and in darkness can we allow God to guide us.
2. We must not rely on any knowledge or experience that we have of God since this blocks true knowledge and God-given experience.
3. We seek perfect union by living in darkness to all objects of sight, hearing, imagination, and understanding—for none of these lead us to God.
4. However impressive our knowledge or feeling for God is, it has no resemblance to God.

CHALLENGES FOR TODAY
- Abandon all previous methods for spiritual life you may have valued.
- Leave aside all that is a natural way of knowing and possessing God.
- What can you contribute to this night of spirit?

DAY 166 *A GLANCE AT THE NATURE OF UNION*
(See *Ascent*, 2. 5)

God is united to our nature as Creator sustaining us in existence. However, there is another union that produces our transformation in God. It is a union of likeness—a supernatural union that results from the conformity and union of our wills and God's. We only achieve this by stripping ourselves of all creatures, actions, and abilities that are unconformed to God's will. God will communicate divine life and union to those who are more conformed to God's will. This supernatural union is not based on our understanding or feeling, but only on the purity and exclusive focus of our love on God.

1. Sometimes we lack conformity of our will with God's, either in the case of a specific action or because of an established habit.
2. We cannot achieve union of wills until everything contrary to this conformity or union of likeness is rejected.
3. Only when we deprive ourselves of all that is not God can we be illumined by and transformed in God.
4. Perfect transformation is only possible with perfect purity.

CHALLENGES FOR TODAY
- You must leave aside everything that is not according to God's will.
- Remember your clearest and best understanding or experience of God is not God.
- This week take special care to make decisions based on God's will.

DAY 167 THE THEOLOGICAL VIRTUES TRANSFORM THE SPIRITUAL FACULTIES
(See *Ascent*, 2. 6)

The union with God is achieved by purifying our intellect, memory, and will by means of the theological virtues of faith, hope, and charity. The three theological virtues cause darkness and emptiness in the spiritual faculties by depriving them of their natural objects. Faith affirms what cannot be understood by the intellect, hope rejects memories and stresses what is unpossessed in the future, and charity abandons all other loves to love God alone. This leads to the transformation we seek. "The soul is not united with God in this life through understanding, or through enjoyment, or through imagination, or through any other sense; but only faith, hope, and charity (according to the intellect, memory, and will) can unite the soul with God in this life" (A.2. 6.1).

1. The intellect must be perfected in the darkness of faith, the memory in the emptiness of hope, and the will in the absence of every affection.
2. This is the active night of spirit because a person does what lies within his or her power to enter this night.
3. The whole spiritual journey can be understood as the transformation of the spiritual faculties by the three theological virtues. This is the darkness that leads to illumination.
4. We must discover these new ways of knowing, possessing, and loving God.

CHALLENGES FOR TODAY

- Think about what you know of God through your intellect and what you know through faith.
- How do you appreciate God's compassion to you because of your memories of God's actions towards you? Then think about God's compassion towards you in your hopes for eternity.
- Which small loves do you need to leave aside in order to pursue the great love of God?

DAY 168 *THE PATH TO UNION IS VERY NARROW* (See *Ascent*, 2. 7)

We journey to union with God by means of a narrow path. In this journey we restrict, or narrow, the focus of our spiritual faculties so that they focus on God alone. Few people are willing to accept the pains of this narrow path, and so few find their way to God. So many people dabble in all kinds of methods that they hope will lead to God. They utilize all sorts of devotions and get nowhere. When the narrow path arrives as the summit of Mount Carmel it opens to the wonders of God's graces and love.

1. Few people have the knowledge, preparation, and desire to commit themselves to emptying the spirit of false values.
2. The journey to God is along a narrow path that climbs high on Mount Carmel. Many people are too burdened with false possessions to make the trip.
3. Some people will try any and every method to lead to God, dabbling in all kinds of petty practices. They do this rather than accept the narrow path that alone leads to God.
4. Many people seek themselves and their satisfactions in the pursuit of God.

CHALLENGES FOR TODAY
- Is your way and method of journeying to God achieving your goals or not? If not, change them.
- Remember John's advice—always choose that which is most difficult.
- How do you follow Christ as he carries his cross?

DAY 169 *NOTHING CREATED OR IMAGINED LEADS US TO UNION WITH GOD* (See *Ascent*, 2. 8-10)

Nothing created or imagined can serve the intellect as a means for union with God. In fact, attachment to what is grasped by the intellect is an obstacle to union. Rather, we know God in contemplation which is a passive gift of God, a secret wisdom beyond the intellect's ability. In this experience the intellect is blind and a person walks in faith. We do not earn or achieve knowledge of God. It is a gift in contemplation and we receive it passively.

1. Everything the intellect can understand, the will experience, and the imagination can picture is completely unlike God.
2. Nothing in this world resembles God. So, we cannot know God by anything this world offers.
3. We need the active nights of sense and spirit to purify all sensory and spiritual knowledge of God.
4. God is darkness to the intellect and faith dazzles and blinds us.

CHALLENGES FOR TODAY
- Has your past life and knowledge of God been focused on the accumulation of information about God?
- Reflect on your image of God to see if it is an idol.
- Pray that the Holy Spirit of truth will lead you to all truth.

DAY 170 PURIFY THE SOURCES OF KNOWLEDGE (See *Ascent*, 2. 11-12)

We must purify those sources of knowledge that really do not help us in our journey to God. Some originate naturally through the senses and we purify these in the active night of sense. Supernatural knowledge which comes to the intellect through the senses must be purified through the night of spirit. These sources are not reliable as sources for true knowledge or divine communications. They cannot serve as a means for union since they have no proportionate relationship to God. We must also divest ourselves of anything that comes through the imagination or phantasy—because discursive interior senses cannot teach us anything beyond what is perceived through the senses. We must instead abide in calm restfulness where God can fill us with peace and refreshment.

1. Supernatural knowledge can diminish faith, impede the Spirit, be sought for the satisfaction it gives, can reduce fervor and God's favors, and open the door to evil.
2. Spiritual knowledge that comes through the senses is not reliable and can easily deceive the person in his or her spiritual journey.
3. God can communicate through the senses but the resulting enrichment does not depend on a person's acceptance.
4. Supernatural knowledge that comes through the senses includes visions, images, heard communications, and sensitive feelings of delight.

CHALLENGES FOR TODAY
- Do not cling to meditation or any image of God.
- Discontinue trying to make particular acts with your faculties.
- Learn to abide in quietude with a loving attention to God.

DAY 171 *SIGNS A PERSON SHOULD DISCONTINUE MEDITATION* (See *Ascent*, 2. 13)

There are three signs that indicate it is appropriate for us to discontinue discursive meditation. 1. We realize we can no longer mediate as we used to with the satisfaction we used to receive from our prayer. 2. We have no desire to apply our imagination to rekindle our prayer, and this used to be the answer when meditation became more difficult. 3. We prefer to remain alone in a loving attention towards God without acts and exercises that we formerly used. When these three signs are present at the same time, then we must remain in peace and follow the lead of the Holy Spirit. This transition is not easy since we are leaving something we knew well and were successful at it and moving to an unknown.

1. Since these indicators can come from sources other than a readiness for contemplation, all three must be present at the same time.
2. The third sign is the surest one—when a person remains alone in loving attention to God without any discursive acts.
3. With the third sign comes peace, rest, and delight.
4. When these three signs are present it is safe to leave meditation and the life of sense and enter that of contemplation and spirit.

CHALLENGES FOR TODAY
- Do not abandon discursive meditation too soon for it is a remote means for beginners.
- From time to time think about whether you are attached to meditation.
- Do you fill your prayer time, afraid of emptiness and quiet?

DAY 172 SOMETIMES WE NEED TO GO BACK TO MEDITATION (See *Ascent*, 2. 15)

When one verifies the three signs referred to in yesterday's reading one is ready to move to contemplation. Experiencing at this time a general loving knowledge amounts to the first steps we take towards the supernatural knowledge of contemplation. This transition does not mean we are never to go back to discursive meditation. At first it is not always easy to enter into this general knowledge of contemplation, and at the same time we are not so far away from meditation that we are incapable of it. So, the need for meditation can continue until we have made a habit of initial contemplation. So, in this transition a person will sometimes contemplate and sometimes meditate.

1. When a person returns to meditation he or she may well feel drawn to remain alone in loving attention towards God.
2. Sometimes a person experiences this loving awareness without any active work of the faculties. Sometimes he or she will need the aid of meditation.
3. In times of loving awareness a person receives God's communication passively without doing anything.
4. When all natural images are purified and driven out of a person, then and only then God communicates supernaturally.

CHALLENGES FOR TODAY
- Do not mix the knowledge that comes in times of loving attention with knowledge in meditation. One is the end and the other a means.
- Are you peaceful with emptiness and seeming idleness? You will need these qualities to be ready for God's transforming presence.
- Check with your spiritual director concerning these signs.

DAY 173 BEWARE OF EXTRAORDINARY COMMUNICATIONS AND VISIONS

(See *Ascent*, 2. 16-19)

John of the Cross was very concerned that we not be misled by communications that we believe come through visions. Some of these are perceptible to us or to other people (corporeal) and some are perceptible by the imagination (imaginative visions). The supernatural representations communicate without directly using exterior senses. Scripture is full of these visions. John insists that people avoid communications and understandings that come to us through these visions and considers them hindrances to true union with God and blocks to authentic revelation of God in faith. John writes at length about these, given their importance in his time. There are contemporary manifestations, places, shrines, people, gurus, and visionaries that people think offer special direct communications of God's message. These can lead people astray from faith. These are all spiritual objects that need to be purified by the night of spirit.

1. There is no advancing in faith without blocking out all that comes through the senses, directly or indirectly, including these visions presented through the imagination.
2. God presents these communications to enrich the person directly, but the person perceives them through the imagination's presentation of the vision. The vision enriches but the imaginative part distracts and deceives.
3. A person must take only the gift God offers and reject the sensory representation and any satisfaction it offers.
4. We must walk exclusively along the road of knowing God through the darkness of faith.

CHALLENGES FOR TODAY

- Give examples of supernatural visions today.
- Are you attached to a place, experience, personal communication, contemporary presentation that has become a spiritual end for you?
- Put no trust in what seems extraordinary communications. Rather, seek God in faith.

DAY 174 DECEPTIVE COMMUNICATIONS
(See *Ascent*, 2. 20-21)

The night of spirit purifies desires for special divine interventions and supernatural communications. Sometimes we desire and then we believe we have received a supernatural communication, but it may not turn out to be true. Sometimes conditions and personal responsiveness may change, and then what we thought to be assured changes too. In the meantime God changes our approach and we no longer need what we asked for. Seeking God's spiritual interventions in life is not a good thing to do. There are boundaries between this world and the next, and we should not seek to transcend them. The desire for knowledge of things through supernatural means is worse than seeking satisfaction and gratification through sensitive means. John reminds us, "Only by means of faith, in divine light exceeding all understanding, does God manifest Himself to the soul" (A.2 9.1).

1. Divine revelations are dependent on human changeable causes and often do not conclude as expected.
2. A person cannot completely grasp the meaning of God's communications without often meeting with some error and bewilderment.
3. Sometimes we yearn to hear a word of support or reassurance from beyond this life, rather than remaining in the darkness of faith.
4. God may give a communication but only because of people's weakness. God does as God wishes, but we should not seek these communications.

CHALLENGES FOR TODAY
- Avoid giving interpretations to what you think are divine communications to you.
- Do not think that seeking special communications from God is a sign of faith. It is not!
- Focus on the life you need to live without seeking supernatural interventions and guidance which by-pass faith.

DAY 175 *THE NEW TESTAMENT'S FOCUS ON FAITH* (See *Ascent*, 2. 22)

In the Old Testament many kings, prophets, and spiritual figures sought divine communications through visions. That was fine then. In the New Testament faith in Jesus Christ is the way to God in this era of grace. Now there is no reason for seeking God's interventions through supernatural means. God has spoken everything to us in the Word, the Son, and has no more to say. We must place our faith in the Gospel's revelation and seek nothing beyond it.

1. Anyone who now questions God or seeks some vision, revelation, or communication, is not centered on Christ as God's final Word.
2. We cannot seek secret truths or special answers that are beyond the Gospel's revelation without showing a lack of faith.
3. We must avoid the satisfactions and gratifications that come when we seek and think we receive special supernatural communications.
4. The night of spirit purifies all objects that come through the spiritual faculties.

CHALLENGES FOR TODAY

- Do not seek answers in special communications as if God's revelation in Christ is not enough.
- Avoid curiosity to know what God has determined we do not need to know.
- Is the Gospel enough for you? What would you like to know beyond this revelation?

DAY 176 WE MUST ALSO AVOID SPIRITUAL INTELLECTUAL COMMUNICATIONS
(See Ascent, 2. 23-32)

There are four kinds of spiritual intellectual communications—visions, revelations, locutions, and spiritual feelings. All four are forms of visions. They are spiritual because they are not communicated through the senses. They are supernaturally imparted to the intellect without any act by the person. These visions are communicated passively. These visions or communications, while spiritual and intellectual, still deal with created objects and consequently are objects of the active night of spirit. We must liberate the intellect from these communications and direct it to the night of spirit. The more one desires darkness regarding possible communications through these visions the greater will be the infusion of faith. "The greater one's faith the closer is one's union with God" (A.2 9.1).

1. The intellect derives knowledge and spiritual vision from these communications without the apprehension of any form, image, or figure of the imagination.
2. We must direct the intellect beyond these spiritual apprehensions and direct it to the spiritual night of faith.
3. Along with faith also comes hope and love, since these three theological virtues increase together.
4. These various visions that John describes in detail can be wonderful but they should never be the object of our aims or desires.

CHALLENGES FOR TODAY
- Do not desire special visions or revelations for you can always be deceived.
- Avoid seeking disclosure of hidden truths or manifestations of some secret or mystery.
- Give yourself entirely to the darkness of faith.

DAY 177 *PURIFYING THE MEMORY AND WILL*
(See *Ascent*, 3. 1)

Book I of the Ascent dealt with the active night of the senses, Book II with the active night of the spirit, the purification of the intellect in faith. Book III deals with the purification of the other two spiritual faculties: the active night of the memory in hope, and of the will in charity. Since the three spiritual faculties depend on each other, the purification of the intellect in faith will simultaneously impact the other two spiritual faculties. However, we must also actively and deliberately purify our memory of its false ways of possessing God, and our will of its false ways of loving God.

1. Let us remind ourselves that we are dealing with the active night of spirit and consequently with our own contributions to this process of purification.
2. The active night of spirit consists in our efforts to purify the spiritual faculties of their false or limited contents and methods of knowing, possessing, and loving God.
3. In our journey to God we are not only burdened by pleasures of sense but also by what we know, remember, and love, and also by how we know, remember, and love.
4. We purify our memory and will of all their false images because they all fall short of who God wishes to be for us.

CHALLENGES FOR TODAY
- How great or small is your image of God?
- Do you rely on your memory to form an image of God's compassion for you?
- What are your greatest loves?

DAY 178 *EMPTY THE MEMORY OF IMAGES*
(See *Ascent*, 3. 2)

God is our teacher and guide in contemplation. We passively receive this illumination and cannot hinder it by sensory and discursive activities of the faculties. So, as with the intellect, we must deprive the memory and will of their natural objects so they can receive an inflow and illumination from God. In the case of the memory we must empty it of all former images so that it is not attached to any earthly or spiritual object. We appreciate God's loving compassion towards us less with memories than with hope.

1. The memory can only be absorbed in hope of God when it lives in forgetfulness of past images and lives without remembrance of anything.
2. We should not store up in the memory objects from the five senses but leave them aside and forget them
3. The memory cannot be united to God and at the same time be united to forms and images that are not God, for God has no form or image comprehensible to the memory.
4. This purification does not lead to the destruction of the memory but to its perfection in hope.

CHALLENGES FOR TODAY
- Compare what you know of God from your memories with what you hope for in union with God.
- Is hope a forgotten virtue for you?
- Pray that God in contemplation will suspend former limited ways of possessing God.

DAY 179 *THREE KINDS OF HARM FOR THE MEMORY* (See *Ascent*, 3. 3-5)

There are three kinds of harm that arise when we do not purify the memory. The first harm comes from the world around us, in so far as relying exclusively on the memory leads to falsehoods, imperfections, appetites, judgments, loss of time, and so on. The second harm resulting from a misdirected focus on the memory comes from evils and delusions that result from false images. The third harm is that memories become impediments to moral and spiritual goods, as we become disturbed by memories and unable to focus on the incomprehensible God.

1. When we focus on memories we can often find an imperfect presentation of facts, people, and God that can lead to sorrow, fear, hatred, vain hope, and vain joy.
2. When we stress ideas and discursive acts of the memory some seem true when they are false and false when they are true.
3. When we become disturbed by memories we lose tranquility and peace of soul and cannot give ourselves to focus on God.
4. Memories are discursive and must be purified in the illumination of contemplation.

CHALLENGES FOR TODAY
- Remind yourself that God is incomprehensible and cannot be understood by accumulated memories.
- Check this week when you remember something to see if you are bothered, annoyed, sad, or joyful.
- Reflect on whether your image of God is dependent on memories.

DAY 180 BENEFITS FROM DENIAL OF MEMORIES (See Ascent, 3. 6)

When we control the negative effects of memories we find three opposite benefits that result from forgetfulness. Instead of the disturbances derived from ideas in the memory we enjoy peace of soul and purity of conscience. Instead of the temptations from evil we find freedom in our thoughts and ideas. Instead of the blocks to moral and spiritual development we discover recollection and forgetfulness and we become disposed to the guidance of the Holy Spirit.

1. Worrying about memories can never remedy the disturbance we feel but only produce further distress.
2. As we try to endure all things with tranquility and peace, so we should respond in this way to memories.
3. We should seek tranquility of soul and peace in all things both in times of adversity or prosperity.
4. Memories make us look back, whereas we should be looking ahead in hope.

CHALLENGES FOR TODAY

- Have you ever thought about controlling your memories?
- Why do you think memories never give a clear image of God?
- Which memories recently disturbed you and why?

DAY 181 HARM RESULTING FROM REMEMBERING SUPERNATURAL COMMUNICATIONS (See *Ascent*, 3. 7-12)

John has reflected on natural imaginative visions recalled by the memory. He now turns to supernatural imaginative communications. These too can become a hindrance to union with God in pure hope. Focusing on these memories leads to a series of harms. 1. A person can be deluded in mistaking the natural for the supernatural. 2. He or she can fall into presumption and vanity. 3. Evil tendencies can deceive a person through these apprehensions. 4. The misdirected emphasis on the memory can be an impediment to union with God in hope. 5. The resulting judgments regarding God will fall short of who God is.

1. No supernatural form or idea held in the memory is equal to God, and we must empty ourselves of these ideas.
2. The more we dispossess ourselves of memories, even supernatural communications and understandings, the more we are left to hope.
3. When we think as we recall our memories that we have experienced a special communication from God we should remember this is not virtue. It is creating an image of God from our memories.
4. Primitives made gods out of stone. Unfortunately, we do the same but from our best images.

CHALLENGES FOR TODAY
- Humility and emptiness turn you to hope.
- Which wonderful past experience blinds you to encounter the true God?
- Does the Church's history present you with an authentic image of God?

DAY 182 BENEFITS THAT COME FROM REJECTING IMAGES IN THE MEMORY
(See Ascent, 3. 13)

The benefits in the case of denying supernatural apprehensions are like those from rejecting natural forms. In addition, when a person rejects all images from the memory he or she enjoys deep spiritual repose and quietude, a peace from the care of having to discern and decide concerning the images, and a freedom from the time consuming discussions with a spiritual director concerning all these images. Memories are discursive and one needs a new kind of insight into God. One of the results of union with God is "forgetfulness of all things since forms and knowledge are gradually being erased form the memory" (A.3. 2.8).

1. Freeing oneself from cares about all these images gives one opportunity to focus on the pursuit of detachment.
2. Since these supernaturally communicated images can come from God why should we reject them? John would tell us to accept the love of God who communicates to us but reject the image as an inadequate portrayal of God.
3. God grants communications passively, we must not deal with them actively.
4. We should only focus on the love of God these communications cause and give no attention to their representations. They could even be recalled for a renewal of love.

CHALLENGES FOR TODAY
- Remember you cannot worship a god made from images in your memory whether natural or supernatural.
- Think often about what you hope for from God.
- Practice prudence and humility in regard to all communications about God.

DAY 183 DISTINCTLY SUPERNATURAL COMMUNICATIONS IN THE MEMORY
(See *Ascent*, 3. 14-15)

In this section of the *Ascent* John considers the third class of apprehensions, namely spiritual intellectual. These are distinctly and supernaturally communicated without corporal image or form. These can be brought back to the memory not with the aid of image or phantasy but through a form impressed on the soul. A person can remember these, not in forms but in the effects they produced, and remembering them can rekindle the former love and also lead to feelings of union.

1. In proportion to our denial of objects of memory our ability to hope increases.
2. There is nothing wrong in using one's memory in daily life, but one should never become attached to images and the gratification they produce, as if they represented God.
3. All religious images have value, even the cult of images, provided there is no attachment that blocks union with the true God.
4. The memory advances by rejecting its normal objects and focusing instead on hope.

CHALLENGES FOR TODAY
- From all images let your heart soar to God.
- Reconsider what if any are your favorite images of God. What should you do about them?
- Hope has been referred to as the forgotten virtue. It is one of the three great powers of your soul.

DAY 184 UNITING THE FOUR PASSIONS TO THE WILL OF GOD (See *Ascent*, 3. 16)

The active night of the spirit includes the purification of the will in charity. This means we must purify the will so that we can employ all faculties, appetites, operations, and emotions towards union with God. The will controls appetites, faculties, and passions, directing them to God in love. There are four passions that direct our lives to God or when inordinate away from God. These four passions—joy, hope, sorrow, and fear—must focus all we do on the will of God and integrating all we do in union with God. We must work to purify each one individually, aware that all four are intimately connected and wax or wane together.

1. John urges us to avoid dividing our will among many objects but to unite it in one single ability and strength directed to God.
2. John suggests that the guiding Scripture reference for the active night of the spirit is "You shall love the Lord your God with all your heart, and with all your soul, and with all your might" (Deut 6:5).
3. When we focus passions on the pursuit of God's will, we learn virtue, when we allow them to focus on what is not God we fall into vice.
4. One passion that gives itself to false goals drags all the others with it.

CHALLENGES FOR TODAY
- Check if you have one great love or many loves.
- How can you bring some unity in your many loves? What integrates them?
- Which of the four passions predominates in your life and why?

DAY 185 JOY (See Ascent, 3. 17)

Joy is the passion and emotion of the will that results from the satisfaction we find in an object we seek. This joy is active, which means we can seek it or not. However, we should only find joy in those things that lead us to God. What we should not do is seek or find joy in objects that lead us away from God. There are many aspects of daily life—God's gifts—that bring us joy, and we can make all these part of our integrated commitment to God.

1. We can find joy in objects that lead us to God or in those that lead us away from God. We must choose only the former.
2. John divides the possible objects of joy into six groups: temporal, natural, sensory, moral, supernatural, and spiritual.
3. All aspects of our daily lives can be integrated in our total commitment, and we can find joy in many ways that are part of our unified God-directed lives.
4. Where we find joy is the goal of our lives. Are we seeking the right goal?

CHALLENGES FOR TODAY
- Where do you find your greatest satisfaction and joy?
- Identify objects of your joy that do not lead you to God.
- Are you a joyful person?

DAY 186 JOY IN TEMPORAL GOODS
(See *Ascent*, 3. 18-20)

We fail when we seek joy in temporal goods such as wealth, status, family, and so on, making them ends in themselves. All these are good in themselves, especially when used in the service of God. However, often we can become attached to them and misdirect our joy to them instead of to God. When we allow ourselves to find joy in creatures as ends in themselves we blunt our dedication to the joy of union with God. If we free our hearts from joy in exclusively pursuing satisfaction in temporal goods many blessings result, including freedom of spirit, clarity of judgment, liberality, peace, and purity of spiritual commitment.

1. Temporal goods are God's gifts and we direct our gratitude to the goodness of God and use these gifts well.
2. When we find joy and satisfaction exclusively in temporal goods we become forgetful of God.
3. Focusing our joy on creatures as the exclusive object of satisfaction weakens our judgment, diminishes our spiritual commitment, and results in lukewarmness to spiritual values. When we do this, we become more committed to creatures than to God.
4. When we detach ourselves from making temporal goods ends in themselves we end up with a new appreciation for them.

CHALLENGES FOR TODAY
- Is the joy you find in temporal possessions dragging you down from the spiritual goals you seek?
- Pay attention to small attachments; they can become great.
- Quantity of goods is not the problem; possessiveness of heart is.

DAY 187 JOY IN NATURAL GOODS
(See *Ascent*, 3. 21-23)

Natural goods refer to all bodily endowments and all rational gifts. We cannot find joy in these for they can provoke vanity rather than gratitude to God. Joy in these natural goods can lead to pride, complacency, sensualness, and flattery. It can result in a dulling of spiritual values, poor judgment, distraction from one's spiritual goals, and lukewarmness to the things of God. If we reply to these natural goods with humility and charity, and then also with appreciation of our neighbors, we can purify our love, deepen peace of soul, withstand temptations, and focus exclusively on what pleases God.

1. Natural goods include beauty, grace, elegance, and so on, as well as intelligence, discretion, insight, and other rational gifts.
2. Joy in natural goods inevitably means focusing on ourselves and not on God.
3. Joy in natural goods involves us in a movement towards sensual satisfaction and away from the life of the spirit.
4. Purification of the will in its pursuit of joy in natural goods includes strengthening the will against sexual threats and temptations.

CHALLENGES FOR TODAY
- Pray to God in gratitude for whatever natural gifts you may have.
- Avoid comparing yourself to others for such comparisons always create problems and harm.
- Why do you think you merit God's love?

DAY 188 JOY IN SENSORY GOODS
(See *Ascent*, 3. 24-26)

Sensory goods refers to all goods apprehensible through the five senses and through the imagination—so through the exterior and interior senses. Clearly we cannot know God as God through the senses. If we misdirect our wills to joy in these sensory objects we hinder our ability to find joy in God alone. If we use knowledge from sense objects as a stepping stone to appreciation for God, then we can profit from them. We must never make joy in sensory goods an end in itself. If we turn from sense objects as ends and use them to focus on God, we become more recollected, spiritually-centered, and find authentic joy in God's many gifts.

1. When we find satisfaction in sense objects but with freedom of spirit immediately raise this to God, then this is good. Many can be greatly moved by sense objects.
2. The person of pure heart finds joy in everything.
3. When we seek joy only in sensory goods, we turn away from God and open our hearts to all kinds of distractions, covetousness, loss of dedication, envy, intemperance, and so on.
4. Until we have controlled the false joy in sense objects we should not expect growth in the spiritual life.

CHALLENGES FOR TODAY
- You can do great harm to yourself by misdirecting joy in sensory goods and so should daily pursue self-control in these areas.
- What are modern sensory goods that distract you?
- Which friends seem to lead you to find joy exclusively in sensory goods?

DAY 189 JOY IN MORAL GOODS
(See *Ascent*, 3. 27-29)

It is not surprising that John condemns the misdirecting of our wills to temporal, natural, and sensory goods, for all spiritual writers do that. Moreover, these goods have no intrinsic value as ends and can harm our pursuit of God. However, John also insists we should avoid directing our wills to joy in moral goods. It is true that these goods have value in themselves and can effect good for others. However, we must avoid joy and satisfaction in possessing them and seek only joy in God's gifts and the good done because of these gifts.

1. Moral goods include virtues, good habits, practice of good works, fasting, almsgiving, obedience to God's law, urbanity, and good manners.
2. A person can rejoice in the exercise of moral goods and God is pleased a person seeks such qualities, but we should avoid joy in simply having and possessing them.
3. When we focus on the possession of moral goods we can easily pass to vanity, comparisons with others, seeking others' approval or praise. These problems then lead to a decrease in spiritual commitment, presumption, and an unwillingness to take advice from others.
4. Avoiding joy merely in the possession of these goods frees us to concentrate on the love of God and engage in a spiritually enriching use of these gifts.

CHALLENGES FOR TODAY
- Rejoice in God's moral gifts to you and pledge to use them for God's honor and glory.
- Remember Jesus' warning that they who do good for others' approval have already received their reward.
- Beware that you can be attached to moral goods just as you can to sensory ones.

DAY 190 JOY IN SUPERNATURAL AND SPIRITAL GOODS (See Ascent, 3. 30-45)

Some of God's gifts to us are for the benefit of others (supernatural goods) and others for a deeper relationship between a person and God (spiritual goods). Again no one should rejoice in the possession of these gifts but only in the good achieved and the love of God encountered and manifested.

1. Supernatural goods would be gifts such as wisdom, knowledge, miracles, prophecy, knowledge, discernment—all goods that bring benefit to others directly and indirectly lead to knowledge and love of God.
2. God grants these supernatural gifts for the benefit of the Church. The key thing is we exercise them for the love of God.
3. Spiritual goods refer to all that aid, motivate, provoke, and direct a person to divine communication and the perfection of spiritual enrichment. These could include statues, shrines, places of prayer, devotional objects, ceremonies, pilgrimages, favorite gurus, preachers, and so on.
4. Spiritual goods can always deceive, and we can become attached to them.

CHALLENGES FOR TODAY
- Never let the extraordinary substitute for the darkness of faith.
- Use spiritual objects if they help, always rising from them to interior devotion and to the praise and love of the incomprehensible God.
- What are the contemporary supernatural and spiritual goods to which you have been attached?

DAY 191 *GOD SPEAKS TO OUR HEARTS*

We frequently speak about our spiritual development as a journey. However, it is a journey that is primarily God's work of drawing us forward, rather than our effort-filled undertaking. When left to ourselves, we seem to spend all our lives travelling without ever arriving anywhere. We remain filled with so many problems to which we do not have any answers. However, God has given us the right perspective on this journey when in Scripture we read, "I shall lead her into solitude and there speak to her heart" (Hosea 2:14). While God leads us, it is still a journey of discovery into the unknown. Every day we make an effort to go to what we do not understand.

1. There are various systems of spirituality. We should consider whether our system is working or not. If not, we should leave it aside and find one that does.
2. Let us think about the major questions that fill our minds and hearts.
3. In the spiritual journey we often keep doing the same things with the same lack of success. Why?
4. Let us ask what is God's will for us as we journey through life?

CHALLENGES FOR TODAY
• Ask God to lead you into solitude and to speak to your heart.
• To hear God's voice in your heart prepare yourself in reflection, silence, and solitude.
• How do you recognize God's voice within you?

DAY 192 *A JOURNEY OF NEGATION*

Sometimes in our spiritual journey it seems we are running out of time, but we are not. There is lots of time. The key issue is how to use it. Answers come from all sides, and God who has the real answers must strain to be heard above the din of our ignorance. This journey is one of negation, and we need to be ready for a call we never thought we would receive. Our call is to denial not achievement, emptiness not accumulation, poverty not possessiveness, and passivity not activity. The spiritual journey implies emptying ourselves of all that is not God so we can attain what is truly of God. An authentic spiritual journey is always through the nights. The night is the death of all false desires, all false gods. The journey through the nights is a journey of purification of everything that comes through our senses, everything that comes from the outside, so that we can be renewed by the life of the Spirit within us.

1. "I didn't know you, my Lord, because I still desired to know and relish things" (S. 33).
2. We become our desires and for the most of us our desires are too small.
3. This journey leads to a drying up of all previous religious devotions that portray an artificial god, because only when we are dry and empty are we ready to be set on fire with God's love and filled with new life.
4. So many people worship a god of their own creation

CHALLENGES FOR TODAY
- Are you ready for a journey of denial and negation?
- What does the night mean for you at this stage in your journey?
- How do you contribute to the effectiveness of the night?

DAY 193 *TWO ASPECTS OF ONE EXPERIENCE*

The active night of sense is the effort to remove faults and sins one can see, but there are lots of faults one cannot see without God's illumination in contemplation. Some writers see the active night of sense as first, followed by the active night of spirit along with the passive night of sense as two parts of the same experience. Then the passive night of spirit follows. However, the experiences of active night of spirit and passive night of sense continue to surface and purify even during any respite or plateau periods.

"However, in the concrete reality of a person's spiritual life there is no real chronological sequence between this (active night of spirit) and 'the passive night of sense' which he treats in Book I of the *Dark Night*. The distinction between these two nights is genuine enough, but it is mainly a theoretical one in which activity and passivity signify two aspects of one experience" (Collings, pp. 67-68).

1. Not everyone experiences the nights in the same way.
2. Teresa and John have different experiences of these transitions.
3. The illumination of contemplation throws further light on more unconscious levels that need active purification.
4. Growth takes place in transitions and crises.

CHALLENGES FOR TODAY
- How do you handle crises?
- Can your spiritual director guide you through the nights?
- Are you actively involved in purifying sense?

DAY 194 DISMANTLING THE FALSE SELF

John of the Cross wants us to endeavor with God's help to purify our failings and learn to engage in profound and continuous recollection. This will enable us to be present to God so that God can train us to be ready for further purification that can lead us to the path of union. "For Christians personal union with Christ is the way to come to divine union. The love of God will take care of the rest of the journey. Christian practice aims first at dismantling the false self. It is the work that God seems to require of us as proof of our sincerity. Then He will take our purification in hand, bring our deep rooted selfishness into clear focus, and invite us to relinquish it. If we agree, He takes it away and replaces it with His own virtues" (See Keating, p. 72). This negation is not an end. It is part of the process of spiritual empowerment.

1. The active night is a discipline the soul must impose on itself.
2. This period of training helps us undertake a difficult climb.
3. John says that if we endeavor to start this journey we must be "fired by love's urgent longings."
4. We are fortunate that God is our personal trainer.

CHALLENGES FOR TODAY
- Remember abnegation is a means; loving union is the end.
- Every renunciation is a gesture of love.
- What part of you needs dismantling?

DAY 195 *THE RIGORS OF SPIRITUAL GROWTH*

"It has been objected by contemporary critics that the demands made by our authors (Teresa and John) are severe to the point of irrelevance for twentieth-century (twenty first-century) people, who find such austerity alien and unacceptable. In fact the teachings of the great Carmelites is at all points rock-rooted in holy writ, and a comfortable determination to water down the wisdom of the gospel is as common, and no less enervating today, as in the sixteenth or the first century of the Christian era" (See Truman Dicken, pp. 369-370). Certainly, there are other easier and more readily accepted approaches to the spiritual journey. The real question is whether they are equally useful in attaining the goals of the journey. John may start in more human negativity, but he reaches greater heights.

1. John's is not an extravagant asceticism, but he does seek a total, relentless commitment to pursue the journey to God.
2. The sacrifice entailed in this journey is not an end in itself, but a manifestation of the loving desire for union.
3. Both Teresa and John opposed excessive self-discipline and asceticism, teaching instead the importance of union of one's will with God's.
4. John teaches the rigors of love and acceptance of the pains of love.

CHALLENGES FOR TODAY
- Does your spiritual life include exaggerations, or is it well-balanced?
- Would you describe yourself as a child in the spiritual life or a mature seeker?
- How do you confront the rigors of love?

DAY 196 TODAY'S LACK OF INTEREST IN ASCETICISM

Christian tradition has always insisted that every Christian must actively seek to remove sinful tendencies from life in order to prepare self for life with God. It is a constant of tradition that we must acknowledge our own sinfulness and undergo conversion before we can begin the journey to God. We know that transformation is God's work within us, but we must ready ourselves for this gift by the removal of sin and the development of virtue. "We don't think much about asceticism these days—not so much in the sense of doing penance for our sins but in the much richer and positive sense of engaging in the struggle to be conformed to God, the effort to free ourselves of everything or anything that keeps us from attaining deep union with God. John of the Cross is no masochistic dualist, a vestige of some bygone spiritual tradition now transcended. No, he is a particularly focused and clear spokesperson for a deep truth that has been experienced by centuries of saints, officially canonized or not" (See O'Keefe, p. 8).

1. We find it acceptable to think of dieting, exercise, jogging, even personal trainers. Why are we uncomfortable about applying this concept to spiritual health?
2. Asceticism can simply mean conforming our will to God's.
3. Several spiritualities emphasize self-fulfillment, neglecting the asceticism that leads to self-fulfillment.
4. Let us discuss with close friends the role of self-sacrifice and asceticism in our lives.

CHALLENGES FOR TODAY
- Describe the key components of your asceticism.
- Reflect on whether your will is centered on God's.
- Do you have an exercise routine? A routine for your spiritual life?

DAY 197 ACTIVE NIGHT OF SENSE AND BEHAVIORAL CHANGE

This is a period of active ascetical choice and commitment; the focus is not merely on prayer and devotions but on a program of self-discipline, correction of faults, living out one's priorities, and a single-minded dedication to God. Clinging to objects, practices, notions, experiences, and causes of religion that once helped us on our journey to God becomes an obstacle to encountering God who is not like any object of sense no matter how spiritual. "The active night of sense deals with the obvious. Its focus is on behavioral change: correcting obvious faults, choosing to mortify our self-centered ego, and exercising restraint regarding sensory pleasures. Though the pleasures may not be sinful in themselves, our inordinate indulgence in them makes us lethargic in responding to God's will. The night of sense consists of 'bridling' our appetites (N.2. 3.1), reining in our desires, and 'pruning' the behavioral branches of our lives (N.2 2.1). The purpose of the active night of sense is not to repress desire but reorient it. It is the soul's first attempt to change its life-organizing principle from the pursuit of pleasure and the avoidance of pain to living a life of virtue by doing God's will" (See Foley, p. 8).

1. Let us reflect on our behavioral changes in recent years.
2. We now understand mortification as re-education or redirection, or reorientation of sense.
3. Our daily behavior must be part of our God-directed lives.
4. What is our life-organizing principle?

CHALLENGES FOR TODAY
- Name your obvious faults.
- Do you have any desires that are out of control?
- Think about what you personally contribute to the active night of sense.

DAY 198 *STRUGGLING THROUGH CRISES*

John of the Cross is one of the greatest guides in times of struggle. His teachings on the two great nights are viewed as essential insights into spiritual life. However, while not everyone deals with the two great transitions of life, we all face the small nights that come often in life. Here, too, John can be very helpful in teaching us that growth takes place in times of crises or transition. "Crisis" comes from Greek and simply means "judgment." In times of crisis we need to make a different judgment about life. We may need to leave aside values from the past and move on to something new. This can be painful. When faced with crisis, even small ones, we must seize the opportunity to struggle through the crisis, make a new judgment, and move on to further growth.

1. We need to see crisis as opportunity for change and growth.
2. We can apply this idea of growth through crisis to family life, Church, and society.
3. We cannot achieve anything worthwhile without a struggle.
4. There is no mysticism without asceticism.

CHALLENGES FOR TODAY
- Are you happy when faced with struggles?
- Is your love strong enough for the struggles ahead?
- Which struggles do you not feel strong enough to face?

DAY 199 *ACQUIRED CONTEMPLATION*

Contemplation is a gift of God. It is an experience that is passive, immediate, ineffable, and infused. It is an intuition that is intense, profound, and very simple. However, the Teresian School of Spirituality insisted since its foundation that there is a transitional experience between meditation and complete contemplation, which they referred to as "acquired contemplation." This is also a gift of God but it includes effort on the part of the individual to prepare himself or herself for deeper union with God beyond meditation. "Teresian theologians have introduced the division of contemplation into acquired and infused. Experimentally infused contemplation is a higher mystical grace, but besides it there is another contemplation, much more common, which is offered to practically all those who are willing to fit themselves for it as they should. It is a contemplation in which a certain divine infusion comes to the assistance of the soul, so that it may hold itself in the presence of God by a gaze of living faith. Hence they name that contemplation active, alluding to the soul's active cooperation, or again acquired, observing how the facility in thus gazing upon God with faith and love is 'acquired'" (See Gabriel, pp. 94-95).

1. Fr. Gabriel sees acquired contemplation as different from meditation and from totally infused contemplation; it is "a contemplative prayer of a lower degree."
2. This acquired contemplation "renders (a person) conscious of the divine activity within." It is "a hidden divine inflowing (that) comes to help the formation of a 'habit' of looking lovingly upon God with the gaze of living faith informed by charity."
3. This early contemplation is common but often unrecognized.
4. Fr. Gabriel's distinctions are not always recognized today.

CHALLENGES FOR TODAY
- Do you find that there is a distinct experience between meditation and contemplation?
- Do you see where you need God's help to form habits to prepare for contemplation?
- What have you done to ready yourself for God's gift of contemplation?

DAY 200 ASCENT AND DARK NIGHT REFLECT JOHN'S INTELLIGENCE

The *Ascent* and the *Dark Night* seen as one integrated work is an exceptional treatise with a logical structure, and rigorous mental applications. This combined work is the fruit of a long experience and personal observation. It is also a strictly biblical work in which every section is introduced by a strong chapter rooted in Scripture. John's presentation is clear, logical, and well integrated. He sees the whole journey and how all parts relate to each other and to the goal. He moves forward with determination without any deviation from his goals. He never shows off his knowledge, but is undoubtedly well grounded, extremely competent, and integrates human and divine knowledge. When we read his works, especially the *Ascent* and the *Dark Night*, we feel we have entrusted ourselves to someone who is well-prepared and knows what he is talking about.

1. This work evidences John's analytical skills and his ability to cut through secondary issues and deal with essentials.
2. John is confident of what he writes and he generates confidence in the reader.
3. John brings the penetrating light of his intelligence to bear on understanding the darkness of the night.
4. John is an expert guide who knows the journey well both from his studies and from his experiences.

CHALLENGES FOR TODAY
- Ask John to guide you further in the spiritual journey.
- Remind yourself of the security you find in John's vision.
- Why are you interested in John's writings?

DAY 201 *TRANSFORMED FROM THE INSIDE OUT*

Many people think John presents a program of mortification, putting to death all desires, passions, and faculties. This is far from the truth. He urges us to redirect or reeducate every aspect of our lives and focus everything on God. "The purpose of San Juan de la Cruz's spiritual practice is a resensitization of the body from the inside out, as opposed to the ordinary path of sensation from the outside in. To achieve this inner transformation San Juan de la Cruz sheds, like so many snakeskins, his habits of ordinary sensation through a spiritual discipline that completely empties him externally and leaves inside a large void, a huge darkness of sensation, a total and absolute dark night of the soul. This total darkness is the result of a dedicated spiritual practice" (See de Nicolás, 57-58). Once totally empty, a person can be filled with God and discover a new set of values, feelings, and practices.

1. Many people experience inner darkness and emptiness, but it is not the result of spiritual practice and transformation, but the absence of it.
2. John's experience of the dark night is not subjective, it is a common calling of humanity.
3. We must long for the time when we can read the "Dark Night," and find that it gives meaning to how we feel.
4. Are you convinced that your current spiritual practice will lead you where you want to be?

CHALLENGES FOR TODAY
- If your day does not have times and places conducive to prayer, find them.
- Is your life influenced from the outside or from the inside?
- Are you excited about your spiritual life and its practices?

DAY 202 *THE NATURE OF FAITH IN JOHN OF THE CROSS*

The future pope John Paul II completed his doctoral dissertation on faith according to St. John of the Cross. He shows how John always speaks of faith informed and vivified by charity. "It is always a question of faith vivified by charity and, indeed, of faith as the means of divine union by reason of its ordination to charity. Faith is treated by St John of the Cross as the means of union of the soul with God; more precisely, as the means proper to the intellect for uniting the soul with God in love. (However) no creature can serve as a proportionate means of union with God, because it lacks the proportion of likeness that is absolutely necessary for union with God. . . . Faith is described as the proportionate means of the union of the intellect with God. . . . The essential likeness of faith to God is the basis for its proportion of likeness, which is, in turn the reason why faith is the proportionate means of union with God" (See Wojtyla, p. 237).

1. Pope John Paul II presented his dissertation to the doctoral faculty of the Pontifical University of Saint Thomas Acquinas (Angelicum) in Rome in 1948.
2. Only faith is capable of uniting our intellect with God for there is no possible likeness between any creature and God.
3. Faith is never abstract but always linked to love.
4. In contemplation God teaches us a new way of knowing through faith which becomes the only way of knowing God.

CHALLENGES FOR TODAY
- How would you describe faith?
- Why is faith linked to charity?
- How has your image of God changed over the years?

DAY 203 CAN LANGUAGE DESCRIBE GOD?

The Christian tradition has generally used two ways to speak of God. One is positive (kataphatic) and uses words, symbols, ideas, and images to describe God. It looks at creation as a reflection of God and so takes the best of creation and applies it in the ultimate to God. Thus, God is wise, just, compassionate, and so on. John uses the attributes or descriptors of God in this way. This is a theology of immanence, it is active, and it tries to say something of who God is. The other approach is negative (apophatic) and insists that nothing in creation can possibly convey anything of God, since God is totally unknowable to human nature. This approach emphasizes the transcendence of God and insists that no image or words can convey anything of God, and so the only thing one can do is empty one's mind, heart, and memory of all former knowledge. It springs from the theology of transcendence and insists on the total separation between the Creator and creation, on the otherness and unknowability of God. Regarding God we live in darkness and this approach tells us what God is not. These two ways of knowing God are complementary and St. John is the inheritor of both traditions.

1. John uses language that reflects both the immanence and transcendence of God.
2. In John's prose we remember that negation is for growth.
3. John always acknowledges his inability to do justice to ineffable experiences using human language.
4. John's poems describe his own intense mystical experiences but cannot fully convey or define them.

CHALLENGES FOR TODAY
- Write a poem describing your own spiritual experiences.
- Which of these two ways has primacy in your life?
- How do you describe God?

DAY 204 INDIFFERENCE TO THE THINGS OF GOD

Almost nothing in our society nourishes contemplative reflectiveness. We are bombarded with commercialized self-gratification at every turn. We give importance to utilitarian approaches to life, to a work ethic, and to a changed approach to filling up time where there is no opportunity for reflection. There often seems a general dulling of the human spirit with its accompanying inability to think of God. We often want ourselves more than we want God, and we block God out of our lives.

"There are naturally recognizable signs indicating that human nature actually exists in a state of depravation. This includes the inability to assimilate and react to facts according to their true value. This inability may either be due to an innate dullness or to a general blunting of the sensibility that has developed in the course of life, or, finally, to an indifference to certain frequently recurring impressions. What we have often heard is quite well known to us and therefore 'leaves us cold'. To this may often be added an excessive preoccupation with one's own individual interests which makes us indifferent to other things. We know that this inner rigidity is wrong and suffer from it. . . . This lack of sensibility is particularly painful in the religious sphere" (Stein, p. 2).

1. The spiritually mature with true living faith see things as they are.
2. So many are surrounded by false inhibitions and rigidity and are unable to see things as they are.
3. Through the nights we can be re-born to this "holy objectivity," and thus react properly to the realities of the world.
4. Our contemporary world is indifferent to the things of God.

CHALLENGES FOR TODAY
- What shapes your life? The realities of life in the vision of God or the false vales of this world?
- Are you indifferent to the call of God deep within your heart?
- Do you have a sensitiveness to spiritual values?

DAY 205 *THE ACTIVE NIGHT OF SPIRIT*

The active night of spirit refers to a process of purification of any satisfaction that comes from the spiritual faculties. It means purifying the intellect in faith, the memory in hope, and the will in charity. In fact, the active night of the spirit consists in purifying one's images of God that come through the faculties. "The active dark night of the spirit consists in the willing and perfect rejection of all understanding, experience, feeling, imaginings, fantasizing, and even supernatural communications. Insofar as possible, the person must place any and all understanding, feeling, imaginings, desires, opinions into a cloud of forgetting to walk the way of naked faith in unknowing. John emphasizes the way to God as one of pure, naked faith. Only such naked faith does full justice to the infinite difference between the Creator and all creatures. The paradox of faith is that it is an excessive light that the person experiences as baffling darkness" (See Egan, p. 179).

1. The active night of spirit includes our "willing and perfect rejection" of what leads us away from God.
2. In the active night of spirit we reject lots of experiences that are good but inadequate.
3. Are there aspects of the contemporary Church that we reject in this dark night?
4. If we deny all our desires, feelings and so on, what is left?

CHALLENGES FOR TODAY
- What does "unknowing" mean?
- Describe an experience of baffling darkness.
- Explain what you understand by the "way of naked faith."

Toledo, looking from the Alcantaran Gate to the castle.
John was imprisoned just beyond the bridge.

10
The Spiritual Canticle

The *Spiritual Canticle* begins and ends John's work as a writer. He wrote the first 31 stanzas of the poem when he was in prison in Toledo (1577-78), and additional stanzas while prior in Granada (1582-84). As far as we can tell he wrote the commentary bit by bit in Granada in 1584, touching it up for two more years until 1586. John worked and re-worked this wonderful book for over eight years. The title is not John's but that of his first disciples and biographers. It does however reflect John's own approach, for the poem follows the imagery of the biblical *Song of Songs*.

For further reading to accompany the reflections in this section, see Leonard Doohan, *John of the Cross—The Spiritual Canticle: The Encounter of Two Lovers*, 2013.

DAY 206 *THE MEETING OF LOVERS*

For the next few days let us focus our daily reflections on the first part of the *Spiritual Canticle*. Stanzas 1-12 describe the anxious commitment of a person who searches for love and union with God. These next days of reflection highlight our need to deliberately pursue our journey to God beginning with appreciation of God's revealing presence in creation and in other people's goodness. It is also a time when we experience painful purification at our inability to get beyond partial and dissatisfying experiences. We realize we will always be restless without God. In the beginning experience of contemplation we catch glimpses of God's love and beauty, feel transformed by the experience, but are left longing for deeper union.

1. In the original Spanish, John never uses adjectives or adverbs in the first 12 stanzas, creating a sense of urgency.
2. One author describes the Gospel of Mark as "a restless rush to the passion." John's first twelve stanzas are a restless rush to the arms of the beloved.
3. These stanzas describe the pain of love.
4. Let us think about how excited we feel when meeting someone we love.

CHALLENGES FOR TODAY
• Do you have a sense of urgency in your pursuit of God?
• Think about what it was like to fall in love.
• Are you willing to invest your time and commitment in this relationship?

DAY 207 SURROUNDED BY GOD'S BLESSINGS (*See Spiritual Canticle*, stanza 1)

There is so much evil in our world, and it can overwhelm us. But we have chosen to immerse ourselves in an awareness of the innumerable blessings of God. However, in this world of blessings, so often God seems hidden from us in spite of our longings. In Jesus' revelation we discover that God is hidden in our own hearts, and our task is to leave aside all false loves that lead us away from God. This means finding new ways of knowing and loving God within our own hearts. This is a painful experience since it implies abandoning our previous immature ways of knowing and loving God through the use of our spiritual faculties of intellect, memory, and will, and letting God teach us how to know, love, and hope in new ways. These are God's ways of purifying and transforming our lives. Thus, we can experience God's love and uncover the mysteries of our faith. In these experiences we are satisfied with God's presence and then left in painful longing by God's absences.

1. Our greatest responsibility as human beings is to seek knowledge and union with God.
2. We need to let go of any previous knowledge, hopes, and loves, and let God transform our faculties of intellect, memory, and will.
3. Deep within each of us there is a zone that is naturally divine, and it is there that we can encounter God.
4. If we wish to make this journey with and to God we must reject everything that is not God.

CHALLENGES FOR TODAY

- Today, spend some time appreciating the blessings that surround you.
- Quietly reflect on the presence of God in your own heart.
- Ask God to teach you to know, love, and hope in new ways.

DAY 208 *OUR EARLY ATTEMPTS TO COMMUNICATE WITH GOD*
(See *Spiritual Canticle*, stanza 2)

We know we cannot communicate directly with God in this life, but hope that God appreciates our desires and affections as signs of how much we long for union with God. When these attempts are imbued with love, God responds with inspiration. Even in the early stages of our spiritual journey we must single-mindedly pursue the love of God making all else secondary. This means leaving aside so much of what we previously valued, especially our former knowledge, memories, and desires. This is painful but it becomes a way of proving our love through this suffering. We see how poor is our knowledge, possession, and desire for God and turn to God asking for communication in faith, hope, and love.

1. Let us make use of whatever channels we can to persuade God of our love and desire for union.
2. We understand that God values love above all else.
3. God always answers our prayers but only when the time is right.
4. Our three greatest spiritual needs—to know, possess, and desire God—are transformed by the three great energies of the soul—the theological virtues of faith, hope, and love.

CHALLENGES FOR TODAY
- Present to God your intense desires and focused affection as signs of your desire for union.
- Reflect on how your image of God has changed over recent years.
- What is the primary interest of your life—is it the pursuit of God?

DAY 209 *LET US DEDICATE OURSELVES TO THE PURSUIT OF GOD* (See *Spiritual Canticle*, stanza 3)

In the initial phases of the spiritual life we can show God the intensity of our desire for union by the practice of virtues and by the spiritual exercises of both active and contemplative life. At the same time we withdraw from any self-satisfaction in the spiritual life, as well as any temptations that weaken our pursuit of God. All forms of attachment to temporal, sensory, or spiritual objects hinder the single-mindedness necessary for our exclusive focus on the search for God. Our contribution in these early efforts is twofold—the practice of good and the rejection of evil.

1. We will never find God except by effort-filled sacrifice of leaving aside all that is not God.
2. The spiritual life is primarily what God is doing in us, but we must show our commitment in whatever ways we can.
3. Our dedication to the pursuit of God requires courageous determination.
4. Enemies of our progress come from the world's false values, temptations from evil in its many forms, and from the natural rebellions of selfish desires.

CHALLENGES FOR TODAY
- John stresses the importance of "all" (todo)—every aspect of life must be given to God.
- John calls you to let "nothing" (nada) block your search.
- Assess your spiritual commitment, that you are not seeking satisfactions from any of it.

DAY 210 WE BEGIN OUR SEARCH FOR GOD
(See *Spiritual Canticle*, stanzas 4-5)

We begin a serious search for God by leaving aside satisfactions that come from anything that is not God-directed, by overcoming temptations, and by fostering self-knowledge. Then we begin to appreciate the presence of God in creation, every aspect of which is a revelation of God's love. The richness and diversity of the created world reflect traces of God's presence and act like mini incarnations of God's grandeur. This is so because God raised up creation in the Son's own incarnation.

1. Let us reflect on how God manifests divine love in creation.
2. How can we learn about God by reflecting on the world's wonders that surround us?
3. Can we think about how Jesus' Incarnation transforms our world?
4. Let us think of creation as a liturgy of praise to God.

CHALLENGES FOR TODAY

- Make an examination of temptations that can block your search for God.
- Think about what you have learned about yourself while reading John of the Cross' works?
- Spend time in praise of creation.

DAY 211 *THE BEAUTY OF THE WORLD INSPIRES US TO LOVE GOD*
(See *Spiritual Canticle*, stanza 6)

The more we see God's beauty reflected in creation the more we are drawn to love God, the source of all this goodness, beauty, and love. Yet simple traces or signs of God's presence are not enough for us, for God seems more absent than present. We long for a deeper union. Partial revelations in creation do not satisfy us, and we discover our desire and longings go unfulfilled. We find this painful and our hope for deeper union grows.

1. We can never be satisfied with partial revelations of God.
2. Creation entices us to think of God, but God leaves us unfulfilled and dissatisfied with only partial knowledge of divine life.
3. Our own images of God are not authentic revelations of God for we often create God in our own image and likeness.
4. Nothing can satisfy us except complete union.

CHALLENGES FOR TODAY
- Find a quiet spot and appreciate the beauty of creation.
- What do you want to know about God?
- Think about your own painful experiences in the spiritual journey and your feelings of inadequacy.

DAY 212 *LEARNING ABOUT GOD FROM OTHERS* (See *Spiritual Canticle*, stanza 7)

In initial phases of the spiritual journey, we can learn much about God from others' experiences. Their commitment to seek God in prayer and contemplation inspires and motivates us. Their intense love and desire for God teach us about how they have witnessed the grace, mercy, and love of God, as they glimpse the greatness of God. But just as creation reveals and hides God, so too do others' experiences, leaving us dissatisfied and in pain at our own unfulfilled desire for complete union.

1. Sometimes what others teach us about God is helpful, but it is often just "stammerings."
2. Commitment to pursue union with God can leave us with the pain of unfulfilled desires.
3. John's concept of impatient love so often reflects our own spirit.
4. There are always good people whose teaching inspires us, even though we must remember this is always partial.

CHALLENGES FOR TODAY
• Think about someone who inspires you and ask why.
• What do you learn from sharing with others in group study?
• What desires do you have in your spiritual journey that are unfulfilled?

DAY 213 EXPERIENCING GOD IN THE CREATED WORLD (See *Spiritual Canticle*, stanza 8)

We gain a partial understanding of the greatness of God through our knowledge and experience of the created world. These experiences can be intense communications that fill us with love, but they can also be overwhelming in so far as they leave us in a painful longing for deeper union with God. As our life becomes more centered on love, we see more clearly how our emphasis on natural life alone is a hindrance to the deeper union we seek. The created world can inspire us and lead us to God. It can also show us how limited and partial everything is in relation to who God wants to be for us.

1. There is a life that is greater than our bodily life with all its restrictions.
2. When we live in God's love it transforms our natural life and gives meaning to our spiritual life.
3. There are two horizons to life—this one we live in each day, and a realm of life beyond this one that gives meaning to the present.
4. God's love penetrates to the very depths of our being and destiny.

CHALLENGES FOR TODAY
- Reflect on what aspects of your life are hindrances to spiritual union.
- Refocus your priorities to center on love.
- How does life beyond this world influence your actions in this world?

DAY 214 *OFTEN WE DO NOT SEEM TO BE GETTING ANYWHERE IN THE SPIRITUAL LIFE*
(See *Spiritual Canticle*, stanza 9)

We all experience pain in our spiritual journey from feeling that our efforts are getting us nowhere and from our inability to sort things out. We run here and there seeking solutions, and we discover that God alone can heal and guide us. However, God attracts us and then leaves us incomplete and painfully dissatisfied. We find life needs total love, and we long to give God our complete love. This means constantly longing for God and never being satisfied in anything other than God. We will always be restless until we rest peacefully in God's love of us and our love of God.

1. Only God can bring us fulfillment in life, and our daily strivings for union are our way of asking God to show us divine love.
2. In these early stages God attracts us to union and then seems to leave us abandoned.
3. When we offer ourselves totally, God leaves us helpless without the union we seek.
4. We know we love God when we do everything to please God.

CHALLENGES FOR TODAY
- John speaks of patient-urgency. Do you need more patience or more urgency?
- Check that discouragement does not weaken your enthusiasm for the spiritual journey.
- Are you doing everything you can to please God?

DAY 215 LONGING FOR THE HEALING PRESENCE OF GOD (See *Spiritual Canticle*, stanza 10)

St. Augustine wrote that our hearts are always restless until they rest in God. Sure enough in our spiritual journey we frequently experience a love-sickness that results from having tasted the goodness of God and finding that our longings remain unfulfilled and our love incomplete. It seems God steals our hearts and leaves us helpless and without the loving response we expected. We find nothing else satisfies us, and we lose taste for anything else. We leave aside all self-interest and seek deeper union in any way we can. But only God's healing presence and transforming love can satisfy us. We long for the wholeness that only a life of dedication to God can bring. Without this it seems we are living in darkness.

1. It is always helpful to identify our own longings for fulfillment and discover they are met in God alone.
2. Life can be full of wearying and annoying distractions that can only be overcome with the refreshing presence of God in our hearts.
3. Love happens within us when we focus ourselves entirely on God.
4. All aspects of life can be integrated in our dedication to God.

CHALLENGES FOR TODAY
- Is there restlessness in your life? Why do you think it is so?
- Give examples of when you think you have tasted the goodness of God.
- In what ways do you need the healing presence of God?

DAY 216 *WE GLIMPSE THE DIVINE PRESENCE*
(See *Spiritual Canticle*, stanza 11)

When we relentlessly pursue the love of God, God responds by revealing insight into the beauty of divine life. However, these glimpses of divine presence intensify our desire for a deeper union and the healing of our profound longings. God is present to us in three ways. First, as creator who sustains us in existence, second, by the transforming power of grace, and third, God is present to us in love when we long for divine union. These are partial satisfactions, for only in the next life can we appreciate the essential presence of God's beauty. In this life we are left with glimpses that do not satisfy. God is health for a love-sick person, and the more love increases the healthier a person becomes.

1. Imperfect love is a sickness that drains us spiritually and can only be healed by God.
2. Only God's love transforms us into who we need to be.
3. The spiritual journey always includes the pain of unfulfilled loves.
4. Unfulfilled love reminds us of the incompleteness of this life and reminds us of a life beyond this world.

CHALLENGES FOR TODAY
- Think about how God is present to you.
- Is there an experience of God that motivates you in your spiritual commitment?
- How do you experience the transforming power of grace?

DAY 217 ARRIVING AT THE BEGINNING
(See *Spiritual Canticle*, stanza 12)

The early part of the spiritual journey includes a period of purification and illumination. A person who receives God's illuminative communication tends to think he or she is rushing headlong to union, and that God is completing the work of transformation. However, a person who longs for union discovers that it comes through faith that is still covered with the restrictions of this life. Faith is a gift, an incomplete communication that awaits fullness of revelation in the next life. So, often in these early stages a person feels he or she is almost there, but that is not the case. He or she feels so close to the love sought, but is still deprived of it. The journey must continue.

1. Now and again we catch glimpses of God's love, are thrilled with the experiences, but must appreciate this is the beginning and not the end.
2. No longer satisfied with mediated experiences of God, through creation and through others, we long for deeper union.
3. We must close the eyes of our intellect and open our eyes of faith.
4. The more we love God, the more the sketch of faith we see will be completed by the vision of love.

CHALLENGES FOR TODAY
- What have you learned in times of purification and illumination?
- Think seriously as to whether you are ready for a major step in the spiritual life.
- Reflect on the strength you gain by humility.

DAY 218 A TIME FOR LOVE

In the next few days we will reflect on stanzas 12-21. These stanzas describe the encounter a person experiences in what John of the Cross calls spiritual betrothal. This is a time of the in-breaking of God's love and includes special communications of God's presence. At this time a person feels protected from disturbances he or she previously experienced but also continues to feel the absence of God. Such a person now sees and appreciates his or her own gifts, longs for transformation of spiritual faculties and yearns for the deeper union with God that only comes in the next stage which is spiritual marriage.

1. These stanzas are now filled with adjectives that describe the richness of the encounter.
2. John's rich descriptions draw us to savor every aspect of this encounter of love.
3. An encounter of love means both find pleasure in the other.
4. Engagement is an exclusive agreement—there can be no other love.

CHALLENGES FOR TODAY
- Taste and see how good the Lord is.
- Remember God is seeking you more than you are seeking God.
- Why do you experience absence in union?

DAY 219 *GOD GRANTS GLIMPSES OF PURIFYING AND TRANSFORMING LOVE*
(See *Spiritual Canticle*, stanza 13)

This period that John describes as spiritual betrothal is a time when a person feels that God is near. This period of engagement is an in-breaking of God's transforming love in a person and includes special communications from God. This is a subtle and delicate knowledge that penetrates to the depths of the soul. It is "an unveiling of truths about the divinity and a revelation of His secrets" (c. 14-15.15). However, such a person still feels the pain of absence and intolerable darkness, both due to the sense of un-fulfillment and of dissatisfaction a person feels at partial communications. However, accepting this pain helps one to appreciate the favors of God and deal with the overwhelming power of these communications. While a person may long for deeper union, he or she is simply not ready yet, human nature cannot cope with it, and continued failures make one unworthy of the deeper communication and knowledge that lie in store. However, this is a time when God grants glimpses of divine love that fill a person with desire for more such experiences. God grants these communications in gentleness, peace, and love.

1. God's treatment of a person at this time is a preparation for strong love that will be needed throughout the rest of the journey.
2. The experiences that God grants at this time are intense but brief for they are also too much for human nature.
3. God grants love in proportion to the person's own love.
4. These communications cause a spirit of love in a person.

CHALLENGES FOR TODAY
- Think of God's gifts and of your own limitations to accept them all.
- Reflect that sometimes the darkness we experience is due to excessive light.
- Prepare to receive in contemplation, appreciating the need for passivity.

DAY 220 *SEEING THE WISDOM OF GOD IN CREATION* (See *Spiritual Canticle*, 14-15)

When God grants a person the union of spiritual betrothal it includes special communication, knowledge, and extraordinary gifts. Previous pain, darkness, and un-fulfilled desires now give way to peaceful love and to many blessings. Noteworthy at this time is the illumination concerning the wisdom of God seen in the harmony of creation. A person appreciates how every creature gives glory to God, and he or she learns so much about God through the revelations of creation.

1. What does creation reveal to us about God?
2. Do we experience more pain or peaceful refreshment in our spiritual lives?
3. What refreshes our spirit and deepens our love of God?
4. We can learn so much from the harmony we see in creation.

CHALLENGES FOR TODAY
* Spend time thinking about all the wonders of creation.
* Express gratitude to God for all the blessings you have received.
* Reflect on how the world is a teacher or guru for you.

DAY 221 VITALLY EXPERIENCING GOD'S ATTRIBUTES (See *Spiritual Canticle*, 14-15, cont)

At this time a person receives a glimpse into divine life, knows God in the vital experience of the divine attributes, and feels God is all this for him or her alone. This is a gentle experience of the power of God. This communication of truths about the divinity is a spiritual revelation given passively to a person. At this time one enjoys being alone with God and personally enjoying the transforming presence of God. This is not a permanent presence, for God still withdraws from time to time, leaving the person alone.

1. How do we experience the qualities or attributes of God?
2. God's self-revelation comes in contemplation and so includes darkness.
3. Do we enjoy being alone with God?
4. After the painful experiences of purification and illumination this period is more peaceful but still has its own pain.

CHALLENGES FOR TODAY
- Focus on one quality or attribute of God and how you experience it.
- Spend some time alone with God.
- Think about what are the greatest desires of your life.

DAY 222 GIVING THANKS FOR GOD'S GIFTS
(See *Spiritual Canticle*, 16)

Anything that is good within us is God's gift. We can offer to God all the goodness and virtues of our lives, giving praise for what God has achieved in us. As we offer ourselves to God, God appreciates this gift even though it is the result of divine transformation within us. However, this is also a time of the disruptive impact of evil that can block the integrity of one's self-gift, and we must be on our guard. In particular a person must unite his or her will to God, wanting only what God wants. Totally focusing our will on God's is our contribution to union.

1. Giving ourselves totally to God in love is one of the best services we can ever perform.
2. Uniting our will to God's is a key value at this time.
3. In spite of growth, let us keep in mind that this is early in the spiritual journey, and we are not yet very mature or strong.
4. Remember we are not striving for a goal of union, rather God is drawing us.

CHALLENGES FOR TODAY
- Offer to God whatever goodness is part of your life and do so in gratitude.
- What evils threaten your spiritual life?
- Is there something that binds you and from which you cannot free yourself?

DAY 223 DEALING WITH PAINFUL DISTRACTIONS (See *Spiritual Canticle*, 17)

Having experienced the closeness of God, a person feels pain when God is no longer near. It is annoying to deal with painful distractions and worse still to suffer from spiritual dryness at this time. A person finds he or she is helpless unless God alleviates these pains. Fortunately, the Holy Spirit can awaken love, refresh our spirit, and refocus our will on God alone. The Holy Spirit also reminds us of God's blessings, helps us control negative tendencies, and leads us to renewed transformation of spirit. Thus, a person can recommit himself or herself to God and rejoice in God's communication and love.

1. When we love intensely we will feel the pain of absence intensely.
2. Let us always remember the blessing of God in our lives transformed by grace.
3. The Holy Spirit prepares us for deeper union.
4. We often cannot appreciate that God is pleased by our love, but God has chosen that this be so.

CHALLENGES FOR TODAY
- Maintain a life of prayer throughout all periods of pain.
- Ask the Holy Spirit to dispel dryness and increase virtue and love.
- Desire and long for the union you seek.

DAY 224 KEEPING WATCH OVER ONE'S HEART
(See *Spiritual Canticle*, 18)

We are always tied down by the limitations of this life. Our strivings for union are always incomplete, imprisoned as we are in our bodies with their tendencies to threaten the peaceful union we seek. Our faculties continually pursue the wrong objects. Rather, we must focus on the spiritual faculties and their transformation in faith, hope, and love. Our interior spirit can always be distracted by exterior senses. We must control these if we wish the Holy Spirit to abide in us.

1. The union of spiritual betrothal is an incomplete union, looking ahead to completeness.
2. This life always has limitations that threaten our spiritual growth.
3. Prayer is a key ally in withstanding the temptations and threats to life in the spirit.
4. We must focus on knowing God in faith, possessing God in hope, and loving God in charity.

CHALLENGES FOR TODAY
- Check to see what are the threats to your spiritual commitment.
- Pray for peace of soul and strength to fight all threats to spiritual growth.
- Spend time in quiet, peaceful passivity.

DAY 225 UNION IN CONTEMPLATION
(See *Spiritual Canticle*, 19)

As a person experiences union, he or she finds that union is restricted by sensory distractions. If union is to grow then divine communications need to be only to one's spiritual part. This is achieved in contemplation that produces an ineffable spiritual communication and brings about a new way of knowing, possessing, and loving God. Thus, it is no longer indirect or through the senses, but a direct communication in the deepest part of the soul. A person wants God to see the transformation divine gifts have achieved and be pleased.

1. Lovers want to be alone and communicate in secret.
2. People who long for union can never be satisfied by indirect communication of intermediaries but only by direct communications.
3. God looks upon the virtues of our lives, appreciates them, and grants deeper communication.
4. Authentic knowledge of God is always foreign to the senses.

CHALLENGES FOR TODAY
• Pray for deeper union and prepare yourself for contemplation.
• What can you do to train yourself to prepare your own body for quiet and stillness?
• Can you be still, be inspired, concentrate, and remain in silence? These are remote preparations for contemplation.

DAY 226 *LONGING FOR SPIRITUAL MARRIAGE*
(See *Spiritual Canticle*, 20-21)

At this point in the spiritual journey, a person longs for spiritual marriage—a stage that requires the complete purification of all imperfections, the total direction of life by the spiritual faculties, and a commitment that includes courageous love. All this in effected by the interventions of the Holy Spirit, who thus enables a person to control all previous temptations and distractions and to direct his or her whole self to God and spiritual values. At this time a person lives in the joy of God's presence where all previous hopes and longings are satisfied. Freed from all negative affects of passions a person can now rest in God's peace.

1. This is a time when a person receives from God purity, beauty, and strength to continue the journey.
2. God helps a person to control fantasy, and bring anger and concupiscence under the guidance of reason. These will not cease but they will be under control.
3. A person also needs courage at this time.
4. It is important that one develop a just balance in the spiritual life without any extremes.

CHALLENGES FOR TODAY
- Celebrate the joy God brings to you at this time.
- Be grateful to God for the control of negative aspects of life that used to hinder the spiritual journey but no longer do.
- This is the time to make a perfect "yes" of love to God.

DAY 227 PERFECT UNION

In the next few days we will reflect on the third part of the *Spiritual Canticle* (stanzas 22-35). This part describes spiritual marriage as a profound transformation of a person. It is a time of the revelation of special secrets and brings the gift of union. It is an experience of peaceful security, mutual surrender, and equality in love. It focuses on love alone in mutual self-gift. God makes all this possible for God is love.

1. At this time a person feels secure in the transforming presence of God.
2. This experience is one of total, complete, mutual surrender.
3. At this time a person can say, "Everything I do, I do with love."
4. This union implies the total renewal of self in which humanity is not destroyed but reaches its full potential.

CHALLENGES FOR TODAY
- Appreciate all the gifts you have received from God.
- Celebrate any growth in your spiritual commitment.
- See yourself as a lover.

DAY 228 SPIRITUAL MARRIAGE
(See *Spiritual Canticle*, 22)

With stanza 22 John begins a description of spiritual marriage. This kind of union only happens—in most cases—after a long period of purification of all evil tendencies. Spiritual marriage is a state of total transformation in love when a person surrenders himself or herself completely to God and discovers that God also surrenders self to the person. It is a time of mutual surrender, communication, and participation. In fact, this is a new level of existence when all aspects of life—temporal, natural, and spiritual—are transformed. A person in this state enjoys security and peace.

1. All growth in spiritual life is God's work within us. We can celebrate whatever growth there is in our lives, and with appreciation we can celebrate the growth in other people's lives too.
2. Our spiritual journey can be filled with struggles and pain, but it leads to peaceful satisfaction at the attaining of our purpose in life.
3. Mutual surrender in love is the goal of the spiritual journey, but smaller experiences of surrender and mutuality occur throughout.
4. In all growth God is our strength, protecting us from evil and controlling all negative tendencies.

CHALLENGES FOR TODAY
- Celebrate the beauty of these gifts that God makes at this time, whether you are at this stage or not.
- Pray that God continue to work within you, transforming all you are into all you can become.
- Spend a few moments expressing your desire for total union with God.

DAY 229 COMMUNICATION OF DIVINE
KNOWLEDGE (See *Spiritual Canticle*, 23)

Spiritual marriage is a time when God communicates an understanding of divine life. This wonderful gift will include new insights never appreciated before, but will also include a deeper understanding of the fundamental mysteries of the Incarnation and Redemption. A person only reaches this state of spiritual marriage as part of the Son's world redemption on the cross. Redemption includes making us companions and achieving union with us in spiritual marriage. The Lord attained this for us in a moment of self gift on the cross, but we strive to receive this gift one step at a time.

1. Redemption is not just from sin but it includes spiritual marriage.
2. God's love is such that it includes raising us up to mutuality and union.
3. John teaches us a more profound and extensive understanding of the purposes of Incarnation and Redemption than we generally comprehend.
4. Jesus' death on the Cross is the moment of spiritual marriage.

CHALLENGES FOR TODAY
- Pray that you may cooperate with God's redemptive and transforming grace in your life.
- Ask God to draw good from evil at every moment of your spiritual journey.
- Reflect on the love that led to the cross and resulted from the cross, especially as it applies to your own life.

DAY 230 SOME OF THE REWARDS GOD GRANTS
(See *Spiritual Canticle*, 24)

The union of spiritual marriage brings with it a profound experience of peace, security, and satisfaction. One sees the many gifts and virtues received from God and appreciates that one now possesses them with permanence and fortitude. A person who reaches this goal enjoys communications from the Son of God—grace, further gifts, protection, freedom from former failures and disturbances, peace, and security. A person who gives himself or herself totally finds God reciprocates and communicates knowledge and awareness of divine life and gifts.

1. This experience is something we eagerly anticipate. It can motivate us in our daily re-commitment to pursue union.
2. The further one pursues union with God—which implies many painful sacrifices and struggles against evil—one finds profound peace.
3. The mutuality of this relationship is amazing, that God reciprocates all our gifts with extraordinary divine blessings.
4. This is a time when a person can experience the greatness and beauty of God.

CHALLENGES FOR TODAY
- You can readily see how the pursuit and attainment of union enriches the Church.
- Think about your image of God and make sure it is not too small.
- Remember that whatever efforts you make, God will outdo you in generosity.

DAY 231 CELEBRATING OTHERS' GIFTS
(See *Spiritual Canticle*, 25)

This is a time when a person praises and celebrates the many gifts God has given to others. A person who is at peace with his or her own life can celebrate how God encourages others, inflames them with love, fills them with charity, and matures their love. A person who is immersed in God can appreciate how God is powerfully present in other people's lives, drawing them to good, centering their will, and enkindling their love. So, one can see traces of God's transforming actions in so many people's lives and celebrate with gratitude.

1. The whole world is aflame with God's transforming presence, and those who see it celebrate with reverence.
2. God transforms the world with love. Sometimes it is just a touch of love here and there, and other times a more permanent presence of transforming love.
3. A profound sense of gratitude is our main response to God's abundant gifts.
4. Since God is so present in others' lives we can learn so much from them.

CHALLENGES FOR TODAY
- Look at others, see God active in their lives, and celebrate.
- Let others' goodness motivate you to greater commitment.
- Try to develop a new way of looking at the world and see always the transforming presence of God.

DAY 232 RESTING IN PEACE AND SECURITY
(See *Spiritual Canticle*, 26)

There comes a time when a person who has dedicated his or her life to the pursuit of God finds that he or she has no interests other than resting in and enjoying the love of God. This is a depth of love unlike any other and penetrates to the very center of one's personality. It is a new level of existence, and while a person does not necessarily experience the intensity all the time, the transformation is complete and permanent. A person now has no interest in anything other than love. The world's affairs and even oneself have no interest for the person anymore. This is the result of a contemplative insight not discursive imagination.

1. This is a new kind of life where only love matters.
2. One's faculties may still be active in old ways and one may still have residues of old useless hopes, joys, sorrows, and fears, but these are all secondary to love.
3. This is the transformation one has been seeking. It is overwhelming and it overflows in love.
4. While generally love builds on knowledge, at this time a person can be so overwhelmed with love that he or she does not understand what is happening.

CHALLENGES FOR TODAY
- There are times when you must love much even without understanding what is happening.
- This week, give priority to love and forget about everything else.
- Are you sure you really want the new life that lies ahead?

DAY 233 *MUTUAL SURRENDER OF SELF AND GOD* (See *Spiritual Canticle*, 27)

Overwhelmed by God's gifts of love a person surrenders himself or herself completely to God. God's surrender to the person who has made this journey is also total and includes communications of secret wisdom given to a person in contemplation. In this way God transforms a person, making him or her ready for union, and enriching intellect and will. In response a person gives self in complete and permanent fidelity, centering every aspect of life on God alone. Such a person has only one overriding desire, namely to give himself or herself completely to God. This motivates him or her in everything.

1. This transformation of intellect and will leads a person to know and love God in new ways.
2. There comes a time when a person focuses on nothing else except knowing how to love and how to give oneself totally to God.
3. This transformation takes place in contemplation.
4. Peace results from the total direction of all faculties to God.

CHALLENGES FOR TODAY
- This week, try to focus all your actions, cares, and desires on God's will alone.
- Think about whether there is an aspect of life that you keep back from God.
- Describe your experience of God's love for you.

DAY 234 NOW MY EVERY ACT IS LOVE
(See *Spiritual Canticle*, 28)

God does not need anything we can offer, but still cherishes all that we do for love of God. In this way like true lovers there develops an equality in love. A person shows total surrender in a life given to complete service of God in love. Thus, God raises the seeker to the level of equality in love. In dealing with God a person dedicates all the soul's energies to love; everything is now done for love (C. 28.7). One's spiritual faculties of intellect, memory, and will, together with all energies of one's spirit are dedicated to God's service. This becomes a habit and continues even when one is not thinking about it. All former activities and occupations give place to a constant attentiveness to the will of God. Now everything a person does is done for love.

1. It is important that a person no longer seeks satisfaction in anything except union with God.
2. At this time one's four passions, natural appetites, and daily cares center on God alone.
3. If a person consistently makes decisions to please God, his or her responses will eventually become automatic.
4. What we formerly valued and treasured lose their importance as God takes over the focus of life.

CHALLENGES FOR TODAY
- Ask yourself why God wants equality in love with you.
- Can you say "now my every act is love"?
- Are you constantly attentive to the will of God?

DAY 235 *BE PROUD OF THE GOD-DIRECTED CHOICES YOU MAKE* (See *Spiritual Canticle*, 29)

We saw that a person arrives at a point where he or she has no interest in anything except the love of God. Now, as a true lover, he or she has no concerns but to be attentive to God and to the exercise of love. This means that everything else becomes unimportant, including previous practices, services, ministries, and good works. All are secondary to the life of love. A person appreciates that "there is no greater or more necessary work than love" (C. 29.1). John knows that "Anyone truly in love will let all other things go in order to come closer to the loved one" (C. 29.10). Others can well criticize this "holy idleness," but a person now knows the secret source of fruitfulness is love alone.

1. In spite of others' reprimands for lack of involvement, a person knows he or she has chosen well in focusing on God alone.
2. Giving oneself to good works is not as effective as giving oneself to love alone.
3. Sometimes a person in love seems lost but actually has found what is most important.
4. People who do not understand the spiritual journey fail to understand the choices others make. We should never be ashamed of the choices we make for the pursuit of God.

CHALLENGES FOR TODAY
- Practice "holy idleness."
- Is every aspect of your life focused on God?
- Remember that no one can serve two masters.

DAY 236 *JOY IN COMMUNION AND LOVE*
(See *Spiritual Canticle*, 30-31)

A person finds much joy, consolation, and happiness in his or her union with God in love. This is also a time of satisfaction in appreciating the virtues and qualities of one's life along with the grateful acknowledgement that they are God's gifts. These virtues are all tied together by love and enrich the Church. Such a person is a reflection of God, since he or she is the embodiment of virtues that are God's gifts. These same virtues manifest a person's strong love, the result of fortitude shown throughout the spiritual journey. Clearly, it is God who has transformed the person, but God recognizes a person's contributions and rewards them with further love.

1. A person realizes that virtues are God's gifts, but also knows God recognizes them as the result of personal development.
2. A life of virtues is bound together by love and without it the virtues would fall apart.
3. A life of dedication is maintained by fortitude which is persevering love.
4. We should look back over our lives to see the struggles and efforts and appreciate God's guiding hand.

CHALLENGES FOR TODAY
- Is fortitude a part of your spiritual life?
- Think about the virtues God has enabled in your life and ask how they are related to love.
- What does strong and vibrant love mean to you?

DAY 237 *ACKNOWLEDGING THAT ALL COMES FROM GOD* (See *Spiritual Canticle*, 32-33)

God's love for a person who has come this far in the spiritual journey is profound. The person takes no credit for the development but rather acknowledges that God gave the love and faith that made him or her worthy of God's merciful love. God loves a person at this time because he or she embodies God's own love. "Thus he loves the soul within himself, with himself, that is, with the very love by which he loves himself. This is why the soul merits the love of God in all her works in so far as she does them in God" (C. 32.6).This transforming love of God removes all that makes a person unworthy of God and enriches him or her with new illumination and transforming grace.

1. It is important that we take no credit for the love within us, since it comes from God.
2. God helps us appreciate how divine love has changed our lives.
3. Even when we have reached this stage we should never forget our former sins but humbly remember from where we came.
4. Let us always give thanks for what God has done for us.

CHALLENGES FOR TODAY
- Reflect on how God's transforming love has changed your life.
- Remembering that your transformation is unmerited keeps you humble, and maintains your life in perspective.
- Keep before your mind that God loves you when you participate in God's own love.

DAY 238 MUTUAL GRATITUDE
(See *Spiritual Canticle*, 34-35)

It is a strange thing that not only does a person express profound gratitude to God for so many gifts, but that God also expresses gratitude to a person who has undergone transformation. God celebrates a person's growth and fulfillment, and he or she can rest in contemplative union, refreshed, protected, and deeply favored by God. At this time, a person finds peaceful solitude in God, rests in contemplative union, and has no need of anything but God's love.

1. God appreciates a person's discovery of solitude, for here it is where one finds true love.
2. The three spiritual faculties of intellect, memory, and will are now all centered on God, knowing, possessing, and loving in God's ways.
3. This is an exclusive relationship, without intermediaries, celebrated in contemplation.
4. This is a mutual love, each in love with the other.

CHALLENGES FOR TODAY
- Spend time alone with God.
- Look back at victories over failures and be grateful for purification, growth, and fulfillment.
- Celebrate what God has done for you and for others.

DAY 239 COMPLETE HARMONY

The next four days' reflections refer to the final stage in the spiritual journey as described in the *Spiritual Canticle*. Here the two lovers long for total union in glory. This period includes immersion in the mysteries of God, delight and gratitude, participation in the life of God, and complete harmony in union with God.

1. People who love each other just want to be together.
2. In one of his poems John says he is dying because he does not die.
3. This section describes longing for a union beyond the restrictions of this life.
4. What is our purpose in this life?

CHALLENGES FOR TODAY

- How intense is your desire to be in God's company?
- Do you think there is harmony in your life?
- Think of the joy you feel in an encounter of love.

DAY 240 *ABSORBED IN GOD'S LOVE*
(See *Spiritual Canticle*, 36)

Lovers like to be alone and enjoy each other's companionship and intimacy away from other distractions. At this stage in spiritual union a person who has journeyed this far—or rather been drawn by God this far—wants to enjoy the love attained, become more like God in love, and learn more about God who loves him or her so much. Having left aside activities in preference for "holy idleness," he or she now wants the depth of love discovered in contemplation to overflow in all his or her actions. Such a person in union with God now wants to see himself or herself transformed and reflected in the beauty of God

1. A person now wants to resemble the Son in all his values so that life is modeled on his.
2. Love longs for deeper knowledge in order to love more.
3. The desire for intimate love takes precedence over all else.
4. John describes the essence of God as beauty, unusual in spiritual writers and mystics.

CHALLENGES FOR TODAY
- Sit still and enjoy being totally present to God.
- Remember there is no growth in love without suffering.
- Ask yourself how you can be more like the Son.

DAY 241 *IMMERSION IN THE LIFE OF GOD*
(See *Spiritual Canticle*, 37)

This present life always has restrictions and limitations, and great mystics often yearn for an ending to this life in order to enter a realm of life beyond this one that has no bounds. Then they can enjoy the profound mysteries of God especially the Incarnation. This is what happens to the person who has reached this stage in the spiritual journey. He or she knows it is not possible to go any further while restricted to this life. However, united to God, a person experiences these mysteries as much as possible in this life, enjoying the attributes, mysteries, judgments, and virtues of God. This mutual knowledge leads to even deeper love.

1. The final stages of the spiritual journey include ever deeper revelations of the mysteries and ways of God.
2. The spiritual maturity described in these stanzas only comes after much purification.
3. This is a time of profound gratitude.
4. We were born to be immersed in the mysteries of God.

CHALLENGES FOR TODAY
- Reflect on these late stages in the spiritual life no matter where you are on the journey.
- Try to think of your life and God's as one.
- How do you think knowledge and love are related?

DAY 242 ACHIEVING WHAT YOU HAVE ALWAYS WANTED (See *Spiritual Canticle*, 38)

Overwhelmed with gratitude, a person wants to love God as much as God loves him or her. Since this is not possible in this life, a person now longs for the next. Such a person's intellect, memory, and will are united with God's, and a person understands, hopes, and loves through the Holy Spirit. While yearning for the fullness of the next life, God grants a person in spiritual marriage an anticipated experience of that ineffable vision.

1. What a person has always longed for is experienced in this concluding state of spiritual marriage.
2. A person now understands, wills, and loves through the Holy Spirit.
3. Lovers always want to love as much as they are loved.
4. This wonderful vision motivates us all to undertake the hardships of the journey.

CHALLENGES FOR TODAY
- Ask God to show you how to love and to give you the strength to love completely.
- Peacefully celebrate whatever God has done in your spiritual life.
- Do not be surprised at God's marvelous gifts; be grateful.

DAY 243 ALL IN HARMONY WITH THE HOLY SPIRIT (See *Spiritual Canticle*, 39-40)

This experience of transformation includes intimacy with God, an appreciation of God-in-the-world, a contemplation of the divine essence, and an immersion in love. John insists a person becomes God through participation—understanding, knowing, and loving in the Trinity, together with the Trinity, and as the Trinity. All this takes place in contemplation. The Holy Spirit has freed a person from all former disturbances and transforms him or her into the life of God. A person appreciates that his or her entire being is now in harmony with the Spirit, and asks that God continue to bestow divine blessings.

1. The Holy Spirit enables us to live this new life of God.
2. A person at this stage returns to God God's own life of love.
3. A person is thus remade in God's image and likeness.
4. All this takes place in a person's inner spirit but the joy of it can overflow to the sensory part.

CHALLENGES FOR TODAY

- Think about your destiny with God.
- Be grateful that God grants these blessings to some for the benefit of the Church.
- Re-read the poem of the *Spiritual Canticle* in its entirety.

DAY 244 *APPRECIATING GOD'S STEADFAST LOVE*

Our world does not seem to have much interest in God and certainly does not think God has much interest in us. Many seek God, but the wrong god—distant, angry, and violent. The fundamental conviction of Christianity is that God is close to us and loves us in such a way that God takes a risk with us. When God sees the world drifting away from divine union in love, God acts unceasingly to bring us back and hold us close in love. A hymn describes this response, "O Love that will not let me go." However, we evidence a lot of conscious and unconscious resistance to God's love and illumination, and we need purification of our actual, habitual, and social sins before we can appreciate that God is love and calls us to a life of union in love. We must tell ourselves that the human heart that seeks meaning and fulfillment can only find them in love. Every day, each one of us can proclaim, "I will sing of thy steadfast love, O Lord, for ever" (Psalm 89: 1).

1. "A soul enkindled with love is a gentle, meek, humble, and patient soul" (S. 29)
2. Which religious movements today have a primitive understanding of God?
3. Let us reflect on our own conscious and unconscious resistance to God's love.
4. What other religions present an image of God as love?

CHALLENGES FOR TODAY
- Give examples of God's steadfast love for you.
- Do you know what are the actual, habitual, and social sins in your life that hinder God's work?
- Why does God take a risk with you?

DAY 245 SURRENDERING TO LOVE

In St. John of the Cross every aspect of life is overwhelmed with love. The pursuit of love of God, or the way of love, is "the single doctrinal line running through all his works" (Fr. Gabriel, p.1). We must respond to this love. Our capacity for love depends on the exclusive and integrated focus of every aspect of our lives. We go beyond our daily devotions to surrender ourselves entirely to God. This self-gift, this more mature consent to God, is our personal commitment. Total transformation is God's work within us, and we contribute nothing to that. We cannot make it happen; we can only prevent it from happening. We can try to prepare ourselves, so we can sing with the psalmist, "May God send his truth and his love. My heart is ready, O God, my heart is ready" (Psalm 56). We love day by day, one step at a time.

1. "How precious is thy steadfast love, O God" (Psalm 36:7).
2. John himself re-found all aspects of life enriched by this journey of love—his poetry, mystical insight, synthesis of life, love of people everywhere—all enriched by the love of this journey.
3. What does surrender mean?
4. Let us reflect on John's own life of extraordinary love.

CHALLENGES FOR TODAY

- Is your heart ready for the fullness of love?
- Can you see changes in your life because of the central importance of love?
- Which aspects of your life are still not affected by love?

DAY 246 OVERCOMING A LOVELESS WORLD

"Where true love is dwelling, God is dwelling there; Loves own loving Presence love does ever share. Love of Christ has made us out of many one; in our midst is dwelling God's eternal Son. Give him joyful welcome, love him and revere; Cherish one another with a love sincere" (Hymn of office readings, week 4, Thursday). God is our future and our hope, overwhelming and overcoming the depressing misery of our loveless world. St. John of the Cross' proclamation of a gospel of love has an intoxicating effect on us, giving us reason to think and believe that love can conquer the hatred, bigotry, discrimination, and dominations of our world. Instead of the small god of contemporary religion, we can say, "Then sings my soul, My Savior God, to thee, how great thou art, how great thou art."

1. How do we prove our love of God?
2. Why does God want to overcome the depressing misery of our world?
3. We Christians must take responsibility for our mission of bringing love to the world.
4. Do you think Christianity is winning or losing its mission of converting the world to love?

CHALLENGES FOR TODAY
- Is your family a model of Christian love?
- Have you ever tried to persuade someone that God is love?
- Pray in gratitude for God's love for the world.

DAY 247 *HUMAN SEXUALITY*

There is a profound, affective, sensuous dimension to John's poetry; it is filled with longing and passion. In spite of his emphasis on purification, John does not propose the destruction of sense but the total unification of affectivity towards God. "In terms of the erotic reading, embodied in his poetry and its world of mutual self-giving, tenderness, intimacy and joy, are important insights into the nature of human love: its beauty, sensitivity and mystery, as opposed to possessiveness, abuse and self-gratification. . . . Western thought has come to separate sexuality and spirituality in a way which tends to cheapen the first and disembody the second" (Thompson, p. 279).

1. Our world separates sexuality and spirituality. John unites them, giving a profound spiritual vision and affirming the highest ideals of Christian teachings on human sexuality.
2. The use of spousal and erotic imagery to describe the union of a believer with God has always been part of the Christian tradition.
3. John challenges everyone to the re-integration of sexuality and spirituality.
4. Often we find that religion has cheapened approaches to sexual love. Why?

CHALLENGES FOR TODAY
- Do you separate your sexual life from religious commitment?
- Do celibates have a better chance of spiritual growth than non-celibates?
- Think about Pope Francis' lament that the world lacks tenderness.

DAY 248 *PASSIONATE LONGING*

It is strange that John who is known for his great asceticism also provides the Church with some of its greatest love poems, filled with passion and sensuousness. "[T]here is an abandonment to all the sensations of love, which seems to me to exceed, and on their own ground, in directness and intensity of spiritual and passionate longing, most of which has been written by love-poets of all ages. These lines, so full of rich and strange beauty, ache with desire and all the subtlety of desire [. . .] this monk can give lessons to lovers" (See Symons, p. 546).

1. John writes with great tenderness, using human love as his point of departure.
2. John's poems are full of intimacy, passion, intensity, sensualness, and longing for union.
3. John quotes 67 times from Scripture's love poem, the *Song of Songs*, a book that never refers to God once; only to human love.
4. When we witness such clumsy and selfish approaches to love today, it is refreshing to read the sensitive, delicate, considerate, sensual, and passionate approaches of John.

CHALLENGES FOR TODAY
- Don't be afraid of passionate longing.
- What lessons on love can this monk give you?
- Are you a guardian of the sensuous?

DAY 249 *THE CALL TO TRANSFORMATION*

We often live an illusion that the life we are living is all there is. However, if we wish to be disciples of Jesus, we must get ready for a call we never thought we would receive. Our lives must be built on Jesus' priorities, and we should become aware that the human search for fullness of life is found in God alone. This is the call to transformation. We all struggle with our personal pain and longing to be who we are called to be—to be our best selves. In doing so we will discover God, and we will also discover ourselves. This journey will always imply collapsing habits from the past, living in faith, abandoning what we previously thought worked and now know does not, and journeying to the unknown, emphasizing Jesus' great priorities. We can make this journey with confidence for it is not our arduous undertaking, scrambling to take a few steps forward. Rather, we are being drawn by the love of God. This transformation is God's work, and we surrender to the divine action within us. We cannot achieve it, but we can prevent it from happening by emphasizing the wrong priorities. There is only one major commitment that a human being can make, to pursue a life of love with the knowledge that nothing else matters.

1. Our commitment begins with the realization of our call, and we must deliberately reflect on this awesome reality. We have a personal calling to union with God in love.
2. To strive for union in love is our enduring purpose in life, and this is what must motivate us in all we do.
3. Let us think about our spiritual calling and the responsibility it implies. This will always require humility at the greatness God has placed before us.
4. Ultimately, spiritual growth is what God is doing in us, and so we will need to appreciate the sense of mystery of our life and surrender to this invitation.

CHALLENGES FOR TODAY

- You must never give in to a reduced ideal of your calling, but be totally committed to the pursuit of Jesus' priorities.
- Spend time alone in contemplative reflection and confront your limitations and your willingness to be too easily content with a half-hearted response.
- What must you reject from your past?

DAY 250 *LIFE IN THE SPIRIT*

One of Jesus' great priorities was that disciples live a new life that would lead them to fulfillment, and we refer to this life in the Spirit as holiness and sometimes as righteousness. In his first sermon Jesus said that those who hunger and thirst after holiness would be happy, even though their commitment to the priorities of holiness would lead them to persecution. For Jesus this birth to life in the Spirit was more than outward practice of virtue or faithful obedience to ritual or to the legalistic approaches of the Pharisees. Rather, he wanted his disciples to seek God's way of holiness before anything else (Matthew 6:33). Holiness is preceded by repentance and conversion to a new way of life. Its real starting point is an awareness of a new relationship between God and disciples. As Jesus' disciples, our journey will be hard and filled with the challenges of the cross. However, faithful obedience to the will of God leads us to build a new world in faith, live in vigilant hope, and be always ready to be judged on our charity. As disciples we strive for the perfect pursuit of the will of God together with a holistic commitment to a covenantal relationship with God in Jesus. Life in the Spirit is the result of the transforming relationship with Jesus. It is not something we earn but a way of life that he gives us. We must hold onto this gift and live out faithfully what we have received. It is a dedication to the Father's will encountered in Jesus. It leads to a new level of existence, new attitudes to life, and a new way of being present to the Lord and to each other.

1. What Jesus and New Testament writers called holiness or righteousness or life in the Spirit, we now refer to as spirituality.
2. God, the Father, the source of all love, reveals to us the divine will through the teachings of Jesus.
3. Our spirituality should lead us to holiness of life, shown in good works and justice, authentic relationships in matters of wealth, power, and sex, and constant effort to produce good fruits.
4. Life in the Spirit allows a person who is in possession of himself or herself to celebrate and develop his or her own uniqueness.

CHALLENGES FOR TODAY
- Have you already left aside the worst about yourself?
- Are you constantly self-critical of your life and values?
- Describe your personal experience of God in faith.

DAY 251 *JOHN AND THE FANTASY OF THE SPIRITUAL CANTICLE*

John's writings, and especially the *Spiritual Canticle,* are filled with richness and beauty that we rarely find in any other spiritual literature. He seems to see beauty everywhere and presents a fantasy of colors in his descriptions in this wonderful book. "A fantasy which gathers together all the beauties of visible creation in meadows, wooded mountains and river banks, night and early morning, love expressed in the whispering of the waters, wounded hearts and white doves, rivers and vineyards, early wild flowers and lions' caves, flames and shepherds, knolls and sheep pastures, abysses and groves of cedars, apple trees and fields of lilies, to weave with threads of light the nuptial cloak of the beautiful bride of love" (See Crisógono, pp. 312-313). When so many people are oblivious to the world around them, this ascetic teaches us how to view things in God's perspective.

1. Only St. Francis of Assisi loves the world as much as John.
2. To write like he does, John must have had an extraordinary sense of beauty and wonderful sensitivity.
3. Let us remember that John writes one of the world's most beautiful love poems when he is immersed in the ugliness of prison in Toledo.
4. John is not striving to show the beauty of his poetry but the beauty of mystical experience.

CHALLENGES FOR TODAY
- Read stanzas 1-22 of the *Spiritual Canticle.*
- Spend a little time away from your normal places of work and home life and reflect on the beauty of God's creation.
- What is it that John wants us to reject of this created world?

DAY 252 *LOVE WITH TOTAL HUMANITY*

John does not like to think that our love can be divided between several objects. One of his favorite passages of Scripture was: "You shall love the Lord your God with all your heart, and with all your soul, and with all your might" (Deut 6:5). "The gift of the sanjuanist teaching is that the key to life is love, and we should love God and humans with the love of a person fully human. This means we love with our head and our heart, our spirit and our body, our intellect and will and our feelings, emotions, and desires. St. John of the Cross reminds us also if we love as a person fully alive it will bring suffering . . . he shows that the very experience of love brings with it a certain amount of suffering and hurt" (See Slattery, p. 30).

1. John's is not easy love. It is strong love, love with every aspect of our humanity.
2. The *Spiritual Canticle* presents one of the most integrated approaches to human-spiritual growth.
3. What we give to God must not be ruined by false asceticism. We must give our best wholistic selves.
4. The *Spiritual Canticle* shows us how spirituality is a striving for a greater share in existence.

CHALLENGES FOR TODAY
- Do not accept a reduced ideal of total self gift.
- Like John of the Cross, seek "all."
- Give every aspect of your life to God.

**This is the door through which John entered to prepare for death.
He would die in this monastery in Ubeda.**

11
The Dark Night

In 1578 John passed about eight months in El Calvario and during that time it seems he wrote the poem "One Dark Night." At this time his own experiences of the night in the Toledo prison would still be fresh in his memory. John probably began the commentary while in Baeza, before the *Ascent* was complete, then worked on both, finishing them in Granada around 1584-85.

For further reading to accompany the reflections in this section, see Leonard Doohan, *The Dark Night is Our Only Light*, 2013.

DAY 253 THE DARK NIGHT

In this section we reflect on ideas from Book I of the *Dark Night*. John calls book one "A Treatise on the Passive Night of the Senses." In this part he presents methods used during the spiritual journey to renounce all attachments to anything that leads us away from God. This part of the journey is a dark night because the purification takes place passively in the illumination of contemplation which is darkness for a person in his or her search. So, the passive night of sense marks the transition from beginners to proficients, from mediation to contemplation. Some truths can only be seen in darkness—a darkness that can be the beginning of newness of life.

1. Purification is achieved by God in contemplation.
2. This passive deprivation of sense is accompanied by a new activity of the spirit, a new prayer, and a new faith (see A.2. 12.6-7).
3. Since contemplation is incompatible with the images of meditation, one who contemplates cannot meditate and generally does not return to discursive prayer.
4. Let us start our journey to a strange new world!

CHALLENGES FOR TODAY
- Try listening to the music of the Night!
- Let go of what you previously valued, and let God become your guide.
- Pray for courage and emptiness.

DAY 254 *THE PASSIVE NIGHT OF SENSE*

The passive night of sense consists in a process of purification caused by the illumination of contemplation by which the senses are accommodated to the spirit. This is a passive night that affects beginners who have been dedicated to God for some time and have been involved in the active night of purification of the senses (see A.1. 13.1). Having found satisfaction in the things of God, they have become detached from things that led away from God and are ready for God's further challenges. Instead of the enjoyment and satisfaction they found in their religious devotions, they now find these same religious practices distasteful, and they feel empty and dissatisfied. Some may respond by working harder than ever at their discursive meditation, but this is not desirable. "They are like someone who turns from what has already been done in order to do it again" (N.1. 10.1). Others show a lot of conscious and unconscious resistance to God's love and illumination, and this needs the purification of actual, habitual, and socially justified sin. We often want ourselves more than we want God, and by clinging to our views of religion we block God out of our lives. So, the passive night of sense marks the transition from meditation to contemplation, the latter being light for the understanding and love for the will. Moreover, this contemplation can be illuminative and delightful, but also purgative and painful.

1. There is unquestionable overlapping between the passive night of sense and the active night of spirit.
2. Before the active night of spirit is complete there are brief experiences of the darkness to come in the passive purification of spirit (N.2. 1.1).
3. The dark night of sense is only the entrance into that of spirit.
4. John does not care whether you are attached to power or liturgy, sex or prayer forms, the only thing that matters is the heart's focus on self-satisfaction.

CHALLENGES FOR TODAY
- Remind yourself today that nothing can adequately represent God.
- Are you attached to something you know leads you away from God?
- Do you keep doing the same practices hoping for a different response?

DAY 255 RIDDING OURSELVES OF IMPERFECTIONS (See *Dark Night*, 1. 1)

We begin our spiritual journey with a resolute determination to pursue union of our will and desires with the will of God. Once we have made this commitment, God takes care of us and begins to draw us to union in divine life. This can initially be a pleasant experience but we need to be careful not to seek the satisfaction and comfort that come at this time. Rather, we need to take courage and intensify our commitment, aware that any growth will need to include the development of virtue and entrance into the dark night.

1. Our love of God is the motivation to begin this spiritual journey.
2. God's love, given in contemplation, helps us control all inordinate desires that lead us away from God.
3. Beginners in the spiritual journey are good people but they are still in a very early stage in the spiritual journey.
4. The consolation and satisfaction spiritually immature people experience at this time can become blocks and hindrances to further growth.

CHALLENGES FOR TODAY

- Reaffirm your resolute determination to give yourself wholeheartedly to the spiritual journey.
- What are some of your faults that hinder growth in your spiritual life and what can you do about them?
- From what you have heard about the dark night, would you like God to place you in it?

DAY 256 *HINDRANCES TO GROWTH —*
SPIRITUAL PRIDE (See *Dark Night*, 1. 2)

Pride is one of the seven capital sins. It stands at the head of most failures that ruin our lives. John of the Cross' originality is that he deals with spiritual pride—a pride that does not result from wealth, position, or power, but from spiritual matters. People at this time see themselves as mature teachers of spirituality after a mere smattering of devotions, feel they should be appreciated as spiritual guides for others, and consider their primitive practices as indicators of spiritual growth. They tout their directors, prayer, gurus, devotions, groups, and programs or ministries as the best.

1. A sign that a person is at the beginning stages of the spiritual life is when he or she is proud of spiritual progress and achievements.
2. Those who are ready to transition to further stages in the spiritual journey recognize the many signs of spiritual pride.
3. We should avoid all comparisons with others except to see our own failures in relation to others' goodness.
4. Let us seek directors who challenge us a lot and praise us little.

CHALLENGES FOR TODAY
- Check to see if you are embarrassed by or oblivious of your own failures.
- Do you find you are getting overanxious about what others think of you?
- Spend a little time reflecting on your knowledge about yourself.

DAY 257 HINDRANCES TO GROWTH –
SPIRITUAL AVARICE (See Dark Night, 1. 3)

Spiritual pride in early stages of the spiritual life leads to spiritual avarice. People want more and more religion and become possessive of religious devotions, practices, people, and experiences. Such people cannot get enough of their favorite religious personality, workshops, ever longer retreats, and the accumulation of the same religiously mediocre books. Their attachment and possessiveness of heart does serious damage to an authentic pursuit of God that should be focused on love of God and neighbor.

1. Devotions and practices can be helpful but must never be absolutized or even given more importance than the simple means they are.
2. Some people can be as possessive of religion's means as others are of money.
3. More religion is not necessarily any better than less. What is important is true devotion that comes from a purified heart.
4. Total purification is God's work, but we can contribute by fighting against possessiveness in religious issues.

CHALLENGES FOR TODAY
* Try to be content with whatever spiritual gift God gives you.
* Evaluate whether you are attached to any particular practice or experience.
* Has someone become too important a guru for you?

DAY 258 *HINDRANCES TO GROWTH —*
SPIRITUAL LUST (See *Dark Night*, 1. 4)

Beginners in the spiritual journey sometimes find gratification from their spiritual experiences, become attached to the physical pleasure associated with such experiences, and seek this arousal in their spiritual commitment. This spiritual lust leads a person away from the pursuit of God. Any inordinate self love will need purification in the dark night. The dark night places these loves in reasonable order, strengthens love of God, and destroys false loves.

1. Religious devotions are means to God and not ends to be enjoyed for their own sake.
2. When our attachment to religious experiences increases, our love of God grows cold.
3. Our bodies eventually enjoy the overflow of love that comes to our spirit, but not in this early stage.
4. The lust experienced in this phase is not spiritual but it proceeds from spiritual experiences.

CHALLENGES FOR TODAY
- Begin early to detach yourself from satisfactions in devotions, practices, and experiences.
- Beware that while you protect yourself from attachments to material things, you can easily fall in to spiritual attachments.
- Ask yourself what you like most about your religious devotions.

DAY 259 *HINDRANCES TO GROWTH — SPIRITUAL ANGER* (See, *Dark Night*, 1. 5)

Beginners in the spiritual journey often become angry when the security and enjoyment they had in spiritual devotions ends. They become angry at the loss of previous satisfaction, and angry at others' presumed lack of dedication. Nowadays, we see so much anger from people who reject others' approaches to Church teachings, liturgy, or ministry projects. There is so much arrogance and resulting anger in religion today. Sometimes it seems that for some the Church has taken the place of God instead of indicating a way to God. It all needs the purification that only comes with the dark night.

1. We have all met people who are unbearable in their arrogant "dedication" to their views of religious devotion.
2. In the spiritual life we must wait patiently until God is ready to lead us.
3. A common danger in life today is when people want to impose their approach to religion on others.
4. Anger is often linked to a fundamentalist approach to religion.

CHALLENGES FOR TODAY
- Be patient with your own imperfections.
- Link a peaceful sense of urgency to your patience in spiritual growth, remembering you do need to grow.
- Review whether you get angry at others who do not see things the way you do.

DAY 260 HINDRANCES TO GROWTH—
SPIRITUAL GLUTTONY (See Dark Night, 1. 6)

When beginners in the spiritual journey begin to find delight and satisfaction in giving themselves to the pursuit of spiritual development, they often cannot get enough of it. So they seek only the comfort, consolation, and satisfaction that involvement in the spiritual life can bring. They accumulate spiritual practices and devotions, spend lots of time in pleasant practices, go here and there for conferences, workshops, and retreats. They always think that more is better!

1. Once we focus on satisfaction in spiritual things it affects all aspects of our commitment, especially prayer.
2. We must always remember our need of purification and the importance of entering the dark night.
3. Satisfaction in religious devotions is not a preparation for the dark night; self-denial is.
4. We can pursue our own will in religious issues just as much as in anything else.

CHALLENGES FOR TODAY
- Check that you practice temperance in religious devotions—without any extremes.
- Remember that spiritual gluttony does not make you more religious but less so.
- When you accumulate religious devotions and practices you become spiritually childish.

DAY 261 *HINDRANCES TO GROWTH —*
SPIRITUAL ENVY AND SPIRITUAL SLOTH
(See *Dark Night*, 1. 7)

The final hindrances to one's spiritual growth that John mentions in this section are envy and sloth. Beginners easily become envious of other peoples' achievements in the spiritual life. Comparing oneself to others always leads to negative selfish reactions. On the other hand, beginners can easily become bored when their self-centered efforts lead nowhere, and they give up further efforts, especially when they lack the sense of satisfaction they formally found.

1. We should identify the good in others' lives and seek to imitate them.
2. Comparing ourselves to others with resulting envy is a forceful failure of contemporary life.
3. Let us remember the diagram of Mount Carmel and John's recommendation that we always choose what is most difficult.
4. We cannot overcome these seven capital failures unless God accomplish it within us.

CHALLENGES FOR TODAY
- Celebrate the successes of others.
- Check whether you have a distaste for sacrifice.
- In all things seek fidelity to God's will for you.

DAY 262 THE DARK NIGHT (See Dark Night, 1. 8)

After beginners have persevered in the practice of virtue and in meditational prayer, God seeks to free them from these primitive practices and lead them to a different kind of communion in the passive night of contemplation. They find they can no longer meditate, experience dryness, and feel former spiritual exercises as distasteful. It seems everything they previously valued is falling apart. God is closing the door on former experiences and preparing them for the passive dark night of sense.

1. There are three positive features of this stage in the spiritual journey: religious fervor, prayer, and mortification.

2. We experience two phases in the dark night of contemplation: the passive night of sense and the passive night of spirit. Here we consider the former.

3. This is a period of passive purification of senses and acceptance of the life of the spirit.

4. Consistency in the spiritual commitment is very important. There must be no backsliding.

CHALLENGES FOR TODAY

- Offer yourself totally to God to be led as God sees fit.
- What is your approach to suffering?
- Does God act in the way you expect? Explain.

DAY 263 *THREE SIGNS A PERSON IS READY TO ENTER THE DARK NIGHT* (See *Dark Night*, 1. 9)

John offers three signs that, when simultaneously present, indicate a person is entering the passive night of sense, which is contemplation. 1. A person receives no consolation either from any aspect of this world or from the things of God. 2. He or she is pained by his or her own lack of service to God. 3. Such a person can no longer meditate, has no desire to apply the imagination, and rather finds satisfaction in a quiet, loving attention to God. When these signs are present together, a person should peacefully leave meditation and follow the spirit.

1. Individually, these signs can come from sources other than a dark night, so one must discern carefully, and all three need to be present at the same time.
2. These experiences dry up the satisfaction and gratification felt in the senses, enable a person to become strong and ready for the service of God.
3. This experience of contemplation as prayer and life produces a desire to remain alone without focusing on anything in particular.
4. At this time a person experiences a new kind of peace that is quiet, delicate, solitary, and satisfying, far from the palpable gratifications of beginners.

CHALLENGES FOR TODAY
- Do not try to force this experience of internal nourishment or you will lose it.
- You may suffer from the loss of security and satisfaction that previously came from what you thought was successful prayer.
- Welcome the emptiness this time brings, and let God fill this emptiness.

DAY 264 RESPOND TO THIS TRANSITION
(See *Dark Night*, 1. 10)

The experience of this transition from a life of sense to a life of the spirit, or from meditation to contemplation, results in a lot of suffering. People who go through this think they have failed God, lost former divine blessings, and that God has abandoned them. With confidence in God a person should let go of mediation and remain peaceful and confident, even if it does not seem he or she is getting anywhere. Such a person should feel peaceful, knowing God does not fail those who seek to complete this journey to light and love.

1. Lack of effort and what seems a waste of time can be very productive times.
2. Contemplation is a secret, simple, peaceful, loving inflow of God in our hearts. We should not hamper it.
3. This is a redirection of our spiritual priorities and is a part of a process of integration. It is a conquering of our inner fragmentation, so that all aspects of our human existence come together in a self-gift to God.
4. At this time, we must willingly surrender ourselves to God's purifying activity.

CHALLENGES FOR TODAY
- Do not go back to the security of meditation and work even harder at it. Rather, let God draw you through emptiness to contemplation.
- Free yourself from too many ideas that become obstacles to a passive reception of God.
- Cultivate detachment, humility, and charity, and leave all else to God.

DAY 265 THE SPIRIT OF LOVE COMES IN CONTEMPLATION (See Dark Night, 1. 11)

Contemplation includes the gift of a spirit of love. This only comes after impurities are removed by means of the night of sense. Moreover, a person often fails to welcome this gift because he or she does not understand what is happening. Eventually, a person becomes aware of God's love without fully understanding what is happening. At this time a person experiences constant solicitude for God, together with a fear of losing God's blessings. This transformation from the life of sense to the life of spirit is God's way of accommodating a person to a new life.

1. God prepares one for love in darkness and dryness.
2. This passive night of sense frees a person from imperfections, moves him or her beyond meditation, and produces virtues for the journey ahead.
3. This is a preparation for the more painful passive night of spirit.
4. We have a responsibility at this time to continue to actively purify our appetites.

CHALLENGES FOR TODAY
- Accept the struggles in prayer and willingly surrender to God's purifying activities in prayer.
- Remotely prepare for prayer by practicing stillness of body, by being inspired by the Spirit, by concentrating with Christ, and by learning silence in God.
- Ask God to grace you with the fortitude needed at this transition.

DAY 266 BENEFITS OF THE PASSIVE NIGHT OF SENSE (See *Dark Night*, 1. 12-13)

A first benefit of the passive night of sense is self-knowledge that includes awareness of our many failures. This leads us to approach God with more respect and courtesy, to appreciate in spiritual humility our own weaknesses, and to celebrate goodness found in others. Among the benefits of the passive night of sense is a thorough reform of former failures based on the seven capital sins. A person begins to live in the presence of God and feels fear at the thought of losing this new knowledge. Then a person finds a new commitment to virtues, especially patience, detachment, and fortitude. God now gives further support, love, and knowledge.

1. This time of emptiness, dryness, sense of loss, and darkness makes us aware we can achieve nothing without God's help.
2. Accumulation of religion gets us nowhere. We must discover our own emptiness. Then God can give us true wisdom.
3. In this transformation a person begins to practice the opposite virtues from former failures in the seven capital sins.
4. People are freed from the three great enemies of evil, the world, and flesh, and are led to acquire the fruits of the Holy Spirit.

CHALLENGES FOR TODAY
- Let go of all self-assurance and see the poverty of all your previous efforts.
- Now is a time to walk with God and desire only what pleases God.
- Welcome the gift of contemplation.

DAY 267 *LENGTH AND TRIALS OF THE PASSIVE NIGHT OF SENSE* (See *Dark Night*, 1. 14)

The passive night of sense ends with a person entering the phase of proficients, the illuminative way. Having gone through many trials, one feels that God nourishes him or her in a new way. However, during the passive night of sense burdensome trials and temptations remain, among them sexual temptations, blasphemy, and scrupulous anxiety. These trials can strengthen and humble a person, thus preparing him or her for what lies ahead.

1. The passive night of sense has different lengths and varies in intensity, depending on each person and God's will for him or her.
2. There are moments of refreshment that occur during this painful period.
3. Most people will have to endure the passive night of sense for a considerable time before being led by God to the passive night of spirit.
4. The passive night of sense leads one into contemplation which is an immediate and direct contact with God. This is an indescribable experience—not in images or words but in love.

CHALLENGES FOR TODAY
- Surrender yourself to God's will for you.
- Be confident that God will not ask you to endure more than you can.
- Celebrate whatever stage you now find yourself in.

DAY 268 *THE DARK NIGHT OF SPIRIT*

We now begin to reflect on what John calls "A treatise on the Dark Night of Spirit." This part of the night focuses on the transformation of the spiritual faculties of intellect, memory, and will by means of faith, hope, and charity. While there are two parts to the night of spirit, namely active and passive, the section of the book of the *Dark Night* which we consider here deals with the passive night of spirit. The passive night of spirit consists in the transition from proficient to union. John's description of the passive night is a profound analysis that shows both John's extensive experience of spiritual direction and his own mystical experience. It is truly a treatise.

1. The passive night of spirit deals with the transition from proficient to union.
2. This is the night of only a few—those who have already been tried and purified.
3. This is the decisive period of life.
4. This dark night of spirit becomes a pervasive inner anguish, as a person feels he or she is no longer on firm ground.

CHALLENGES FOR TODAY
- Don't feel bad at the loss of past good things.
- Be ready for a new approach to faith, a new mode of hope, and a new depth of love.
- Think about your own creatureliness and human failings.

DAY 269 EXPERIENCES OF PROFICIENTS
(See *Dark Night*, 2. 1)

Generally, people spend many years in the stage of proficients with its sense of freedom, satisfaction of spirit, and interior peace, before some will move on to the passive dark night of spirit. Having left aside meditation, these people enjoy the calm experience of loving contemplation. Purification is still needed and pain can be more intense—although often interspersed with times of serenity and peace. For a select few, who have appropriate strength and capacity, a prolonged experience of this night leads to purification along with enjoyment of the delights of God.

1. Following the night of sense God gives people who need it a period of tranquility prior to entrance into the night of spirit. This is a period of rest, satisfaction, and delight.
2. The purification of sense is still not complete and even during the night of spirit a person must uproot former failures.
3. There are some whom God decides cannot face the full force of the night of spirit, and so God lets them experience the night in stages with periods of rest to sustain them.
4. Unusual physical experiences can occur at this time. They indicate the body's inability to cope with the new life of the spirit.

CHALLENGES FOR TODAY
- Contribute whatever you can with efforts to purify the spiritual faculties of their false or limited content and methods of knowing God.
- Think about your image of God. Has it changed in recent years? How?
- Spend less time remembering God's past compassion to you and more time reflecting on hope of God's future blessings for you.

DAY 270 IMPERFECTIONS OF PROFICIENTS
(See *Dark Night*, 2. 2)

There are two sorts of imperfections in proficients—habitual and actual. The former are imperfect habits that still remain after the partial purification of the night of sense. These failures need to be uprooted and not just pruned. Moreover, proficients still have the natural dullness of a distracted and inattentive spirit, indicating they have not fully given themselves to God. The hardships of the night throw light on these bad habits and help remove them. Then there are the actual failures of proficients that result from overemphasis on the satisfactions they receive at this time—in the peace following the night of sense—satisfactions that can lead to vanity and arrogance.

1. After the purification of the night of sense, a night that is "bitter and terrible to the senses," comes the night of spirit that is "horrible and frightful to the spirit."
2. The night of spirit digs out the roots of former failures, as well as preparing a person for the union ahead.
3. People who reach this transition think they have achieved more than they have, and can become bold and arrogant regarding their presumed successes.
4. Spiritual direction is particularly important to counteract the natural dullness that can still remain and to keep whatever little growth there is in perspective.

CHALLENGES FOR TODAY
- Be attentive so as not to become too attracted to the transitory blessings that follow the pain of this night.
- Reflect on John's diagram of Mount Carmel and its many challenges.
- Think about your own habitual and actual failures at this time in your life.

DAY 271 REAL PURIFICATION IS THE WORK OF THE SPIRIT (See *Dark Night*, 2. 3)

The real purification even of the senses begins with the spirit. In the passive night of spirit both sense and spirit are jointly purified. Proficients are still rather lowly in their communication with God. The night of spirit deals with the transition from proficients to union, it gets people ready for union, and it refocuses all faculties and affections to center on God alone. However, first in this night everything around us falls apart, God no longer seems real to us, faith loses its challenge, and the Church and its teachings seem irrelevant. This leads to inner anguish as a person no longer feels he or she is on firm ground.

1. The passive night of senses is just a reformation and a bridling of the appetites rather than a full purification.
2. The night of spirit is essentially a transformation of the spiritual faculties—the intellect experiences darkness, the will aridity, and the memory emptiness.
3. Those that are willing to leave aside the initial blessings of proficients are ready to enter the dark night of contemplation.
4. During this time God will not act as we expect.

CHALLENGES FOR TODAY
- Accept the sense of loss and helplessness that now visits you, as you feel deprived of the security and joy of past good things.
- Ask God to lead you to a new way of knowing, possessing, and loving.
- Think about the awesomeness of God, your role as a creature, and ask why God wants your love.

DAY 272 *THE PASSIVE NIGHT OF SPIRIT*
(See *Dark Night*, 2. 4)

The journey to union with God consists in our spiritual experience of how God teaches us to know, possess, and love God in new ways—in the ways God wants us to. The passive night of spirit is the period when a person, no longer experiencing his or her former supports, now in darkness of the intellect, distress of the will, and affliction and anguish of the memory, journeys in darkness to pure faith. The intellect moves from human, natural knowing to divine wisdom, the will from a lowly manner of loving to divine love, the memory from a dead past or falsely imagined future to hope.

1. We must all leave aside former ways of acting and choose God's ways.
2. We strip ourselves of previous ways of knowing, seeing how poor our former understanding was.
3. This is a painful abandonment and rejection of what we used to cherish.
4. We discover that we cannot know God by accumulating information from the intellect, we cannot possess God by accumulating memories, and we cannot love God by accumulating desires and small loves. We encounter God in faith, hope, and charity.

CHALLENGES FOR TODAY
- You cannot be filled with the vision of God until you are empty of everything else.
- Let go of what you think you know, possess, and love of God and be taught by God in new ways.
- Are you in any way resisting God's purification of you?

DAY 273 NATURE OF THE PASSIVE NIGHT OF SPIRIT (See Dark Night, 2. 5)

God teaches us how to love through the illumination of contemplation. This illumination is so bright we are thrown into darkness and suffer from the pain that comes because our human nature cannot cope with this new revelation. So, this illumination purifies a person by plunging him or her in his or her own miseries. A person feels he or she has lost all past favors and supports, rejected by God and unworthy of future blessings.

1. The darkness of the night is caused by illumination—like looking into the headlights of an oncoming car.
2. We want this revelation but suffer because we know we are unworthy of it.
3. The brighter the light, the more it hurts our unprepared sick eyes. Weak intellects are darkened by God's illumination.
4. God's aim in this painful experience is not to chastise but to grant more profound favors.

CHALLENGES FOR TODAY
- Do not worry if you feel empty. Rather, rejoice that God can now fill you with wisdom.
- Once again, remember you are not journeying forward through unknown darkness, but God is lovingly drawing you towards the light.
- Do not run away from suffering; savor it.

DAY 274 AFFLICTIONS IN THE PASSIVE NIGHT OF SPIRIT (See *Dark Night*, 2. 6)

When a person who has sought to give himself or herself to God sees more clearly than ever his or her miseries and failures, it can be so overwhelming that he or she feels the loss of self completely. Suddenly such a person feels God is not just absent but has rejected him or her. It is equally common that such a person feels forsaken by other people, even friends. Also at this time a person feels empty of everything that used to please and bring satisfaction. Instead he or she experiences immersion in failures, aridities, abandonment, and darkness. Feeling torn apart, oppressed, empty, and worthless, it seems the end is near. And it would be, were it not for a few moments of relief.

1. This experience leads to the death of old ways and moves on to a new birth.
2. The most painful part of this experience is that a person feels God has cast him or her into darkness away from divine life.
3. Contemplation is illumination. At first we experience it as darkness because we are overwhelmed by the brightness of God's revelation and cannot bear it.
4. John describes this experience as one of poverty and nakedness. We must become ever poorer regarding our own knowledge and daily strip ourselves of all false understandings of God.

CHALLENGES FOR TODAY
- When in pain remember "the night is God's most beautiful creation" (Charles Péguy).
- Pray you can bear the pains of transformation.
- Check to see of what are you possessive.

DAY 275 OTHER AFFLICTIONS OF THE DARK NIGHT OF SPIRIT (See Dark Night, 2. 7-8)

A person feels without consolation or support, helpless and without solutions or remedy, immersed in desolation. However, God is humbling, softening, purifying, and readying a person for union and love. Often a person who undergoes this ongoing purification is convinced that something still remains to be done, for he or she feels there is still an enemy within. Now and again, the full force of purification returns. This is a time to simply endure the purification patiently, to be content to find no satisfaction in anything, and to remain calmly in darkness and emptiness.

1. This experience can last several years.
2. At this time people know they love God but feel God no longer loves them and that they have no relief from this affliction.
3. Praying is not easy at this time, but even if one manages to pray it does not seem God hears.
4. People undergoing this experience can easily feel out of it, forgetful, unable to concentrate, incapable of attending to spiritual or temporal matters.

CHALLENGES FOR TODAY
- Learn to endure patiently whatever trials God sends you.
- Think often about how much you want to love God and how much God loves you.
- Savor the emptiness of these times.

DAY 276 THE DARK NIGHT GIVES LIGHT

(See *Dark Night*, 2. 9-10)

The night of contemplation darkens only to illumine, humbles only to exalt, impoverishes and empties so one can enjoy all earthly and heavenly things. The spirit must be totally purified in order to receive divine communications. The dark night helps us get rid of all lesser, useless ways of seeking God. It purifies intellect, memory, and will to ready a person for rebirth to the life of the spirit.

1. Contemplation is a divine inflow of love. It does not produce pain. It is a delightful illumination.
2. The transforming light of the passive night of spirit has the same effect on a person that fire has on a log—it dries up, purifies, sets on fire, gives heat and light, transforms, and consumes.
3. The passive night of spirit involves many fears, struggles, a sense of being lost, and a feeling that all former blessings have now gone.
4. Eventually, this experience brings true peace.

CHALLENGES FOR TODAY

- Be grateful for the transformation that God has in store for those who love God.
- Is your image of God an idol created from your own experiences or do you let God be who God wishes to be for you?
- Compare the ways you know, possess, and love God—past and present.

DAY 277 *THE DARK NIGHT ENKINDLES LOVE*
(See *Dark Night*, 2. 11-12)

The love that God grants a person at this time is more profound than previous gifts of love, for this is felt deep within one's spirit and not in the sensory part. A person may not understand what is happening but he or she experiences being transformed by a powerful divine love. This only happens after God has purified a person of all false loves and has given him or her capacity to receive this union in love. Now a person has integrated the whole of life in the pursuit of the love of God. Aware of the power of God's love and not possessing it fully leads to intense painful longings.

1. This night purges and enkindles, cleanses and illumines by love.
2. Because total purification is not complete a person receives this love with distress and longing.
3. In these times of painful longing a person experiences a certain companionship with God and an interior strength.
4. Contemplation now infuses love and wisdom, and removes ignorance as it transforms the spiritual faculties.

CHALLENGES FOR TODAY
- Keep in mind you may not understand what is happening to you but you will experience a transforming love within you.
- Pray for the courage needed during this experience.
- You do not need to do anything except receive this love and let it transform you and overflow to others.

DAY 278 DELIGHTFUL EFFECTS OF THE DARK NIGHT OF SPIRIT (See *Dark Night*, 2. 13-15)

The dark night of contemplation transforms the will in love and illumines the intellect with mystical knowledge. The person longs for this loving knowledge with burning passion. This thirst of love is far greater than any previous love, for it is felt in a person's spiritual part, but the suffering is also intense for a person now appreciates the incomparable good that is lacking. The thought that one has lost God causes fear and anxiety that God is not pleased. Later, with further gifts of love a person gains strength, courage, boldness, and longing.

1. Immersed in darkness and a sense of the absence of God, a person is filled with impatient love.
2. In the dark night of spirit one's actions, passions, and appetites are purified and put to sleep, as one becomes free of the control of the senses.
3. One does not lose one's way in the dark night, for God is drawing a person to security, safety, and salvation.
4. God is teaching us to love authentically.

CHALLENGES FOR TODAY
- You can still be bold in your search for God even though feeling unworthy of God's love.
- Look at the good God has wrought in your inner spirit.
- Remember that leaving aside everything for love of God will not leave you empty but full.

.

DAY 279 *THE DARK NIGHT OFFERS SECURITY*
(See *Dark Night*, 2. 16)

In the dark night of spirit a person walks with security because all his or her senses and spiritual appetites, previously enslaved, are now controlled. A person feels free, liberated from all previous evil tendencies, and now walks in darkness and emptiness. Such a person walks in security for he or she is no longer concerned about evils, but rather rejoices that appetites and faculties are focused only on the gift of union with God. This person may feel in darkness but God is personally guiding him or her. God grants fortitude, so that a person becomes determined not to offend God, nor to omit any service for God.

1. This person is advancing securely because he or she is getting lost to what was known and tasted and going by a new way.
2. To reach an end along an unknown road we cannot guide ourselves. We need God as our guide.
3. We can walk securely in contemplation for we are illumined as to what leads to God and what leads away from God.
4. A person is filled with vigilant care and solicitude for the things of God.

CHALLENGES FOR TODAY
- Realize you do not earn security; it is God's gift to you.
- Focus on a new vision of life in which all that leads to God brings peace and security.
- When you feel in darkness remember you are not alone.

DAY 280 CONTEMPLATION IS A SECRET COMMUNICATION (See *Dark Night*, 2. 17)

Let us remember that contemplation is a communication we receive passively. God infuses it in us in love. This communication is a secret to the intellect and to other faculties because it is an ineffable gift that transcends everything sensory. It is secret because the one who receives it cannot explain it to others. Moreover, it is secret because it envelops a person in love so that he or she sees how lowly and base everything else is. Finally, this dark contemplation is secret because it is the way of unknowing—a way to a hidden God.

1. In contemplation God leads us away from everything we knew and leads us through unknowing to a new wisdom based on faith.
2. A person does not understand how this communication happens. It is a secret even to the person who receives it.
3. This illumination in contemplation leads a person to a deeper desire to receive the wisdom of God.
4. This contemplative purification and transformation endows a person with love of neighbor, submissiveness to God, a correction of failings, and a clear sense of direction in life.

CHALLENGES FOR TODAY
- You can welcome God in contemplation by never being a hindrance to divine interventions through activities of your faculties.
- In this experience learn more about yourself and how you never make progress without God's help.
- Let go of what you formerly cherished.

DAY 281 *CONTEMPLATION IS A LADDER OF LOVE* (See *Dark Night*, 2. 18)

The steps on a ladder go up and also go down; we can ascend and descend with the same steps, gaining or losing height. As one ascends, one learns how to ascend more. As one descends and loses ground, one can descend even more. There are ten steps on this ladder of love. John calls knowledge of these steps "a science of love."

1. This ladder of love presents the steps to follow to rise to God.
2. You cannot remain stationary on this ladder; you either go up or you go down.
3. This ladder describes the science of love.
4. Climbing is always a challenge—you need preparation, courage, endurance, and perseverance.

CHALLENGES FOR TODAY
- Reflect on this ladder. It is a shortcut to union with God in love.
- What have you learned from your previous efforts on this journey?
- Choose a peak to strive for.

DAY 282 *THE FIRST FIVE STEPS ON THE LADDER OF LOVE* (See *Dark Night*, 2. 19)

John proposed ten steps in the "science of love," which he saw as a wonderful short way of reaching our destination. The first step on the ladder of love is when God gifts a person with the sense of dissatisfaction and sickness with the way things are going in life. The second step develops from the first and consists in a person's relentless pursuit of God, seeking only God in every aspect of life. The third step is when he or she performs good works as part of his or her total self-gift to God. The fourth step is an important development of love, for one now pursues God without fail, in spite of any sufferings that may come in the way. Step five on the ladder of love is when a person receives from God an impatient desire and an ardent longing for God.

1. This love of the ten steps transforms a person and fills him or her with love of neighbor too.
2. John had an important guiding principle for all we do; "Where there is no love, put love, and you will draw out love" (L. 26).
3. This ladder of love as a way to our destination is a wonderful opportunity to reaffirm our conviction that love is the gift, the motivation, the goal, and the reward of this journey.
4. The pursuit of love leads to pain as we see more and more how much God deserves and how little we give.

CHALLENGES FOR TODAY

- See God in all things.
- Give examples of where and how you think you have climbed higher on the ladder of love.
- Apply the concept and teachings of the ladder to your love of family and friends.

DAY 283 *STEPS SIX TO TEN ON THE LADDER OF LOVE* (See *Dark Night*, 2. 20)

The fifth step on the ladder of love leads into the sixth when the person's hope invigorates him or her to further purification and love in the pursuit of God. The seventh step is an ardent boldness when one is no longer satisfied with a moderate response to God and does not want to hold back development in any way, but receives courage to respond with boldness. The eighth step happens when a person is united to God in love even though not continually. In this intermittent, actual union, such a one now senses that he or she can reach out for God or be drawn to God by the infusion of love. The ninth step is when the Holy Spirit causes one to sense the presence of God's love in his or her life. It is a time of satisfaction in the blessings of God, and a person feels this is what he or she has been longing for—habitual union. The final step is one's union with God in afterlife, as he or she is totally purified and transformed by God's love.

1. In a world that lacks love the pursuit of love requires courage.
2. One does not climb this ladder with determination and effort. One must be receptive as one is drawn upwards by God's love.
3. It is interesting that when mystics and spiritual writers of every generation are asked for the central value in the development of spiritual life, they emphasize love.
4. These ten steps are our program of action in our journey through life.

CHALLENGES FOR TODAY
- Look at today's news and see where love is lacking.
- Where are you on the ladder or love?
- Are you convinced that love is the one thing necessary in spiritual development?

DAY 284 *THE DISGUISE A PERSON WEARS DURING THE DARK NIGHT* (See *Dark Night*, 2. 21)

A person disguises himself or herself for two reasons: first, to curry favor with a lover as in the fun of a carnival, or second, to hide from enemies who can no longer recognize the person. The same disguise achieves both results in the dark night of spirit. In this experience a person disguises himself or herself in three colors—white for faith, green for hope, and red for charity. These same three colors that please God also hide one from all enemies. The white of faith overcomes the restrictions of the intellect. The green gives courage and strength to turn from past memories to focus on the hope of eternal life. The red of charity protects, strengthens, and invigorates all other virtues.

1. A person loses interest and satisfaction in the limited knowledge of the intellect, limited possessions in memories, and limited love in petty desires.
2. These disguises are three gains built on three losses.
3. These three qualities of a person in the dark night of contemplation imply a person now has no interests or concerns except God alone.
4. These three parts of a person's disguise help prepare for union while opposing all that is evil.

CHALLENGES FOR TODAY
- If someone looked at you what disguise covers you and why?
- Assess yourself against these three elements of the life of a dedicated person.
- Do you know or believe, remember or hope, desire or love?

DAY 285 *A PERSON'S HIDING PLACE IN THE DARK NIGHT* (See *Dark Night*, 2. 23)

During the dark night of spirit a person journeys "in concealment," hidden from all former threatening evils. He or she experiences contemplation as a passive infusion without any involvement of the sensory part and so hidden from all obstacles these faculties can cause. Contemplation also gives concealment by giving strength against all attacks of evil. A person can suffer from some threats both sensory and spiritual, and God allows this for further purification. But God's blessings will increase, bringing peace and union in the highest degree of prayer.

1. The more spiritual this communication, the more remote it is from the senses and from all that is evil.
2. When a person is under threat from evil at this time, he or she enters more deeply into his or her inner spirit without knowing how or why. God thus leads him or her to concealment.
3. In the dark night of spirit a person lives alone with God in peace and security, undisturbed by the world's false values.
4. Temptations can continue at any time in this life.

CHALLENGES FOR TODAY
- God allows you to face temptations in order to strengthen your dedication.
- Live in and treasure solitude.
- At any and every stage in life you need to live in concealment from evil.

DAY 286 THE PERSON IS NOW AT PEACE
(See *Dark Night*, 2. 24-25)

By means of the dark night of spirit a person is at rest in appetites and faculties and goes to divine union with God through love, with peace in both sensory and spiritual parts. Thus united to God, purified, quieted, and strengthened, a person is made ready for union in the possession of love. This is the result of God's vigorous detachment and radical purification. A person can now rejoice, having been led by God through solitary and secret contemplation. Free of all sensory obstacles, he or she is now guided by love alone to the heights of union with God.

1. At this time a person finds a new bond with God in the possession of love.
2. Contemplation leads to renewal of life, to a wisdom in our knowledge of God, and to union with God in love.
3. John complements these ideas on contemplation in the *Dark Night* with insights into union in the *Spiritual Canticle* and the *Living Flame of Love*.
4. The dark contemplation of the night of spirit produces forgetfulness of self, a desire to do God's will, and a commitment to the service of others.

CHALLENGES FOR TODAY
- Welcome the peace and quietude God brings to you.
- Give glory to God for the transformation God has wrought in you.
- In every aspect of daily life make sure love alone guides you.

DAY 287 *IN DARKNESS WE FIND ILLUMINATION*

Our spiritual journey takes us not only through the active nights of sense and spirit but most especially through the passive nights of sense and spirit. This part is very difficult for all of us, for it means we have to learn passivity while living in a world of action, ministry, community, and spiritual techniques. When we look back over the history of spirituality we find that all great figures had to pass through solitude, darkness, emptiness, and the desert in order to find answers to the most profound questions of humanity. Only when we have the courage to face and enter the passive nights can we deal with our own meaning and destiny. It is darkness that brings illumination; that thick darkness where God dwells (Exodus 20:21). The thought of living, learning, and growing in darkness seems so strange to us. But, John of the Cross disrupts our way of thinking, valuing, viewing religion, and understanding our own destiny. To be in darkness does not mean that you cannot see or that you have no vision. It is a call to see in a new way and to look at things in a new way.

1. How do we learn passivity in our world where it often seems only action is valued?
2. We must surrender to a new way of seeing our lives—in darkness.
3. Can we think about living in a totally different way?
4. "Let your mind start a journey through a strange new world. Leave all thought of the world you knew before. Let your soul take you where you long to be" (See "The Music of the Night," in *The Phantom of the Opera*, by Andrew Lloyd Weber).

CHALLENGES FOR TODAY
- Name some great figures that passed through darkness in their life's journey.
- Can you let go of the life you knew before?
- How has John of the Cross disrupted your way of thinking about life?

DAY 288 *THE JOY OF COMING INTO THE LIGHT*

"I will lead the blind by a road they do not know, by paths they have not known I will guide them. I will turn the darkness before them into light, the rough places into level ground. These are the things I will do, and I will not forsake them" (Isaiah 42:16).

"If I say, 'Surely the darkness shall cover me, and the light around me become night,' even the darkness is not dark to you; the night is as bright as the day, for darkness is as light to you" (Psalm 139:11-12).

So often we think we see, appreciate, and know God; we accumulate information from reading, studying, discussing, and sharing. But we can never know God unless God enlightens us and grants us knowledge of divine life. This takes place in the nights of contemplation. However, the joy of coming into the light is never as great as when we have been in darkness. In darkness we find how small our image of God is, and we discover the absolute conviction of divine transcendence.

1. "[N]ow that you have come to know God, or rather to be known by God" (Galatians 4:9).
2. In the nights God leads us away from our childish understanding to a mature vision of God.
3. We should never be discouraged in the nights. We are not struggling in an unknown situation, but God is drawing us through the nights.
4. We are pilgrims seeking encounter with the otherness of God.

CHALLENGES FOR TODAY
- Have you ever thought how small your image of God is?
- Remember this darkness is illumination.
- Pray for courage to make this journey.

DAY 289 *DARKNESS OF CONTEMPLATION*

John of the Cross in his book on the *Dark Night* of the soul presents us with "a few principles which shed a wonderful light on the mysterious way of God, and clearly explain the disconcerting sides of His sanctifying action" (Fr. Gabriel, xii). It is mysterious how we gain illumination in darkness. In the darkness, we can easily feel helpless, abandoned, and no longer standing on firm ground, until we realize it is the brightness of God's revelation that blinds us. The hymn for the office of readings in week four, Saturday, puts this well: "Great Father of Glory, pure Father of Light, . . . O help us to see Tis only the splendor of light hideth thee." In the darkness of contemplation, which is an intimate experience, we gain knowledge of God, and this knowledge is the goal of all spiritual exercises.

1. The purification of the passive nights comes in contemplation when God reveals the divine life to us.
2. We need to get used to the fact that God does not act towards us in ways we expected.
3. How does each of us understand "the disconcerting sides of God's sanctifying actions"?
4. Let us reflect on how God is currently trying to transform our lives.

CHALLENGES FOR TODAY
- Describe an experience of intense darkness in your life.
- Are you surprised at how God treats you?
- What are your expectations in prayer?

DAY 290 *NIGHT AS A PERSONAL AND SOCIAL EXPERIENCE*

Journeying through the nights is a painful and bewildering experience. People experience it in varied ways, although it will eventually affect every aspect of one's personality—psychological, spiritual, mental, emotional, and even physical. While it is not the same for any two people, it does manifest itself in some common experiences of darkness, pain, emptiness, abandonment, poverty, and nakedness. It is a dispossession of everything we held dear and a reshaping and redirection of the principal energies of the soul—the three spiritual faculties of intellect, memory, and will.

However, nowadays the metaphor of the night has expanded beyond a personal experience to include social, ecclesial, and political elements that affect us every day. So, we now speak about dark nights in society and in the Church. At times, we experience a loss of previous values that we held dear in society and in the Church and a great void, emptiness, and lack of conviction that what we thought was so valuable no longer is. We experience a darkness that we cannot remove, but know that only God can do this for us.

1. There is no easy access to God that would bypass the nights.
2. Let us think about Jesus' experience of the dark night.
3. Why are our social and political lives filled with darkness today?
4. Describe a situation in the Church in which former secure values no longer sustain us.

CHALLENGES FOR TODAY
- What are or were the worst aspects of the night for you?
- Describe an aspect of the Church's dark night experience.
- Who are people who have dealt well with the nights of their lives?

DAY 291 NIGHT MORE LOVELY THAN THE DAWN

The simplest way of understanding John's system of spiritual growth is to say there is a beginning in our own sinfulness and an end in union with God in love. Between these two is the one and only means—journeying through the nights. Everything else is secondary. So, for John, the critical component in spiritual growth is entering the dark night. We find that John is enthusiastic about this, both because his own experience showed him how important it was, and because he has seen its effects in his spiritual direction. He knows it is important. When we read John of the Cross' *Dark Night* it seems he is filled with enthusiasm and excitement, more so than in any of his other works. John gives the impression that the doctrine of the nights is his favorite topic and spiritual insight.

1. For John, the teaching on the dark night is the critical component of spiritual development.
2. If we only face the smaller nights and crises of every day, week, or month, John teaches us how to deal with them.
3. The dark night is our only light.
4. Perhaps John writes with such enthusiasm since he appreciates how his own dark night in the Toledo prison led him to love and union.

CHALLENGES FOR TODAY
- Do you value the dark night?
- Can you face crises with excitement?
- Think about a night experience you had.

DAY 292 NO SUBSTITUTE FOR GOD

John is always aware of the limitations of our ways of speaking about God or describing experiences of God. All can get in the way of encountering God as God is. The differences we see in the Church between various interpretations of doctrine, or pronouncements from progressive or conservative groups regarding what they think is authentic teaching would probably leave John unimpressed. God is total mystery, unfathomable and unknowable. We must never substitute any idea or understanding for God, no matter how wonderful we think our interpretation might be. "Throughout his works, but particularly in *The Ascent of Mount Carmel* and *The Dark Night of the Soul*, John draws out the radical implications for Christian spirituality of a familiar theological principle: that no creature, no human feeling or experience, no idea or dogma, no vision or spiritual ecstasy, no matter how profound, can ever represent or communicate the full reality of God as God is (cf. Ascent II, 4, iv). Therefore we can never afford to become fixated on such things to the point where we confuse them with the divinity to which they should lead us." (See Payne, p. 251)

1. Can we fall in love with someone we don't know?
2. What can we learn from contemporary portrayals of God?
3. If all portrayals are partial, what is our best hope?
4. What are contemporary religion's worst portrayals of God.

CHALLENGES FOR TODAY

- Do you have a favorite experience of God? Is it a help or a hindrance?
- Beware of anyone who claims to know God.
- Which image of God do you need to let go of?

DAY 293 *LET GO OF IDOLS*

In the experience of the dark night there comes a point when everything we formerly valued seems to be falling apart. At this time, we simply do not know what to do; we feel lost and without a sense of direction, nor does God intervene to help us out. In fact, it seems God has abandoned us or even rejected everything about us. This is not only a description of our own personal journey, but a more than adequate description of the struggles many have in the Church today. The ongoing crisis of the Christian Churches is a long dark night that calls out for a passive night of purification. In the dark night our image of God dies, and God then gives us a new image of divine life. Likewise, with profound sadness we see that for many believers the former image of the Church is dying, and many in the Church are attached to sense objects and appetites that need purification as a first step to renewal. It is easy to say the Church is always wonderful and always sinful, but for many nothing seems to change. Rather, they see a helpless clinging to old ways that needs a passive purgation of a dark night for leaders and followers alike, so that the Church can once again satisfy the yearnings of the human heart.

1. Let us think about contemporary dark nights in the Church and society.
2. The dark night represents the purification of images.
3. Which images in Church life no longer speak to us?
4. We always walk in darkness, guided by faith.

CHALLENGES FOR TODAY
- Think back to the idols you worshipped in earlier life.
- What do you need to help you walk in darkness?
- Let go of something you know you have been clinging to.

DAY 294 *IS THE DARK NIGHT NECESSARY FOR EVERYONE?*

John states clearly that unless God places a person in the dark night, he or she cannot purify self of all imperfections nor prepare for union. He also points out that not everyone moves on to the passive night of spirit, for such development depends on God's sovereign will. John says it is God's desire to place people in the dark night so that they can move on to union, but for one reason or another they do not respond. Sometimes they do not want to enter; then again they may be without suitable spiritual directors to help them. At times God makes people advance without their help or cooperation, but then their progress is slow. Some go so far as to hinder God's efforts. What John does insist on is that purification is necessary for union with God. One who prepares himself or herself for entrance into the dark night takes a short cut to progress. Those who do not will need to face long times of gradual purification in this life and in the next before they are ready for union with God in love. John wants this transformation for everyone, and to ask John whether we can get by with less would be outside his interests.

1. We must always remember that John was an all-or-nothing kind of person and his goal is very clear—union with God in love, the best of which a person is capable.
2. The dark night of spirit is not essential to individuals' journey to God. However, the purification that comes with the dark night is necessary in one way or another for union with God in love.
3. God has created each of us with a longing that only God can satisfy and with a capacity for union with God. Until these yearnings are satisfied we will always be incomplete. This purification requires the dark night or something like it.
4. Although John hopes for peoples' growth, he even suggests that the stage of beginners is permanent for some.

CHALLENGES FOR TODAY
- Endeavor to accept whatever trials come your way.
- Do you hinder God's work within your spirit?
- Would you like to be everything of which you are capable?

A la tarde te examinaran en el amor aprende a amar como dios quiere ser amado y deja tu condicion.

In the evening of life we will be judged on love.

12
The Living Flame of Love

In this section we turn our attention to reflecting on the *Living Flame of Love*. The *Living Flame of Love* describes the goal, the peak of the spiritual journey. Everything else about the journey gets its meaning from this encounter. It is the final part of John's vision of the spiritual life. The *Ascent* and the *Dark Night* led us through the journey of faith and the purifications of sense and spirit required for union. The *Spiritual Canticle* described the journey of love from early longings to betrothal and spiritual marriage. The *Living Flame* presents four aspects of the final stage in spiritual life—spiritual marriage. It is not itself a further stage in spiritual life but a deeper appreciation of the transformation experienced in spiritual marriage and of the quality of love that becomes more intensified at this time. This is a book for everyone, including those who have not reached these later stages of spiritual life, for its vision fills readers with enthusiasm for the goal and motivation for the journey.

For further reading to accompany the reflections in this section, see Leonard Doohan, *John of the Cross: The Living Flame of Love*, 2014.

DAY 295 *A STORY ABOUT SPIRITUAL MARRIAGE* (See *Living Flame*, Prologue)

Many people are reluctant to read this book of St. John of the Cross, since it deals with the most intimate and advanced experiences in the spiritual life. John himself was reluctant to write about them for he felt inadequate to explain such profound gifts of God. The *Living Flame* deals with four aspects of the final stage of spiritual development which John dealt with in the last section of the *Spiritual Canticle*. This poem and commentary describe what it is like to reach the mountain top. It can challenge and motivate all of us to strive for the peaks.

1. The poem deals with a very special quality of love.
2. No one can pass beyond spiritual marriage in this life, but with time and practice one can experience a love that is deeper and more intense.
3. This is the time of inner transformation when a person feels united to the fire of love.
4. The Trinity always promised to abide in the hearts of those who loved God.

CHALLENGES FOR TODAY
- Open your heart to hear of God's love for you.
- Celebrate those in the Church who have attained this level of love.
- Review your own life to make sure love motivates you in all you do.

DAY 296 *THE LIVING FLAME OF LOVE IS WITHIN US* (See *Living Flame*, 1. 1-8)

The flame of love is the Holy Spirit who dwells within us as a fire that consumes, transforms, and enflames us. This experience is so transforming for anyone, "it makes the soul live in God spiritually and experience the life of God" (F. 1.6). The Holy Spirit is within us as a permanent habitual presence of transforming love and at the same time as an experience of enflamed love acting within us as a result of the permanent habitual presence. The former is like a log burning intensely, while the latter is like when the log bursts into flame. At this stage in the spiritual life, a person no longer acts on his or her own, but the Holy Spirit takes over a person's actions, making them divine.

1. Only people who are purified of failures and filled with love can hear the voice of the Holy Spirit within them.
2. This intense experience is a foretaste of the love of union in eternal life.
3. Love is never idle; it is always growing and intensifying.
4. One feels possessed by God and desires to be in complete union which is only possible in the next life.

CHALLENGES FOR TODAY

- Ask the Holy Spirit of love to fill you with all love.
- Spend time expressing as intensely as possible your own love of God.
- Think about a time when you were overwhelmed by God's love.

DAY 297 GOD DWELLS IN THE CENTER OF OUR HEARTS (See *Living Flame*, 1. 9-17)

This union of love takes place in the deepest center of the human spirit away from all influences of sense and of evil. In the interior of a person whose life is totally given to God, God now takes over a person's activities, making them divine. This activity of the Holy Spirit is greater than any other communication and transformation of love. In this transformation a person is drawn to his or her greatest capacity and strength. It also includes communication of divine knowledge and the renewal and refocusing of the spiritual faculties to concentrate on God alone.

1. Love motivates a person to move to God. The deeper the love, the deeper one can center oneself in God.
2. The Holy Spirit's transforming love must reach a person's deepest center.
3. These experiences seem incredible, but God is generous in love.
4. This love generates a vision of peace, glory, and tenderness.

CHALLENGES FOR TODAY
- Purify your life of all that is not for the love of God.
- Rekindle your faith in the desire of God to dwell deep within your heart.
- Pray to the Holy Spirit to come and transform your heart to be a heart for God.

DAY 298 *LOOKING BACK TO THE NIGHT OF SPIRIT* (See *Living Flame*, 1. 18-26)

This is a digression in the poem in which John looks back to earlier stages in the spiritual life. During the passive dark night of spirit the Holy Spirit seeks to purify a person's imperfections in order to prepare him or her for the transformation in love that comes later. The same fire of love that will transform and unite must first purify a person in aridity and darkness and let him or her appreciate more in self-knowledge the wretched state of his or her life. Thus one sees the need to remove so many weaknesses and see his or her desperate need of transformation.

1. At this time the Holy Spirit is not gentle but afflictive.
2. There is a war going on between the virtues and goodness of God and a person's negative habits.
3. The brightness of the Holy Spirit as living flame throws light on the darkest regions of a person's inner spirit, causing confusion and pain.
4. The passive night of spirit is an experience of oppression, abandonment, darkness, and intense suffering.

CHALLENGES FOR TODAY

- Look deeply at your own weaknesses and see your need of change.
- Think about whether you are hard, dry, and unfeeling in relation to the pursuit of God. Can you change this yourself?
- Welcome the purification the Holy Spirit brings, for later the Holy Spirit will lead you to union in love.

DAY 299 *SEEKING UNION BEYOND THIS LIFE*
(See *Living Flame*, 1. 27-36)

The union of love that God brings to the deepest center of a person's spirit is intense but still leaves a person yearning for total union that only comes later in the next life. A person now sees he or she is ready for union with God and knows the rich gifts received from God have prepared him or her so well. Such a person wants no further delays and moved by the fire of love longs for the transition from this life to the next. A person at this point perceives the power of the next life, views everything as God does: "All things are nothing to it, and it is nothing in its own eyes; God alone is its all" (F. 1.32).

1. In spite of the wonderful experience of spiritual marriage a person still feels incomplete as he or she yearns for fullness of union beyond the restrictions of this life.
2. The Holy Spirit grants such intense acts of love to a person that he or she cannot do anything else except long for the total union that is now just glimpsed.
3. There are three hindrances to total union. i. The temporal one of creatureliness. ii. The one caused by natural appetites and affections. iii. The third hindrance refers to the restrictions of this life, only breached by death.
4. The communication of the Holy Spirit rouses and invites the person to maintain his or her focus on what lies ahead.

CHALLENGES FOR TODAY
- Seek joy in always fulfilling the will of God.
- What do you expect in the next life?
- How does the hope of union with God in love motivate you in all you do?

DAY 300 IMMERSED IN THE LIFE AND LOVE OF THE TRINITY (See *Living Flame*, 2. 1-15)

The second stanza of the poem proclaims that it is the Holy Trinity who effects the divine work of union. The Holy Spirit is a powerful fire of infinite love that transforms a person. The gentle hand refers to the Father, generous and powerful, always ready to bestow gifts on the person. The only begotten Son of the Father is the delicate touch that wounds and cauterizes to bring this healing love. This fire of the Holy Spirit does not burn to destroy but it cauterizes to heal. This experience is truly a contemplative communication of the divinity, who heals by wounding with love.

1. In the stage of spiritual marriage, which John of the Cross describes in the *Living Flame of Love*, the living flame is the Holy Spirit, who is a fire that consumes, transforms, and enflames a person.
2. Although this fire is intense it does not consume or destroy or afflict the person. Rather, it transforms, divinizes, and delights.
3. A person who enters this experience feels on fire with the love of God and experiences in the depths of his or her being that he or she is enflamed with the love of God.
4. A person now experiences union of wills, of hearts, of actions in conformity with the will of God, and of service and love of others.

CHALLENGES FOR TODAY
- Remind yourself of the importance of receptivity and passivity in your relationship with God.
- Unite your will in total obedience to the will of God.
- Pray that the Holy Spirit burns away your many imperfections.

DAY 301 *TOUCHED BY THE GENTLE HAND OF THE FATHER* (See *Living Flame*, 2. 16)

The gentle and loving hand of the Father touches a person, wounding but bringing life and healing. It is a gentle and loving hand that wounds in order to heal, kills to give life. The merciful and omnipotent Father treats each one with a gentle hand. Although nations tremble before the power of God, God treats each one with extraordinary gentleness. This gentle hand causes death and gives life, wounds in order to cure, and puts to death what makes us lifeless. "You are friendly and gentle with me, how much more lovingly, graciously, and gently do You permanently touch my soul!" (F. 2.16).

1. The second stanza of the "Living Flame" emphasizes how the Trinity transforms into itself the person it touches, changing every aspect of death into life.
2. The death that comes from the Father's gentle hand concerns old ways of thinking, possessing, and loving, as the Trinity transforms the three spiritual faculties.
3. God is the source of all development in the spiritual life, drawing people forward to divine life and taking the initiative at every stage.
4. It is amazing that God treats us with such gentle care, since there is no reason or possibility of a reason why God should.

CHALLENGES FOR TODAY
- In prayer respect God's sovereign will, knowing that you do not understand God's ways.
- Wonder at God's gentle care of you.
- Think about the many gifts God has bestowed on you.

DAY 302 *THE SON BRINGS HEALING THROUGH A DELICATE TOUCH* (See *Living Flame*, 2. 17-22)

The Word, the Son of God, touches a person and penetrates his or her very interior depths of being, transforming him or her in God. Although terrible and strong, the Son touches a person with gentleness when he is permanently hidden within a person who is then refined, cleansed, and purified. Thus, the Son withdraws the person from all other interests to focus on himself alone, pervading the very interior point of the human spirit. This touch is so special that it gives a taste of eternal life, as inexpressibly profound as is possible in this life. This experience can be so deep that it overflows into the body that then shares in these delights.

1. The person tastes here all the things of God, since God communicates to it fortitude, wisdom, love, beauty, grace, and goodness.
2. This touch of the Word is not yet perfect, but it anticipates eternal life.
3. This is a touch of the substance of God in the very interior substance of a person's heart.
4. Even the body can delight in this anointing.

CHALLENGES FOR TODAY

- Ask the Word of God to draw you away from all other interests in order to focus on God alone.
- Are you sure you want God to dwell within you?
- What are the secondary interests that hinder your total concentration on God?

DAY 303 *PURIFICATION OF SPIRIT*
(See *Living Flame*, 2. 23-31)

This is John's second digression, as he looks back to earlier times. Undergoing purification of spirit is proof of fidelity. It is a time when God reforms us through the flame's purifying action. Generally no one reaches the experiences described in the *Living Flame* without having passed through many trials. These trials include temptation from the world, afflictions of the senses, and trials in the spirit. Through these trials and suffering a person acquires virtues, strength, and perfection.

1. The trials of the purification of spirit are a necessary preparation for union.
2. Only those who have served God, shown great patience and constancy, and have endured many hardships can advance along this road of purification.
3. Purification pays every debt and leads to a delightful experience of union.
4. This purification of sense and spirit leads to the union God wants for each of us.

CHALLENGES FOR TODAY
- Are you willing to endure this purification?
- How earnest is your desire to advance?
- Rejoice when you are chosen for purification.

DAY 304 THE HOLY TRINITY CHANGES DEATH TO LIFE (See *Living Flame*, 2. 32-36)

John of the Cross's mysticism is eminently Trinitarian. This is his distinctive way of speaking about God and of explaining our participation in divine life. While John's focus on the Trinity permeates the entire poem and commentary of the *Living Flame*, it is particularly pronounced in stanza two. The Holy Trinity acting as one changes death into life. There are two kinds of life; that which comes after death and consists in the vision of God, and that which comes from purification that leads to the possession of God in the union of love. In this latter case, a person brings death to the old life, and through union with God he or she lives the life of God. A person has passed from death to a new spiritual life.

1. A person is unable to live the new life God offers if the old life continues, focused on values that lead away from God.
2. The three spiritual faculties must center on God, and natural appetites must now find fulfillment in God alone.
3. The person becomes dead to all he or she was and alive to God and moved by the Holy Spirit.
4. God so acts within a person that he or she becomes God through participation.

CHALLENGES FOR TODAY
- Rejoice in the renewal God gives to you.
- What kind of life do you desire—this world's or the next's?
- What aspects of the old life still linger in you?

DAY 305 TRANSFORMED BY GOD'S ATTRIBUTES (See *Living Flame*, 3. 1-8)

God reveals the divine self to a person by means of the divine attributes—justice, mercy, beauty, love, etc. These descriptors become like many lamps in the person, each one distinctly and all of them together giving light, knowledge, and enflaming him or her in love. The person delights in this experience, as each attribute burns in love and enlightens and enflames all the other attributes. Thus, the person enjoys all attributes together, and each one separately, but always enriched by all the others. So, God loves the person with the full power of all the divine attributes—loving with justice, mercy, liberality, absolute humility, and so on. In this way God reveals and communicates the divine self in this union, while a person is transformed through participation in God and in God's attributes. The communication of the vital interrelationship of all these attributes is wonderful. They are not just illuminating but loving, and "the soul perceives clearly that love is proper to eternal life" (F. 3.5).

1. Absorbed in the love of these attributes, a person becomes more alive in love and perceives that love is the essential aspect of eternal life.

2. A person experiences that God is wise and loves with wisdom, is infinitely good and loves with goodness, is holy and with holiness loves, and so on with the other attributes.

3. God is all these attributes in simple oneness of being, and the person experiences these attributes in one simple act of union.

4. God communicates the divine life to a person's faculties through the revelation and experience of the divine attributes.

CHALLENGES FOR TODAY

- Think about how you experience the love, compassion, justice, mercy, etc. of God.
- Why is love the essential aspect of eternal life?
- How do you learn about God?

DAY 306 GOD COMMUNICATES DIVINE LIFE THROUGH THE ATTRIBUTES (See *Living Flame*, 3. 9-17)

God's attributes communicate special knowledge to the person. John refers to this loving knowledge that comes from experiencing God's attributes as reflections of the splendors of God and also as overshadowings of God's protection. This illumination is based on the nature of each of the attributes. Thus, the communication that God's beauty casts over the person will be another beauty based on God's beauty, God's fortitude another fortitude, God's wisdom another wisdom, and so on with the other attributes. Since a person cannot comprehend God fully in this life, his or her understanding will always be a reflection or a shadow of God's beauty, wisdom, fortitude, and so on. However, the person experiences God in the divine attributes, and understands and experiences God in each of these splendors or shadows—a reflection or shadow of omnipotence, wisdom, and goodness.

1. A person experiences illumination when in union with each divine attribute and is then transformed into each of these qualities.
2. The Holy Spirit grants this illumination in order to lead people to deeper life.
3. This communication is not just deeper knowledge. Rather, it is a vital experience.
4. Each attribute is experienced distinctly, yet each one throws light on the others.

CHALLENGES FOR TODAY

- Open your mind and heart to let God reveal to you something of each descriptor you know of.
- Which quality of God is most important to you and why?
- Pray for the illumination that only God can give you.

DAY 307 NO GROWTH WITHOUT PURIFICATION (See *Living Flame*, 3. 18-22)

In stanza three of the "Living Flame" John presents a digression which is similar in content to the second book of the *Ascent*. It calls for the purification of the three spiritual faculties of intellect, memory, and will through faith, hope, and love. Through the trials and suffering described in the digression a person acquires virtues, strength, and perfection, as God purifies and strengthens him or her for union. Moreover, this purification helps a person appreciate that one cannot know God by the accumulation of knowledge, or possess God by the accumulation of memories, or love God by the accumulation of small loves and desires. A person must focus life on faith, hope, and charity.

1. Few people reach the state described in the *Living Flame* because they are unwilling to endure this purification.
2. This is a critical moment in the spiritual life when a person gives himself or herself totally to God, and God prepares the person for special communications.
3. This digression looks back to times that included one's active involvement and efforts to purify the three spiritual faculties in the active nights.
4. There is no other way to union except purification.

CHALLENGES FOR TODAY
- Meditate once again on your need of purification of your ways of knowing, possessing, and loving God.
- Try to appreciate the importance of emptiness.
- Think of purification as a gift.

DAY 308 TRANSFORMATION OF THE SPIRITUAL FACULTIES (See *Living Flame*, 3. 23-26)

The three spiritual faculties suffer when they are empty, but they must be emptied of false values in order to be filled with new ways of knowing, possessing, and loving God. When they are empty and purified they feel intense pain at their own emptiness and yearn for what they lack, namely God. The intellect thirsts for divine wisdom. The will hungers for the perfection of love. The memory seeks the possession of God in hope.

1. The experience of emptiness in the spiritual faculties normally occurs towards the end of a person's illumination and purification.
2. Without purification we can become burdened by bits of knowledge, useless memories, and small insignificant loves.
3. We often think our sins block a deeper experience of God but so do our limited knowledge, superficial memories, and small loves.
4. The whole spiritual journey can be summed up as the purification and redirection of the spiritual faculties in faith, hope, and love.

CHALLENGES FOR TODAY
• What do you know about God?
• Is your life centered on wonderful memories or future hopes?
• What do you want from divine illumination?

DAY 309 OBSTACLES TO GROWTH IN THE SPIRITUAL LIFE (See *Living Flame*, 3. 27, and 57-67)

When God bestows gifts on people they need to be prudent in guarding themselves from exposure to obstacles that can block growth. Three obstacles in particular need careful attention and watchfulness. John calls these obstacles "blind guides," and he refers to an unqualified spiritual director, the distractions of evil, and the person's misunderstanding of what is happening to him or her.

1. Unqualified spiritual directors often interfere in a person's spiritual journey by supplanting the guidance of the Holy Spirit, or by imposing activities when detachment and receptivity are what one should be doing.
2. Once a person has reached quiet recollection in which the functioning of the faculties cease, it is not only useless to repeat former efforts, it is harmful.
3. A person impedes God's work in solitude, thinking that doing something is better than waiting in solitude for God's gifts.
4. God wants a person in silent quietude, but the person often desires to act through his or her own efforts with the intellect and imagination.

CHALLENGES FOR TODAY
- What are the major obstacles in your life?
- Do you rely too much on your own understanding of what is happening in the spiritual life?
- Can you be still and do nothing?

DAY 310 REMEMBER GOD IS THE PRIMARY AGENT OF SPIRITUL GROWTH
(See *Living Flame*, 3. 28-44)

When a person seeks God, he or she needs to be aware that God is seeking more than he or she is. When such a person directs desires to union with the will of God, then God gives grace to draw him or her to divine life. Thus, God prepares a person until he or she merits union in God and transformation of spiritual faculties. A person must realize that God is the principal agent in advancement. The person's responsibility is not to place any obstacles in God's way of guiding it. It is always important that we keep things in perspective, especially when faced with the trials and sufferings of the nights. We are not struggling to pursue God in spite of all the trials we must face. No! It is God who is drawing us through the hardships of life towards the goal we both seek, union in love.

1. Once a person becomes accustomed to spiritual things and endowed with fortitude and constancy, God weans him or her away from the focuses of beginners and places him or her in the state of contemplation.
2. Later, a person must stop meditating and seeking the satisfaction it can give. Rather, he or she should remain passive waiting for God with loving attention.
3. When a person chooses to act he or she utterly hinders God's work of transformation.
4. It is even important to leave aside the practice of loving attention to God to be available for whatever God desires.

CHALLENGES FOR TODAY
- Seek places and times of solitude.
- Try to avoid using intellect, memory, or will; just open your heart to passively receive.
- Do not re-live stages already passed and achieved.

DAY 311 LEARNING HOW TO DO NOTHING

(See *Living Flame*, 3. 45-62)

God works within us in recollection and solitude. We must avoid any activity that threatens this solitude and recollection that God wishes to achieve in us. We must do nothing and let God work within us, leading us to greater solitude, tranquility, and freedom of spirit. The soul accomplishes a lot when it learns how to do nothing; then it is ready to advance. So, if it empties the faculties, it becomes free to receive new communications from God. Then God graces the person by bringing him or her to solitude and emptiness regarding faculties and activities, for God wants to speak to a person's heart. God values this passivity, tranquility, solitary sleep, and forgetfulness.

1. When people are in emptiness they should not go back to former actions and satisfying religious devotions, for thus they will lose ground and suffer needlessly.
2. As one progresses he or she does not need to make acts of love, for God takes over and fills the person with divine love. God does this only when the will is empty of all other loves.
3. A person is united to God in faith and not in knowledge; possesses God in hope and not in memories; loves God in charity and not in desires.
4. We will need to withstand contemporary preferences for activity, rather than passivity.

CHALLENGES FOR TODAY

- Ask God to take the initiative in your spiritual life.
- Set up a place, maybe in your home, where you can rest in quite solitude.
- If you have a spiritual director make sure he or she is knowledgeable about the spiritual life.

DAY 312 EYES COVERED WITH A CATARACT CANNOT SEE CLEARLY   (See *Living Flame*, 3. 68-76)

Prior to the purification of the spiritual faculties, a person cannot raise his or her eyes to God's divine light for it has never seen it before and does not know where to look. Naturally it desires only darkness because that is what it knows. With the light of God's grace a person is transformed and illumined so that God's light and the person's light become one. Until this time it seems that a person's spiritual eye is covered by a cataract and cannot see God clearly because of the covering over the eye. This cataract blocks a person from knowing God in faith, possessing God in hope, and loving God in charity. Rather, all the person sees are intellectual knowledge, empty memories, and useless desires. In transforming the spiritual faculties, God penetrates the very substance of a person, thus preparing the faculties for union with God.

1. The faculties are only satisfied when they are possessed by divine knowledge, love, and glory.
2. Through these faculties a person gains power and capacity for experiencing and tasting the deep knowledge of the attributes of God.
3. It is impossible for a person without purification to judge the things of God.
4. Even small attachments obstruct a clear vision of God.

CHALLENGES FOR TODAY
- Examine your life and values to make sure you want only what God wants.
- Remind yourself that you attain nothing in the spiritual life—it is all gift from God.
- What according to you are the really important things in the spiritual life? Would your director agree?

DAY 313 TOTAL SURRENDER
(See *Living Flame*, 3. 77-85)

Once the spiritual faculties are transformed and surrender themselves to God, they become enkindled in love and reflect their new knowledge to God and to others. Whatever the attribute of God that is revealed, the spiritual faculties now reflect that quality back to God. So, according to the excellence of the divine attributes that God communicates, a person, with God's grace, gives them back to God with the same excellence. So, receiving love, the person gives back love, receiving justice, he or she gives back to God a life of justice, receiving compassion, the person returns a life of compassion to God, and so on. Through this substantial transformation the person relates to God as God does to him or her. As God gave self totally, so the person gives himself or herself totally to God. Thus, the person gives to God all that God gave, and thus repays love with a suitable gift.

1. In this transformation God re-surrenders to the person, and the person loves God as if again.
2. This reciprocal love is like a spiritual marriage in which the goods of each are possessed by both.
3. A person is now conscious of his or her inheritance as an adopted child and acts accordingly.
4. God accepts these gifts as if the person were giving something of himself or herself, even though it is all God's gift.

CHALLENGES FOR TODAY
- In a special place and time surrender yourself totally to God and to the divine will for you.
- Ask God to love in and through you.
- Express your gratitude to God for what God has achieved in you.

DAY 314 *AWAKENING TO A NEW VISION*
(See *Living Flame*, 4. 1-13)

The final stanza of the *Living Flame* describes a person who has searched for divine union and now celebrates God's gifts in gratitude and deep love, thanking God for the effects produced from this union. These include an awakening of the person's spirit in gentleness and love and the breathing of God in the person. So, the person experiences an awakening of love in the very center and depths of his or her being, and feels so captivated and aroused in love that it seems the whole world participates in this intense movement of love. In this experience a person sees the beauty of everything in the world, and he or she appreciates how all creatures find their life and strength in God. "And here lies the remarkable delight of this awakening: the soul knows creatures through God and not God through creatures" (F. 4.5).

1. God reveals to the person the divine life and being and the harmony of every creature in that divine life.
2. So, a person sees God in essence and God in relationship to all the creatures of the world.
3. Through this cosmic awakening, a person sees God and God in creation at least partially.
4. A person is aware that all creation is distinct from God, but now knows all things better in God's being than in themselves.

CHALLENGES FOR TODAY
- Ask God to awaken you from the sleep of a natural vision to a supernatural vision.
- Spend time appreciating the wonders of God's creation.
- What does creation tell you of God?

DAY 315 *THE INDWELLING OF GOD*
(See *Living Flame*, 4. 14-16)

What a person knows and experiences of God in this awakening described in comments on the final stanza of the "Living Flame" is beyond words. It is the communication of God's excellence to a person's inner substance. This awesome revelation is one of terrible and solid array of divine power, but a person is made gentle and charming with all the gentleness and charm of creatures. Of himself or herself, a person does not have the capacity and strength to deal with such an experience, for here the person faces God filled with the graces of all creatures, awesome in power, glory, and excellence. However, such a person no longer fears, for God acts in a friendly way towards him or her. God reveals divine power with love and goodness.

1. In this experience God communicates strength, love, admirable virtues, and charity.
2. God now transforms a person with the vital experience of the divine attributes.
3. There is no need for fear in this awesome revelation for God reveals the divine life gently.
4. Something happens under the transforming power of God's love that opens the way to a new vision of God and of a new transformed humanity.

CHALLENGES FOR TODAY
- God rests within you; celebrate!
- From time to time withdraw from all activities and rest in God.
- Read prayerfully verses 1-5 and 14-15 of the *Spiritual Canticle*.

DAY 316 CELEBRATE (See *Living Flame*, 4. 17)

At the end of the spiritual journey God dwells within a person with an embrace that is close, intimate, interior, and pure. The person experiences this intimate embrace sometimes in enjoying God in quiet passivity, sometimes in an awakening when God communicates knowledge and love. However, in the person striving to be perfect all is perfect, and the awakening and in-breathing of the Holy Spirit is strangely delightful. God breathes the Holy Spirit into the person and produces an awakening of divine knowledge, thus absorbing him or her in God and rousing love. This breathing of the Holy Spirit fills the person with good and glory and enkindles him or her in love of God.

1. In this awakening a person experiences the power of the Son of God who captivates a person in love.
2. The Holy Spirit dwells within us, bringing us love, teaching us love, and loving within us.
3. God dwells within us when we have controlled all appetites and affections.
4. People who reach this state in the spiritual journey bring glory to the Church; let us be grateful to them.

CHALLENGES FOR TODAY
- Celebrate God's presence in the mystics of the Church.
- Renew your joy in where you are in the spiritual journey and rekindle a sense of urgency to move ahead.
- Offer to God in prayer all the efforts of members of the Church who pursue union with God in love.

DAY 317 LOVERS LOOK AT THE WORLD DIFFERENTLY

The world has generally been viewed as one of the three great enemies of a person's spiritual growth. Ascetics fled the world. John also concerns himself with our disordered attachment to the world when we make it an end in itself. Men and women can become enslaved to the world's values and instead of possessing the world become possessed by it. As we journey to God along the path that John presents, we find a new freedom in dealing with the world and see it as God's gift. For John, it is the development of the journey and life of love that makes things different and enables us to look at the world in a different way. "Romance transforms the way lovers look at the world around them; suddenly the whole world becomes more beautiful, more vibrant, more wonderful" (See Cheryl, p. 13).

1. All the world speaks of the presence of God's love.
2. Love makes us see everything in a new way.
3. The whole world looks wonderful to lovers.
4. Stripped of false values creation is great!

CHALLENGES FOR TODAY
- Does love make you see things differently?
- Does your spirituality include an ecological dimension?
- Read a section of Pope Francis' encyclical, *Laudato si*, on the environment.

DAY 318 TRINITY IN DAILY LIFE

Stanza 2 of the *Living Flame* focuses on Trinitarian theology, in which each of the Persons acts separately and they all act together. So, the cautery is the Holy Spirit, the hand is the Father, the touch is the Son, yet all three form part of the transforming actions of the poem. John's descriptions of each of the three functions include so many powerful and practical ideas. For example his approach to the symbol of the hand includes a fine balance of problematic issues we often face in theology. "He concentrates into the single image of the hand, so often symbolic of divine action in the Bible, many of the most problematic theological issues: how power and gentleness, judgment and mercy, omnipotence and sweetness can coexist" (See Thompson, p. 258).

1. John's spirituality is eminently Trinitarian.
2. The Trinity's inner life of love is the beginning and end of all our spiritual efforts.
3. We think of the separate actions of the three Persons, but the Trinity always acts in unison.
4. The coexistence of seeming opposite qualities brings balance into our understanding of God.

CHALLENGES FOR TODAY
* Think about the role of the Holy Trinity in your daily life.
* Which is most significant for you—cautery, hand, or touch?
* This week try to bring a Trinitarian focus to your prayer.

DAY 319 LET THE SPIRIT OVERFLOW TO THE SENSES

"[P]eople often assume that the spiritual life grows from the outside to the inside. The assumption is that a person will advance through force and activity, and that the movement is from the senses to the spirit. But John says the reverse is true. To reach this peak the senses have to be set aside. And then the spirit may overflow to the senses. . . . The love of God, experienced within, flows out to the senses. Mysticism precedes asceticism." (Welch, *Gods Die*, p. 49) This is a powerful reminder that we do not earn transformation; it is a gift that results not from efforts but from God's love. Fr. Gabriel puts it simply and powerfully. "The end whither St. John directs us is a union wherein the ascetic meets the mystic, wherein to the soul's perfect giving of itself to God corresponds God's perfect giving of Himself to the soul" (See Gabriel, p. 12).

1. We often try to add on to our spiritual life, but growth takes place from the inside out.
2. We are not destroying the senses but giving them life from the spiritual inside.
3. Let us think about the phrase "the ascetic meets the mystic."
4. Do we give too much emphasis to force and activity in our spiritual lives?

CHALLENGES FOR TODAY
- Does your giving to God correspond to God's giving to you?
- Does the love of God flow out from you? How?
- Look within to discover the source of growth.

DAY 320 *LIVING IN A REALM OF LIFE BEYOND THIS ONE*

There is more in life than meets the eye; there is a world that is not immediately apparent. Our experience teaches us that there are two horizons to life, and they are intimately linked. We discover in ourselves a zone that naturally yearns for transcendent reality, and we live at this level of mystery, where we are enthralled by enduring truths. Everything we think and do is transformed by this awareness of a relationship between our everyday life and a realm of life that gives meaning to this one. As people dedicated to spiritual growth, we should naturally identify with the transcendent. Deep within each of us there is a yearning for union with God. This process of discovering the potential for growth that lies within us includes distancing ourselves from the accumulation of religious devotions and entering with simplicity into our own hearts. No one paints a great cathedral, one sandblasts it. Likewise, we seek the richness of life not by adding on more religious practices but by touching ultimate goodness and love that lie within us. Encountering the everlasting call of God in our own hearts, we then see that our experience guides the course of life. We need to pay attention to the connections between our own yearnings for fulfillment and the call of another realm of life, for we live here in this world while always being elsewhere too.

1. While appreciating two horizons of life, we must gradually integrate both into one total way of life.
2. We speak about living in the presence of God, or enjoying the fullness of the present moment; to do this we must integrate both horizons at the same time.
3. We live in this world having already been elsewhere in our prayer; living here is always different because of efforts to be elsewhere.
4. Having experienced God's love, and integrated both levels of life, we commit ourselves to what is real and true.

CHALLENGES FOR TODAY
- Does your knowledge of being elsewhere affect how you live in the here and now?
- Think of an experience of when you caught a glimpse of a realm of life beyond this one.
- Share suggestions on how to make faith more real in daily life.

DAY 321 *HARMONIOUS HUMANITY*

John described the essence of God as absolute beauty. This was not an analogy with nature but an inner beauty of the being of God. In other words John refers to a metaphysical beauty, or what we would probably call the beauty of the inner being of God. In our spiritual journey to union in love we find that our own being finds inner harmony in God, and then we relate to others and to the world with similar harmony. "The intimacy with God apparently allows a person to function in a beautifully human way; and that human way of functioning, of knowing and loving, is now in total accord with God's will, with God's knowing and loving this world. Through the loving union with God the person is free to be the creature God created. . . . Because this person is knowing this world with God's knowing, and loving it with God's loving, he or she can be passionately related to this world, be committed to it, without the heart being fragmented or enslaved, and without distorting the world. This person loves with a freedom of spirit, without clutching" (See Welch, *Transformed Humanity*, p. 106-107, 109).

1. John's teaching leads people to develop extraordinarily well integrated lives.
2. Some people live without a "why," and others live without a clue (p. 108).
3. Give examples of how we are passionate about this world.
4. Christians are called to transform the world not reject it.

CHALLENGES FOR TODAY
• Are you the person God wants you to be?
• Do you live in accord with God's will?
• What affect do you have on the world around you?

A statue of John in Avila.

13
Some Significant Challenges in John's Teaching

There are few spiritual writers who challenge their followers as much as John of the Cross does. We have seen that he speaks with honesty and forthrightness about the most important aspects of our spiritual journey. He presents us with the goal of spiritual life and clearly identifies the means to achieve it. His writings abound in challenges that are part of reaching the fulfillment that calls us and for which we yearn. These next several days present us with some of these challenges.

DAY 322 *APPRECIATE THE HIDDENNESS OF GOD*

In his major works John of the Cross describes a person's search for God. He or she becomes aware that God will always be somewhat hidden while we remain in this life. Even in the union of love to which John leads us, God is still hidden as long as this life lasts, for we are on pilgrimage to an awareness of the absolute otherness of God. God visits us and thus raises us up, then withdraws into hiddenness and leaves us in pain. We may appreciate God's beauty and love in creation, and through others, but these are merely traces of God's presence and a partial understanding of God who always remains hidden. Even partial revelations of love and of the divine presence enrich us, but also leave us aware that God is really still more hidden than revealed. Partial presence feels like absence. Even the deeper relationships that come later in the journey are surrounded in darkness for this is still "dark, for it is contemplation" (C. 14-15. 16), and "Truly a hidden word" (C. 14-15. 17). Finally, the experience of mutual love and sharing in union has no name (C. 38.6), for it is unexplainable, undiscoverable, and hidden.

1. It seems that God is absent because of our failings.
2. God is not really hiding, but actually seeking us.
3. Often we find God is hidden because sometimes we make mistaken interpretations of God's presence.
4. Even the revelation that comes with faith still leaves God hidden and us hungering for the real thing—the fullness of God .

CHALLENGES FOR TODAY
- In what ways do you experience God as hidden?
- Is God's hiddenness frightening to you?
- Give examples of how you love someone who seems partially hidden to you.

DAY 323 *FIND WHERE GOD IS HIDDEN?*

If God is hidden where can we find God? First and last, we find God in the revelation of the Son. When we seek God we find that God always seems distant when we want to be close. God is hidden but we can find God as long as we understand that even when we find God it will still be in hiddenness. God is never absent from us, for in each of us there is a center which is naturally divine. God is even hidden in the divine gifts of presence, whether by essence, grace, or spiritual affection, but even these are partial revelations. God's hiding place is within us not outside us, so, we should not go searching for God elsewhere, outside of ourselves, but find God within. God is sometimes hidden in the communications we receive and in the concepts we have. While the full revelation of God only comes in the next life, God is within our hearts but we cannot comprehend God completely. We find God still hidden in faith, and we continue to seek God in faith, love, and unknowing, leaving aside all former knowledge, understanding, activities of faculties, and satisfactions.

1. The Trinity is hidden by essence and presence in the innermost being of the soul (C. 1.6).
2. "God does not reveal himself as he is, since the conditions of this life will not allow such a manifestation" (C. 11.3).
3. "You yourself are his dwelling and his secret inner room and hiding place" (C. 1.7)
4. To find God we must leave aside every other interest, thus uncovering both God and our true selves.

CHALLENGES FOR TODAY
- Remember that "Only by means of faith . . . does God manifest Himself to the soul" (A.2. 9.1).
- This week search for ways to find how God is present to you.
- In your prayer search for God's hiding place within you.

DAY 324 ENCOUNTER A HIDDEN GOD

In seeking God we need to foster an awareness of our failures and sense of emptiness without God, cultivate a longing for God, and seek God in faith, love, and unknowing which is the virtue of hope. We must be aware that God is not like any understandings or experiences we have of God, and God does not act as we expect. We should accept dryness, darkness, and emptiness, and reject addictive sensory satisfactions that can get in the way of the pursuit of deeper spiritual values. We should rejoice in the discoveries we make, maintain a sense of urgency in the search, and center everything on love, leaving aside any affection and desire for anything other than God. We must go deep within ourselves in recollection and hide away with God in the depths of our own inner spirit, leaving aside whatever takes us away from God. We can never cling to what we understand or experience of God but welcome what we can neither understand nor experience. It is in darkness that God reveals divine life, especially in the dark night of contemplation, and this requires of us discipline of life, a single-minded dedication to God, priorities that focus all life in the pursuit of God, and careful correction of our faults. Then we can ready ourselves for God's illumination as we are enlightened in the dark night.

1. "Faith and love are like the blind person's guides. They will lead you along a path unknown to you, to the place where God is hidden" (C. 1.11).
2. For this search we will need a heart that is open and surrendered to God, strong, and free (C. 3.5) and a clearly developed self-knowledge (C. 4.1).
3. Part of our contribution is to engage in a relentless search, doing all that is possible in a journey away from our false selves and towards God.
4. This search can include an appreciation of the wonders of God's love in creation (C. 4.3), insofar as this can awaken us to love God more.

CHALLENGES FOR TODAY
- Do you ever feel empty? Why?
- Is hiddenness abandonment?
- Remember the joy you feel when you find something that was hidden.

DAY 325 *KNOW GOD IN SILENCE*

St. John of the Cross tells us that God's communication comes in tranquility and solitude (C. 14-15. 23). He says that in the spiritual journey there comes a time when we are surrounded by silent messengers who communicate a thousand graceful things about God. We discover that God's communication is not "out there" but within our own hearts in contemplation. There, in quiet, we get beyond the incomprehensible stammerings that pretend to communicate but convey very little. In contemplation we discover a new communication of God, not just reflected in creation and essentially visible in its wonders, but when God communicates and we vitally experience the attributes of God. In silent contemplation, we appreciate all the tranquility, rest, and quietude of the peaceful night; and receive new knowledge in God. This communication in tranquility and quietude is now in silence and in secret where the soul receives "hidden wonders, alien to every mortal eye" (C. 19.3).

1. In union with the Son we find rest, recreation, refreshment, and strange knowledge of God (C. 14-15.4).
2. The soul experiences communication as "a whisper," the voice of a gentle wind, a revelation that is silent music and sounding solitude.
3. So, John urges solitude, quiet, simplicity, and poverty of spirit, focusing exclusively on love for God.
4. We must leave noise behind and never underestimate the value of silence.

CHALLENGES FOR TODAY
- What are the silent messengers who communicate to you?
- Do you find quiet time each day in a busy world?
- Have you established periods of alone time?

DAY 326 WELCOME TRANSFORMING SILENCE

God communicates in silence, teaching us very quietly and secretly. Part of our understanding of the divine nature is that God communicates love internal to the Trinity and in constant gift to the world. Humanity often cannot or will not listen, but God's communication is everywhere. To aid in this communication we must choose solitude, that quiet and peaceful solitude in which we can rest alone, focusing on love for God and for our neighbors. When we learn to rest in quiet solitude, God communicates in silence. In many ways we hunger for this silence. Our lives are filled with noise and clutter, and in our spiritual lives, for the most part, we wander around disoriented, at best adding a new coat of paint to our spiritual lives now and again. John of the Cross presents an entire remaking of the spiritual system. He challenges us to leave aside everything from the outside and only listen to what is within. He emphasizes a silent resting in the Spirit. In silent attentiveness and inner recollection, we open our hearts to the transforming presence of God.

1. "In contemplation God teaches the soul very quietly and secretly, without its knowing how, without the sound of words" (C. 39.12).
2. In contemplative silence we can quiet the sensible dimensions of life and focus our spiritual vitality on God's love.
3. In fruitful emptiness God guides our spiritual activity.
4. As an English hymn reminds us, "The whole world is aflame with God but only they who see take off their shoes."

CHALLENGES FOR TODAY
- Ready yourself for divine interventions in your lives.
- Every day needs a period of silence.
- Think about a former special experience in silence.

DAY 327 *LEARN HOW TO LISTEN IN SILENCE*

As we focus our attention on God we must choose what to listen to so that we are not distracted by our cluttered world. We need a mature focus on what priorities we choose to pursue. This means deliberately choosing what we will set our hearts on, what we will tolerate, what we will heed. Clearly in all of this, we must listen to our hearts, for God speaks to our hearts. This includes living detached from all that is not God. We also listen to God's messengers in our inner spirit, to those who share our values, to creation that reveals traces of God's presence, to others who teach a thousand graceful things of God. All tell us something about God, the divine presence in our world, and the unceasing divine love that calls, heals, challenges, and fulfills. John's life evidences a relentless pursuit of union with God through early growth, reform, persecution, abandonment, and death. Is what he achieved unusual or is it the desirable outcome for more of us?

1. "God speaks to the heart in this solitude. . . in supreme peace and tranquility, while the soul listens" (F. 3.34).
2. John is a perfect example of a person who listens to God's call to total transformation.
3. The fact that John attains what he does tells us that human beings are capable of this human growth and potential.
4. We are oppressed by artificial listening, especially in our consumer society.

CHALLENGES FOR TODAY
- How do you show that you have the skill of listening?
- When you are quiet, what do you hear?
- Can you listen to the yearnings of your own heart?

DAY 328 *STRIVE TO PURSUE LOVE*

John urges those who truly love God to strive never to fail in the pursuit of love (see C. 13.12). We can make this journey with confidence for it is not our arduous undertaking, scrambling to take a few steps forward. Rather, we are being drawn by the love of God who is always the "primary Lover." We cannot achieve it, but we can prevent it from happening. This will be a painful journey for God does not love like we do, and our journey is learning how to love as God wills. Our commitment begins with the realization of our call, and we must deliberately reflect on this awesome reality. We have a personal calling to union with God in love. If we have not thought of this before, then it implies a new perception of our life, identity, and destiny. This sense of identity and enduring purpose comes from the inward journey into our hearts to discover our hopes, dreams, and deepest longings. Ultimately, spiritual growth is what God is doing in us, and so we will need to appreciate the sense of mystery of our life and surrender to this calling to pursue a life totally given to love.

1. We must match God's gift of selfless love with our own choice to focus exclusively on a life of love.
2. To strive for union in love is our enduring purpose in life, and this is what must motivate us in all we do.
3. The fathers of the Church defined a human being as "capax dei," capable of God.
4. This transformation is God's work and we surrender to the divine action within us.

CHALLENGES FOR TODAY
- What is currently blocking God's actions within you?
- What is the one thing in life that you pursue more than anything else?
- Is your life organized to pursue love?

DAY 329 *SEEK TO SATISFY DESIRE*

Desire is not easily satisfied. When John speaks of desire he is describing an attitude of the whole person, an existential yearning or longing to be who we are called to be, who we need to be in order to find peace and fulfillment in life. The desire he describes is the cry of humanity for fulfillment in the union of love. In the spiritual journey our desire centers on union with God, and as this desire is only partially fulfilled it also brings pain. This desire can only be alleviated in God and implies the loss of interest in all else. We respond to this desire within our own hearts. The desire John presents is the human heart seeking meaning and fulfillment and finding them in love. It is no use seeking fulfillment in the accumulation of desires outside ourselves. So, we fulfill our desire in the interior recollection of our own hearts, for God resides within. While our desire seems at times to burn us up, we also quickly see it is God who desires the love relationship and is the first Lover. So, God visits a person frequently during the desire-filled search for God and re-enkindles our desires for fullness of life.

1. The *Spiritual Canticle* is a poem of lovesick desire, wounded desire, and love-filled desire.
2. Desire is not only for greater union but also to be rid of temptations and disturbances.
3. Desire always remains the guiding power in our lives.
4. When John speaks of desire he is describing what is at the core of our humanity.

CHALLENGES FOR TODAY
- What do you desire more than anything else?
- Do your desires define you?
- What desires would you like to have?

DAY 330 MAKE DESIRE EFFECTIVE

We all try every means to satisfy desire. Desire by itself is not enough, we must do something about it, we must do all we can to satisfy it. Only when we do everything that is possible to prepare ourselves for union is our desire authentic. Among the primary means of authenticating our desire are the uprooting of false loves, the practice of virtues, and the spiritual exercise of active and contemplative life. Everything that is not focused on desire for God is a distraction. We must be careful for we become our desires and for the most of us our desires are too small. Fortunately, the dark night is the death of all false desires, all false gods. Our desire must be for greater love and union, from the early stages of love and excitement in pursuing union with God, through periods of pain and loss at God's absence, and on to early stages of union. At times we are filled with impatient love that allows no rest, no delays in the ongoing pursuit of greater love. Desire for deeper love and union is what propels and motivates us in our spiritual journey in our ceaseless pursuit of the goal of this journey.

1. Let us evaluate our various desires and make appropriate decisions.
2. Have we thought about setting ourselves greater desires?
3. Will the pursuit of our current desires lead us to fulfillment?
4. Let us remember that false desires are false gods.

CHALLENGES FOR TODAY

- Think of times when you experienced pain at unfulfilled love.
- What should you desire?
- Are your desires too small?

DAY 331 *NURTURE DESIRE*

We should always identify the desires of our lives. Desire is the human response to what will make us complete. It shows us the direction of a pilgrimage we undertake to find fulfillment, to find ourselves, to find the love for which we were created. Once we identify the desire of life, it becomes the motivating force for all we do. As we pursue desire with single-minded dedication, we must first of all purify our desires. Our desires define us. At times, we seek something or someone so intensely that it takes the place of God. When we abandon all false desires, false gods, we lose our false selves and find our true selves (C. v.29). We must undertake this journey with excitement and enthusiasm and let nothing digress or distract us. Some grow weary in this journey and many abandon the effort. We must follow our desire unceasingly, with deliberate and intense longing. Desire is placed in our hearts by God who longs to satisfy our hopes more than we do, and we are immersed in God's love. Even our own initial desires, and more so as they grow, act as messengers showing us both what our hearts yearn for and also what God wants from us.

1. Only a life of love satisfies desire.
2. John makes us aware of deep desires that we have, a hunger that cannot be satisfied except in this journey of love.
3. As we follow our desire, God teaches us to love with the very strength with which God loves us (C. 38.4).
4. God is the prime Lover who has placed this yearning within us.

CHALLENGES FOR TODAY
• What will make you complete?
• Identify your greatest desires.
• Let your heart be drawn by God; remove all obstacles.

DAY 332 CALLED TO STRONG LOVE

The spiritual journey is a journey of love, and one who makes this journey will need strong love, and as we journey we come to realize that we were created for this love. During the experiences of this journey our love will mature as we learn to let go of false loves and to discover new ways of loving (C. 1.2). However, from the first step we must do everything under the powerful motivation of strong love (C. 1.2). We need readiness to persevere in this love and sacrifice and do everything to gain or receive it (C. 1.13). To the initial determined self-gift and self-forgetfulness needed to start this journey, we add acceptance of the burning pain that love causes. Intense love such as this requires freedom and fortitude, as we seek to surrender ourselves to God, to love God in every way we can, and to continue to prepare ourselves to love more purely and intensely. The *Spiritual Canticle* presents us not with the struggles of a seeker but with those of a lover.

1. John tells us that spiritual betrothal is the time of deeper love and mutual surrender.
2. In this growth of love and self-surrender we need "a singular fortitude and a very sublime love" (C. 20-21.1).
3. God shows us genuine love, the tenderness and truth of love, supreme and generous love.
4. The total surrender that John refers to is caused by God, it is a gift of consuming love that includes the desire that every expression becomes an act of love.

CHALLENGES FOR TODAY
- Pray for steadfastness, courage, and perseverance.
- Don't let anything disturb you or fill you with fear.
- Is your love strong enough?

DAY 333 *SURRENDER TO STRONG LOVE*

The *Ascent* and the *Dark Night* purify in view of a union of love. They describe a transformation that takes place in contemplation when we become receptive to God's activity within us, when God purifies our false desires, false loves, and false gods and fills us with an inflow of love. Our capacity for this love depends on the exclusive and integrated focus of every aspect of our lives. This is a time of mutual surrender, profound communication, and total dedicated devotion to God's service. John tells us that God values this love because it is strong. A major change has taken place in this communion of love; from now on the person's love will be God loving in the person—this is the work of the Holy Spirit. As a person is thus transformed, all his or her actions cease to be his or her own, for it is the Holy Spirit who now makes them and moves the person to union with God.

1. "Everything I do I do with love, and everything I suffer I suffer with the delight of love" (C. 28.8).
2. God communicates a new way of living and loving, and establishes an intimate relationship with each of us.
3. It is this stronger love and more unitive love that leads the person to God.
4. John tells us that a person feels this love in the very substance of his or her soul, in the deepest center of the human spirit.

CHALLENGES FOR TODAY
- Why do you think your love is strong?
- What have you surrendered to prove love?
- Give examples of people who have strong love.

DAY 334 ENJOY THE BEAUTY OF GOD

For John, sin is the absence of beauty, and he looks at it with sadness rather than being judgmental. The spiritual journey is God's progressive revelation of divine life and the communication of special knowledge. John agrees with theologians and philosophers that we know God primarily through the divine attributes, and he lists them in both the *Ascent* and the *Living Flame* (A. 2. 26.3, F. 3.2). Mystics rarely add to the traditional list of divine attributes, but John singles out one attribute that was very special to him—divine beauty. He uses this word to describe God, always using the noun form *hermosura* (beauty) rather than the adjective *hermoso* (beautiful). This unusual description is not used analogically from the beauty of nature, but rather is clearly intended to refer to the inner being of God; "his beauty, his divine essence" (C. 11.2). So, for John beauty is a divine attribute equivalent to the divine essence; it does not refer to external beauty but to internal, metaphysical beauty or inner harmony of being.

1. In two passages John seems swept off his feet when he thinks of God's beauty (see C. 36.5 and C. 11.10).
2. Even in the early illuminative phase of contemplation God communicates glimpses of his divine beauty (C. 11.4).
3. The world calls us to God and urges us to appreciate the hidden presence of love that surrounds us.
4. Let us think about the ugliness of our world which contradicts God's call to love.

CHALLENGES FOR TODAY
- What does God's beauty mean to you?
- Where do we see reflections of God's beauty?
- What for you is the major quality of God?

DAY 335 *APPRECIATE THE WORLD*

John enjoyed time alone in the cave in Segovia, loved to take his friars for walks at El Calvario, and saw beauty all around him in Granada. He was a man of sacrifice and detachment who also appreciated the world around him. When you view the world through a different lens, everything changes. For John, love made him see everything in a new way, in a real way. In the ascetical phase of the journey "the consideration of creatures is first in order after the exercise of self-knowledge" (C. 4.1) for it helps us appreciate the greatness of God's love and generosity in creation, and this awakens our love for God (C. 4.1, 3). "Only the hand of God, her Beloved, was able to create this diversity and grandeur" (C. 4.3), and we become "anxious to see the invisible beauty that caused this visible beauty" (C. 6.1). Later, in God all is transformed, and one can return to the beauty of everything in God, for all the world now speaks of the presence of a loving God. "[W]ith his image alone, [he] clothed them in beauty" (C. v.5).

1. John is always showing us how to discover openings into the inner world of God's love; one of the openings is creation.
2. Creation is now an efficacious sacrament of God's love.
3. Creation is beautiful because God gazed on it, and when we look at the world in contemplation we encounter the loving actions of God.
4. As we look on the world today, we see God's wisdom and judgment in the wonders of all around us.

CHALLENGES FOR TODAY
- Spend some quiet time celebrating creation.
- Remember you are also the fruit of God's creative touch.
- What can you contribute to the beauty of this world?

DAY 336 *FINDING ONE'S IDENTITY BEYOND SUFFERING*

John saw his sufferings in prison in Toledo as darkness before the dawn, a glad night that led to transformation in love. As he welcomed his transformative sufferings, John became a different person because of suffering. Christians have always believed in the redemptive value of suffering when linked to love, and Christians of every age give a special authority to suffering for love. John had no interest in suffering for its own sake. On the contrary, contemporaries affirm that he had a very pleasant personality, enjoyed life and people, loved the outdoors, and delighted in friendships. John also practiced discretion in austerities and criticized those who "burden themselves with extraordinary penances" (A.1. 8.4). However, he pursued love and was willing to do whatever was necessary to achieve his goal; this is a fundamental pillar of John's vision of life. Again, suffering is for love, and when motivated by love "you will not notice whether you suffer or not" (L. 17). So, a person finds his or her own identity beyond suffering and only because of suffering. One's authentic calling can be appreciated only in suffering which becomes the beginning of a newness of life.

1. "What profit is there in anything that is not the love of God?" (A.3. 30.5).
2. When suffering is the result not of love but of hatred, then each one must confront it, remove it, never forget it, and respond to it in love and service.
3. John gives the impression that if a person is not pursuing love then he or she is involved in something that is part of the sufferings of this world.
4. Early Christians chose the crucifix as an image of the essence of Jesus' life and teachings.

CHALLENGES FOR TODAY

- Part of facing up to suffering is confronting the consequences suffering has on others wherever we find them.
- Do you frequently remember the Lord's passion?
- What role does suffering play in your spirituality?

DAY 337 *FIRED WITH LOVE'S URGENT LONGINGS*

The purpose of the *Dark Night* is to describe a person's conduct "along the spiritual road that leads to the perfect union with God through love" (N. Title). Of course, one only undertakes this journey when one is "fired with love's urgent longings," and one travels "with no other light or guide than the one that burned in my heart." At the end of the journey, it is "love alone," that makes one soar to God (N.2. 25.4). Perhaps we could describe the spiritual life as the journey of strong love (N.2. 11.3; see C. 31.4). From start to end John's approach is to affirm "nor have I any other work now that my every act is love" (C. v. 28), and overriding every other conviction is "When evening comes you will be examined in love" (S. 60). The major transformation of love in contemplation empowers a person to see the whole world through the lens of love.

1. John is always concerned that human love can be divided into thousands of affections and desires. What he wants is complete unity of affective life, totally directed to God.
2. In our contemporary world where a continued lack of love threatens to burst frozen hearts, John's vision of a world dedicated to love is revolutionary.
3. John has a guiding principle for all we do; "Where there is no love, put love, and you will draw out love" (L. 26).
4. "The ultimate reason for everything is love" (C. 38.5).

CHALLENGES FOR TODAY
- Is love the guiding quality of your journeying?
- Are you fired-up with enthusiasm?
- Do you put love where there is no love?

DAY 338 *CLIMB THE LADDER OF LOVE*

We saw in previous reflections that John describes the asceticism of love as a ladder that has ten steps. These are the ten steps of the "science of love." These ten steps start with longing and restless pursuit and go on to include good works, dedication to the removal of faults, and the acceptance of sufferings in life. Gradually one's desire for God becomes an impatient longing. While we must make some effort on our part, the ascent of the ladder is primarily God's work within us, and God's gifts of love draw a person to higher steps. Seeing God's work within, a person becomes encouraged in the journey and even bold and daring. So, the person becomes united to God although not continually, begins to experience a permanent sense of the presence of God, and moves to union. The intensities of this journey through the dark nights open people to the loving service of others. At the end of the nights love is strong. Love is the gift, the motivation, the goal, and the reward of this journey.

1. This languishing in pain is partly due to an awareness of one's own failings, but it also includes a yearning for a changed life.
2. During the journey one leaves aside any image of God of one's creation and searches in love for the true God.
3. Giving oneself to pleasing God at all costs implies being committed to self-control and ready to pay the cost of love.
4. What would our designed ladder of love look like?

CHALLENGES FOR TODAY
- Do you want only what God wants?
- Has your love grown this year?
- Think about a next step you could take.

DAY 339 *HOW TO FIND FULFILLMENT*

In his own journey of faith and love, John was ever dedicated to the two-fold goal of union with God and total renewal of self. For John, personal transformation and fulfillment were byproducts of the search for union with God, but both went together. John himself experienced the benefits of this transformation, as we see in the beauty of his poetry, his perceptiveness in spiritual direction, his warmth and affection in dealing with others, his empathy for his directees, and the peace and resignation of his last months. The goal of spiritual development includes the profound enrichment of life. This is a journey to human fulfillment. We find fulfillment in life by reaching our full potential in lives given to God. When so many contemporary lives, even those of religious people, are absorbed in trivial ideas, hopes, and loves, John challenges us to be who we are capable of being, to let our lives be filled with the greatest thoughts, hopes, and loves that human beings can attain.

1. This is a journey in which we come to realize that God has already always been with us drawing us to fulfillment.
2. The journey through the nights does not drain us of our humanity but refines and redirects it.
3. The journey is more foundationally about God's love for us rather than our love for God.
4. Human fulfillment is found only in God—this is what life is all about—a striving for knowledge of and hope in God permeated with love.

CHALLENGES FOR TODAY
- Has religious commitment made you a better person?
- Who do you know who seems diminished by religion?
- Do you consciously accept God's transforming love in your life?

DAY 340 CELEBRATE GOD'S GIFTS

One of the great contemporary problems we face is indifference to the life of the spirit, as we immerse ourselves in the superficiality of religious devotions, thinking we can earn growth. We must be aware of our own emptiness, as we daily realize that we grow primarily by receiving and cherishing the gifts of God. These gifts are not little supports here and there on our journey to God. So, we need to think about life as gift and calling to respond to God's gifts; this is our goal, this is God's hope for us. Salvation history describes God's strategy of love for us all, and it tells us how God constantly takes a risk with us, filling us with gifts, sharing and inviting us to love. Moreover God's gifts of love are not just for a small elite group. John seems saddened to acknowledge that some do not relish the gifts of God; others just do not understand these gifts and find it incredible that God treats them so generously.

1. "Who can free themselves from lowly manners and limitations if you do not lift them to yourself, my God?" (S. 26).
2. God's gifts transform us into who we are intended to be.
3. John reminds us that God "is not closefisted but diffuses Himself abundantly, as the sun does its rays, without being a respecter of persons" (F. 1.15).
4. John insists that God grants these favors and does so according to the divine will.

CHALLENGES FOR TODAY
- Which of God's gifts are special to you at this time?
- Name some major ways in which God supports you.
- Do you show enough gratitude to God?

DAY 341 MOVE FROM DEATH TO LIFE

John of the Cross has a wonderful grasp of the spiritual life and balances ordinary everyday values with insights into the most extraordinary communications of divine life. John's entire system centers on God whom he sees as the principal agent in spiritual life, drawing people forward, and taking the initiative at every stage. God's love precedes all human response, purifying, illuminating, supporting, sharing, transforming, and intervening in extraordinary ways. The Trinity transforms into itself the person it touches, changing every aspect of death into life. The whole of the spiritual journey is a movement from death to life; in fact, God uses death to gain life. The death that the Trinity brings about concerns old ways of thinking, possessing, and loving. Of this transformation each person can say, "You have put to death in me what made me lifeless, deprived me of God's life in which I now see myself live. You granted this with the liberality of your generous grace" (F. 2.16).

1. "Let it be known that what the soul calls death is all that goes to make up the old man" (F. 2.33).
2. "All this is the activity of the old life, which is death to the new life of the spirit" (F. 2.33).
3. This is our living of the Lord's death and resurrection.
4. This transformation is not just for individuals, but for societies and churches too.

CHALLENGES FOR TODAY
- What do you still need to die to?
- Do you have balance in life?
- Describe how you think you have moved to new life.

DAY 342 *FIND SATISFACTION IN GOD ALONE*

Sooner or later, human beings must arrive at the awareness that they can never be fulfilled except in union with God. From the earliest times of his life, John of the Cross was deeply aware of this. "I no longer live within myself and I cannot live without God, for having neither him nor myself what will life be? It will be a thousand deaths, longing for my true life and dying because I do not die" (Stanzas of the soul that suffers with longing to see God, 1). This is not a confession of faith by John but an experience, a deep awareness of the reality of life and God. Finding satisfaction in God alone includes mutual knowledge, mutual surrender, and equality in love; in other words total mutual sharing where each keeps back nothing. At this time one understands that there is no greater or more necessary work than love, and so he or she is constantly attentive to love in all he or she does with no concern for anything else. Rather, a person loses interest in everything else. Finding satisfaction in God alone means desiring only what God desires, loving as God loves, and seeking mutuality in every aspect of life. It means total faithfulness, conforming one's will to God's in self-gift and obedience, accepting everything that comes from the will of God. A person contributes, but even the little he or she does is because God has bestowed these desires on the person.

1. This love is based on deeper knowledge, an intimate sharing of each one's deepest hopes and longings.
2. A person's longing to find satisfaction in God alone arrives at a place where "All things are nothing to it, and it is nothing in its own eyes; God alone is its all" (F. 1.32).
3. We seek to possess God but find we are possessed by God; we seek to love and find we are loved totally by God; we seek union and realize it is a gift.
4. John emphasizes the spiritual reality that finding satisfaction in God alone is a gift.

CHALLENGES FOR TODAY
* Ask yourself what satisfies you.
* Do you still feel unfulfilled yearnings? Why?
* Do you really believe God satisfies your desire for fulfillment?

DAY 343 *PERCEIVE LOVE IS ESSENTIAL TO LIFE*

John describes the goal and end of the spiritual journey. It describes the experience of a person who has journeyed to the center of his or her humanity and there discovered the revelation of God's love. In this life-giving experience one is no longer oneself as before but a new self, transformed in God's love. In this encounter or experience of God a person knows, possesses, and loves God in new ways. In this experience a person "perceives clearly that love is proper to eternal life" (F. 3.5). John teaches us that love is the very reason why we were created (C. 29.3), the ultimate reason for everything in life (C. 38.5), and that at the end of life we will be judged on love (S. 60). He also insists on the priority of love in every aspect of life. However, John's teaching gives an unusual and contemporary focus to our understanding of the nature of love. God reveals love in the communication of divine attributes. God loves with the full force of each of the attributes and with all of them influencing each other. This becomes one of the richest explanations of love in the whole of spiritual literature. In this the person sees that "love is proper to eternal life."

1. As we journey to God we perceive that love is the essential component of life.
2. This vision is also a very clear project of action for Christians in their ministries throughout the world.
3. Our journey to God is the gradual acquisition and understanding of the nature of love.
4. Love is who God is. and it is our own goal in life.

CHALLENGES FOR TODAY
- What do you think is essential to life besides love?
- Does love have priority over all else for you?
- What role does love play in your work and profession?

DAY 344 APPRECIATE CREATION

John loved the beauty of God's creation not just in general but with a particular appreciation for each one of God's creatures. There are four points to John's approach to creation. First, the temporal veil of all creatures must be renounced if one is to seek union with God. Creatures, in spite of their beauty, cannot become ends in themselves. John is not opposed to nature, but knows it can become a block to union with God when people are attached and possessive of things. The second point in John's approach is to appreciate that during the ascetical period of the spiritual journey creatures can lead one to God. This is important for it helps us appreciate the greatness of God's love and generosity in creation and can thus awaken our love for God. The third point in John's approach is when in contemplation all is transformed in God a person sees God in every aspect of creation, and discovers the inner world of God's love, in a new vision of the cosmos. John moves from renunciation to seeing reflections of God's beauty in creation, to an appreciation of the sacramental quality of creation, and moves on to a wonderful conclusion, his fourth point; that a person knows creatures through God and not God through creatures.

1. "Only the hand of God, her Beloved, was able to create this diversity and grandeur" (C. 4.3).
2. At first, a reader can easily feel disoriented when reading John's forceful opposition to all created things, and then see his love and enthusiasm for the same.
3. A person now knows all created things better in God's being than in themselves.
4. This is a new supernatural vision of the relationship between God and creation.

CHALLENGES FOR TODAY
- What role does creation play in your spirituality?
- Can you express your deepest feelings in any way other than through created life?
- How do you appreciate yourself as a creature of God?

DAY 345 AWAKEN TO A NEW SPIRITUAL VISION

John disrupts our way of thinking and understanding of God's role in our lives. Something happens under the transforming power of God's love that opens the way to a new vision of God and of a new transformed humanity. In this awakening, a person sees everything integrated into a unified vision of all reality. The person becomes conscious of how all creatures find their meaning only in God, and he or she sees the whole world in one unified vision of God. This awakening, this contemplative glance of reality, changes everything. John says that in this awakening a person arises from the sleep of a natural vision to a supernatural vision. As God does this a person begins to see the entire plan of God's love for the world and God's strategy of love for humanity. John pointed out that a person now "has God's view of things, he regards them as God does" (F. 1.32). No wonder John says this vision captivates him and arouses a response of deeper love for God (F. 4. 3).

1. So much of life is compartmentalized but in John it is integrated.
2. The entire world needs an awakening such as John suggests.
3. Can Christianity awaken the world to a new vision?
4. Is our vision of reality old or new?

CHALLENGES FOR TODAY
- Is your vision of life like God's?
- Do you have a strategy of love?
- Describe the spiritual vision that captivates you

John's original tomb in Ubeda. His body would eventually be moved to Segovia.

14
A Few Simple Qualities
and Practices

There are many qualities we will need to respond to John's challenges and make the spiritual journey successfully. John mentions several indispensable attitudes that at first seem opposed one to the other, but they are not. At one time one quality is needed and at a different time another one. Let us keep clearly before our minds and hearts that the journey is a cooperative venture; some of the qualities mentioned here emphasize God's role and others ours. Let us look at a few of these, with the hope that they might help us as we respond to the challenges we have seen in John's life and writings. He also suggests several practical spiritual practices that help focus our commitment during this journey.

DAY 346 *PATIENCE—URGENCY.*

We will need patience on our spiritual journey, lots of it! Because slow maturing is an essential aspect of human growth. We will need to be patient in continuing to make daily efforts with equal enthusiasm even when we never seem to be getting anywhere. On the other hand, patience is not enough; time will not have a magical effect in spiritual growth. We must make constant effort; effort with a sense of urgency and fidelity will be a daily need. John pointed out that those who lack patience "grow angry with themselves in an unhumble impatience. So impatient are they about these imperfections that they want to become saints in a day" (N.1. 5.3). On the other hand many people have too much patience when dealing with the spiritual life and spend years without making any significant progress. So, while these two qualities at first seem opposed, they are not. Both are indispensable, and can mutually correct each other and maintain our commitment in balance. We must be patient to be where God wants us to be, and always filled with a sense of urgency to move towards deeper union in love.

1. Never focus on the pain of the struggles, but the joy of success.
2. "[Many beginners] do not have the patience to wait until God gives them what they need when he so desires" (N.1. 5.3).
3. Some "are so patient about their desire for advancement that God would prefer to see them a little less so" (N.1. 5.3).
4. Let us keep in mind that spiritual growth is the great priority of life.

CHALLLENGES FOR TODAY
- Do you emphasize patience or urgency?
- Describe your efforts to achieve the goals of this journey.
- What do you wish was different in your life?

DAY 347 PERSEVERANCE—FLEXIBILITY.

At each stage in the spiritual journey we will need perseverance. For example if we discover suitable means to aid us in our journey we must stick with them, utilizing them as much as possible. Once we have identified these means by spiritual direction or discernment then we should persevere in their use. At the same time, we must be always ready to change when it seems appropriate, for we can never become attached to any means, for that is what we would find listed in the two broad valleys of earthly and heavenly goods. Spiritual practices can become the greatest deception of all, and people can easily start clinging to their good practices thereby blocking any genuine advancement to God. Let us remember what John said in the prologue to the *Ascent*: "Some people—and it is sad to see them—work and tire themselves greatly, and yet go backwards; they look for perfection in exercises that are of no profit to them, but rather a hindrance. Others continue to make fine progress in peace and tranquility" (A. Prologue. 7). Nevertheless, there are times when perseverance is needed. "[T]hrough perseverance in its spiritual exercises without consolation or satisfaction, the soul practices the love of God, since it is no longer motivated by the attractive and savory gratification it finds in its work, but only in God" (N.1. 13.5). So, perseverance and flexibility are not mutually exclusive; there is a time when each will be needed.

1. Never forget the value of checking with a spiritual director or mentor to revise together the emphases you give in your spiritual life.
2. Avoid all temptation to put your journey on hold or to take a break; pursue the goal with constancy.
3. In some of the most important moments of life, you are on your own, at times lonely in your struggle, but you must go on; God will always be there close by.
4. There are times when one quality is needed and times when what seems its opposite may well be useful.

CHALLENGES FOR TODAY
- Maintain balance in your life and avoid extremes.
- Are you attached to some spiritual practices?
- Which spiritual practices you are currently using that you honestly think are a waste of time?

DAY 348 DETACHMENT—INTEGRATION

These two qualities are really two aspects of the same approach to the spiritual journey. It is true that John uses the first component much more than he does the second, but he lived at a time when the focus of the spiritual life was to see a certain opposition between this world and the next. However, the Second Vatican Council, among its many achievements, defined the autonomy of earthly realities, insisting that the world was good in itself. This had been John's position too, but he came in a different historical period. So, when we read John's works, especially his poetry, we cannot miss the fact of how much John loves the world that comes from God's love. John only ever wanted his disciples to detach themselves from possessiveness of heart regarding anything that is not God. Put another way, he wanted people to unify the whole of life in one great self-gift to God. So, the more modern interpretation of John's approach to detachment is to say that he seeks integration of the whole of life from all who seek union with God.

1. Ascetics fled the world to prepare for afterlife (fuga mundi).
2. John also appreciated people, God's most beautiful creation, as much as nature.
3. We should not detach ourselves from values that we need to integrate into life.
4. Every aspect of our lives and world is God's gift except sin.

CHALLENGES FOR TODAY
- Is your life well-balanced and integrated?
- Examine your own life regarding this double quality.
- Evaluate how you can integrate what you thought you should detach yourself from.

DAY 349 *FORTITUDE—EMPTINESS*

One would not generally put these two qualities together, but in John's approach they are intimately connected. In our spiritual journey we will need both. We generally think of fortitude as a quality that grows from strength to strength, but it is not. Rather, it is a gift from God that descends on a person like the fire of Pentecost on the Apostles (C. 14-15.10), and it results from emptiness, as long as we understand that emptiness is not weakness but strength. The spiritual journey demands fortitude which is often lacking in beginners (N.1. 7.4), but it is a quality needed throughout the journey. Unfortunately, some people never reach the end of the journey because "They were in need of greater constancy and fortitude than they showed" (F. 2. 27). The fortitude needed for advancement in the spiritual journey comes in the night of sense where "it draws strength from weakness. . . and thus becomes strong" (N.1. 13.5). It continues throughout the rest of the spiritual journey. We will always need fortitude to persevere in the journey with its darkness and emptiness. However, emptiness is also an important quality and is caused by the purification of the passive night of sense in contemplation. In fact, without this emptiness a person cannot achieve true peace and satisfaction. Emptiness is the requisite for union with God, and "a person should possess fortitude in order to remain in emptiness and darkness regarding all creatures. . ." (A.2. 24.9). God rewards emptiness with the fortitude needed to persevere in this challenging journey.

1. God only draws a person from the prayer of beginners to contemplation "when the soul evidences adequate fortitude and constancy" (F.3. 32).
2. The way of entering the night is "desire to enter for Christ into complete. . . emptiness" (A.1 13.6).
3. In the spiritual journey we must always hope in the midst of emptiness for the blessings the Lord has in store for us.
4. We will not grow through personal strength but by being more deeply rooted in our own emptiness.

CHALLENGES FOR TODAY
- Pray for fortitude which is an attribute of God.
- Can you make every effort to become spiritually empty?
- Review your life to see if you have the emptiness needed for fortitude, or the fortitude needed to be aware of your emptiness.

DAY 350 *SOLITUDE—COMMUNITY*

John of the Cross lived in daily interaction with many people. He had a very busy life, and lived and cherished community. But he also treasured solitude, and loved to go off on his own to quiet places at El Calvario, or the cave in Segovia, or the gardens of the monasteries with the conviction that God communicates in tranquility and solitude (C. 14-15. 23). Aware of the many distractions bombarding us from all sides, we need to choose our own space of solitude. In the spiritual journey, the desire for solitude grows, and we must create opportunities where we can listen to God speaking in our hearts. So, for John, community and personal solitude went together. If we are very occupied in activities, even ministry, then we should also "spend at least half of this time with God in prayer. . . [we] would then accomplish more with less labor" (C. 29. 3). So, please let us balance commitment to community growth with personal solitude.

1. There comes a time in the spiritual journey when one prefers "holy idleness" rather than the noisy accomplishments of active life and ministry (C. 29.3-4).
2. Seeking solitude becomes harder in our noisy world.
3. God communicates to us in solitude and through others.
4. Building community and praying in solitude are both services to the Church.

CHALLENGES FOR TODAY
- Do you have a quiet place for solitude?
- Can you balance solitude and community?
- Which of these two services do you think God wants from you at this time?

DAY 351 *LIVE HERE—LIVE ELSEWHERE*

Having reflected on John's life we can readily appreciate that he was totally immersed in the ups and downs of life in sixteenth century Spain. He lived amid problems and tensions not unlike those we face in our contemporary world. At the same time he was engaged in leadership roles that demanded community building skills, business skills, financial management, foundation planning, collaboration with different and at times divergent authority figures, extensive travel, and involvement in both civil and ecclesiastical politics. He was very busy and involved in fulfilling God's will in the here and now. At the same time he always tried to create space for himself, sacred space if you will, in which he could always stay rooted in the values of life beyond this one. Living elsewhere is not just for the afterlife, rather it begins in the here and now, starting especially when one moves from meditation to contemplation (A.2. 14.2). This awareness of God's presence within us—this call to live on two horizons of life at the same time, means we travel everywhere in the presence of God, maintaining a constant loving attention to the divine presence (S. 53, 88). We will always be restless until we discover the peace of living in the presence of God (C. 6.2); traveling with God extinguishes the difficulties of the spiritual journey and refreshes the soul (C. 10.6).

1. Amidst all John's commitments, he strove always to live the fullness of every moment in the presence of God.
2. Let us reflect on how the next life influences us now.
3. What happens at death gives motivation and meaning to life in the present.
4. Never separate the challenges of this life and those of the next; integrate them in your total self-gift to God.

CHALLENGES FOR TODAY
* "Preserve a habitual remembrance of eternal life" (S. 83).
* At death, how would you have hoped to have lived?
* Try this week to live in awareness of God's presence to you.

DAY 352 ALL—NOTHING

We must give the "all" of ourselves, if we wish to gain the "all" of God. Let's remember, that John's sketch of Mount Carmel has two wide valleys that list possible attachments to goods of earth and goods of heaven. On the other hand the straight and narrow valley in the middle that leads directly to the top of the mountain and the gifts of God John highlights with seven "nothings" (nada), suggesting that the speedier way to the top is a journey of denial. Some readers have misunderstood John, even calling him "doctor de las nadas," thinking that his aim was to emphasize the denials of the journey. This is a superficial interpretation. Rather, John was focused on the goal and was willing to do whatever was necessary to get there. An athlete does not stress the training but the victory at the end of the ordeal. That is where the attraction lies. John pursued love ("todo") and was willing to do whatever was necessary to achieve the goal ("nada"). John wrote in one of his letters: "For he who is poor in spirit is happier and more constant in the midst of want, because he has placed his all in nothingness, and in all things he thus finds freedom of heart" (L. 16).

1. "Whoever knows how to die in all will have life in all" (S. 160).
2. Let us strive to keep both targets—the all and the nothing—in balance.
3. Do we do enough training to gain the "all" we seek?
4. "All for you and nothing for me" (S. 111).

CHALLENGES FOR TODAY
- Are you willing to pay the price of success?
- What do you want out of life, and what are you willing to do to get it?
- What does "all" mean for you?

DAY 353 SEEK GOD THROUGH THE NIGHTS

This is the only authentic way of journeying to God. It is our version of living the passion of Jesus. There are many times in life when we may be peaceful and satisfied with ourselves and even with our spiritual progress, but these are not times of assured growth. We may look at ourselves with satisfaction without seeing the real picture of our need of transformation. Living in the dark night is the only guarantee that we are being guided along the narrow valley that leads to the top of Mount Carmel. The dark night is a glad night, a guiding night, a night more lovely than the dawn, and a night that unites the lover with the Beloved. The dark night is one of those experiences that sucks the life out of us, bringing us pain like we have never known, but it is drawing out of us false values that will always corrupt our lives until we change them. The same night with its destructive force will also bring us to new life that will enable us to become our true selves. When we look back, we will give thanks for the night experiences.

1. The journey through the nights leads us to union in love.
2. If the Church would seek God through the nights what would it have to change?
3. We do not grow by adding on more values but by getting rid of false ones.
4. "Let Christ crucified be enough for you, and with him suffer and take your rest" (S. 92).

CHALLENGES FOR TODAY
- Think about a time in your life that resembles a dark night.
- Why do you accept the darkness of this journey?
- Are you convinced that only darkness brings illumination?

DAY 354 *PURSUE CHOICE FOCUSED LOVE*

Many people in the spiritual life make decisions of accumulated love. They do one good thing today and another tomorrow. These kinds of decisions are good but they cost very little. More important is what we could call decisions of choice-oriented love which imply a significant choice for God. Accumulated love rarely implies renunciation; it is just another gesture of love for God, added on to many others. But, the capacity for renunciation is a distinctive quality of authentic love. When we make a decision, a choice for love of God, it often means renouncing what up to that time we valued; now we leave it aside and choose differently. In fact, we may find that in renouncing what up to that time we valued, and leaving it aside, does not mean that we disdain it, but we feel called to make a decision for something better, in this case life with God. Accumulated love is easy, and it does not characterize our lives nor refocus our personality; choice oriented love does. The journey to God is made up of decisions of choice-oriented love. In the spiritual journey we make a series of choices for a totally new direction in life, and these decisions change us.

1. We need to fill our lives with serious decisions for good, not small ones.
2. We often accumulate small acts of love when God wants something much more serious.
3. If we were really dedicated to the spiritual journey, we would make important, life-changing decisions.
4. God gives us the needed strength for choice-focused love.

CHALLENGES FOR TODAY
- What serious decisions have you recently made for God?
- Evaluate your main decisions this week.
- Give an example of a big choice you know God wants you to make.

DAY 355 *MAKE PURPOSEFUL CHOICES*

The bride in the *Spiritual Canticle* decided to lose herself purposely, because she desired to be found (C. 29.10). We must deliberately decide to leave aside what is not God in order to deliberately and purposely seek God alone. In all decisions on the spiritual journey we are always free to make them and free to refuse our consent (A. 1. 11.3). Without purposeful decisions we can easily "fall from happiness and firmness in [our] spiritual exercises and end up by losing everything" (A. 1. 11.5). So, we should always make purposeful decisions, endeavoring to choose to deal with that which is most difficult. In John's diagram of Mount Carmel those people who cannot make the hard decisions but immerse themselves in secondary ones are they who walk with religious enthusiasm through the valley of earthly goods and the valley of heavenly goods—the ways of the imperfect spirit. We must always be ready to make hard, purposeful decisions for God and loving union and nothing else, nothing that leads us astray, nothing that distracts us, nothing that is merely partial, nothing that weakens our pursuit, and so on.

1. The *Spiritual Canticle* reminds us it is critical that we be ready to make purposeful choices.
2. We must develop a habit of mind that enables us to choose wisely.
3. We need to be always suspicious of our motivations, and we should strive to move away from self-centeredness.
4. One of these purposeful choices is to climb the ladder of love (N.2 19-20).

CHALENGES FOR TODAY

- Make purposeful decisions always!
- Which choices are you weak in pursuing?
- Can faithfulness to this year's readings be a purposeful choice?

DAY 356 *IMMERSE YOURSELF IN THE JOY, PEACE, AND LOVE OF GOD.*

This is our purpose in life, and it is also the end of our spiritual journey as an anticipation of life in the world to come. It seems always difficult for us to grasp the fact that there is more to life than meets the eye. Nevertheless, it is our call to live in union with God that gives meaning to this present life. We encounter the everlasting call of God in our own hearts, and we need to pay attention to the connections between our own yearnings for fulfillment and the call of another realm of life. This is one of the foundational experiences of our spirituality. The world in which we live only has meaning because of a realm of life of which we catch sight from time to time. However, when we look at that other realm of life beyond this one, we find that God's life of loving union internal to the Trinity is the model of our life and the goal of this life too.

1. As we journey through life we catch a glimpse of a horizon of life beyond this one.
2. Deep within each of us there is a yearning for union with God; when satisfied it brings us peace.
3. There is a restlessness within us that is a longing for our true life.
4. When we live in God we live in peace.

CHALLENGES FOR TODAY
- What would your life be like without God?
- Is spiritual growth a primary or secondary goal for you?
- Are you pleased with the quality of your spiritual commitment?

Avila at night.

Conclusion
Some Final Thoughts As We End This Year with St. John of the Cross

DAY 357 *LET US LOOK BACK TO WHERE WE STARTED*

We live today in dark times. Throughout his writings John often looks back, and he reminds us that before God's illumination we were once obscure and blind. John summarizes how things were when he says we went from darkness to darkness, guided by that darkness. No matter our dedication, it often seems we just cannot see things in the way God sees things or in the way God wants us to see things. John says we live with cataracts that cover our spiritual eyes! Anyone who has had cataract surgery will acknowledge the brilliance of this example. Whatever you look at you see through the cataract—it puts a filter over everything. In fact you get to the point where you begin to think that what you see is all there is to see! John reminds us how God drew us out of this darkness. From time to time it is worth remembering where we were, for the joy of coming into the light is never as great as when you have been in darkness. God leads us out of this darkness, through the pains and trials of the spiritual journey.

1. When we do not seem to be getting anywhere it can be useful to look back at where we came from.
2. God guides us by the hand and trains us to see in a new way.
3. Looking back, what do you think God has done for you?
4. What are contemporary filters that cover your eyes?

CHALLENGES FOR TODAY
- Do you look at things through a filter?
- Give examples of where and when God drew you from darkness to light.
- What do you see and know about God that you never did years ago?

DAY 358 MAY A VISION OF LOVE CONDITION ALL WE DO

John teaches us that love is the very reason why we were created (C. 29.3), the ultimate reason for everything in life (C. 38.5), and that at the end of life we will be judged on love (S. 60). We must maintain the priority of love in every aspect of life throughout our spiritual journey. Whenever we think about the qualities of God we find that God reveals divine love in the communication of every divine characteristic. God loves with the full force of each of the attributes and with all of them influencing each other. Thus, God loves each of us with justice, goodness, mercy, and so on. When we seek to know and experience God, we discover that God's personal love for us is imbued with every one of the divine attributes. The person thus sees that "love is proper to eternal life." We can describe the spiritual journey in several ways, but included among them is the understanding that our journey to God is the gradual acquisition and understanding of the nature of love. As we journey to God we perceive that love is the essential component of life.

1. When we use qualities to describe God, every one of them is permeated by love.
2. We remind ourselves that we are created in the image and likeness of God. But God is love.
3. Let us think seriously about why we were created.
4. Which divine attributes are most important to us and why?

CHALLENGES FOR TODAY
- How do you experience God's love?
- Think about your understanding of love; has it changed?
- How does love permeate your daily life?

DAY 359 *OUR ROLE IS TO RECEIVE*

John tells us over and over again that God is the agent of all spiritual growth. God is the principal lover, leading us along the road to union. No matter how much we think we are seeking God, it is always God who takes the initiative in seeking us. Our responsibility is to place no obstacles in the way of progress. In the spiritual life there should be no dabbling, experimenting here and there with various systems and practices. We must be single-minded in our commitment, persevere in a chosen way, and prepare ourselves to receive. God does all the work. We need to learn the importance of passivity and receptivity. John suggests here and there that a person even withdraw from active life to focus exclusively on "the attentiveness of love towards God." He then speaks about "solitary love . . . the end for which we were created," and refers to this as "holy idleness." While John is firm on the priority to be given to solitary love and union with God, we should also remember that John was very active in dedicated ministry as his own mystical union gave rise to intense apostolic activity in the service of others.

1. God "acts as the blind man's guide who must lead it by the hand to the place it does not know how to reach" (F. 3.29).
2. We are often too active in the spiritual life.
3. John tells us; "The person accomplishes a lot by learning to do nothing" (F. 3.47).
4. We should frequently ask if our ministry involvement is an overflow of our contemplative silence.

CHALLENGES FOR TODAY
- Do you give priority to doing or being?
- If you are involved in ministry does it overflow from your spirituality?
- Do you train yourself to be receptive?

DAY 360 LEARN PASSIVITY

Sometimes it seems in our desire for spiritual growth that we are running out of time. We are not! There is lots of time if we have the right perspective and realize it is God who is acting within us. If we are willing to leave aside our own natural ways of acting and place ourselves in a receptive attitude towards God, then God places us "in solitude and in the state of listening." Then we should enter "this simple and idle state of contemplation," "this idle tranquility," with a spirit that is silent and detached. Lest we think we are not doing our part, we should remember that God is working in us. We often think we advance by our own willpower and efforts, purifying sense activities to earn a spiritual approach. John requires the purification of sense, but then insists it is God's love that leads a person to a life of the spirit that overflows and transforms sense. Although we read that it is best to do nothing, the texts really mean it is best to do nothing except to love God and neighbor. Nothing else is important. "It is sufficient for it [the soul] to possess one degree of love, for by one degree alone it is united with Him through grace" (F. 1.13; see also S. 12).

1. Many contemporary spiritualities are too active.
2. We always find it very hard to accept that we are really doing very little during the spiritual journey.
3. Do we live in a state of listening and receiving?
4. Effectiveness in ministry comes from passivity in prayer.

CHALLENGES FOR TODAY
- Do you give too much emphasis to your willpower and efforts?
- Try to give God some empty and open time.
- Do you have the right perspective on your spiritual efforts?

DAY 361 MAY OUR UNDERSTANDING OF GOD INFLUENCE ALL WE DO

We have seen that a spiritual person always lives on two planes of existence; he or she lives in the here and now while at the same time living elsewhere. Every human being now and again catches a glimpse of the life beyond this one, and this becomes the foundation for faith. John says that only a very thin veil separates us from the life of the world beyond this one. This awareness changes the way we view our world and its values. The life beyond the present one that gives meaning to our existence, influences all of us in the way we live in this world while yearning for the world beyond. This is a new level of consciousness. A person sees the power of God to transform his or her life, appreciates that God is the principal actor, and realizes that growth and readiness for the next life is the result of God's work within us.

1. The "here and now" is conditioned by the "there and then."
2. There is no more important a question for anyone seeking God than to ask what happens at death.
3. Give examples of when you glimpsed life beyond this one.
4. While a person longs for union, he or she is primarily concerned to accept God's will for life or death.

CHALLENGES FOR TODAY
- When do you catch a glimpse of life beyond this one?
- How do you link the two horizons of life?
- Do you make decisions in light of death?

DAY 362 *LOOKING AHEAD*

John gives us hope in his call to transformation and to union with God in love. He tells us what can happen to humanity under the transforming power of God's love. We all struggle with our personal pain and longing to be who we are called to be—to be our best selves. We are all called to search for union with God. In doing so we will discover God and we will also discover ourselves. This journey will always imply collapsing habits from the past, living in faith, abandoning what we previously thought worked and now know does not, and journeying to the unknown. As we look ahead let us remember that love is the very reason why we were created (C. 29.3), the ultimate reason for everything in life (C. 38.5), and that at the end of life we will be judged on love (S. 60).

1. What is happening to us because of God's love?
2. Let us revisit key moments in this year that gave us insights into ourselves and God.
3. Let us strive to maintain any gains we have made.
4. What illusions do we live under?

CHALLENGES FOR TODAY
- Are you living a reduced ideal of your calling?
- Look ahead and decide what you want to do and who you want to be.
- What are your next goals?

DAY 363 *MAY THE END DRAW US TO JOURNEY WITH ENTHUSIASM*

John tells us that a person's experience of God is indescribable and that it touches the very inner substance of a person. It is a taste of eternal life and "pays every debt," tribulation, trial, or penance a person has undergone to get to this point (F. 2.23). John says several times that he feels he cannot do justice to describing how wonderful this experience of love and transformation is. The purpose and destiny of each of us is to be in union with God in love in eternity. Everything else is secondary. Most of us will end up taking the broad valleys of earthly and heavenly goods that John describes in his diagram of Mount Carmel. Many of us will make the journey long, laborious, and only partially successful in attaining the goal. John shows us the end of the journey and reminds us and encourages us to take the shortcut of the direct, but steep and narrow way to the top of Mount Carmel. His descriptions are so powerful and awesome that they become motivation for each of us to undertake this journey with enthusiasm. We will always be restless until we rest in God.

1. "The appropriate language for the person receiving these favors is that he understand them, experience them within himself, enjoy them, and be silent" (F. 2.21).
2. What enthuses us in our spiritual commitment?
3. Do we take a short cut or go the long way to our goal?
4. What is the greatest motivation in our lives?

CHALLENGES FOR TODAY

- When you think of the afterlife are you happy or sad?
- In which of the three valleys do you spend most of your time?
- What role does the Trinity play in your daily life?

DAY 364 REMEMBER THERE IS NO EASY ACCESS TO PERFECT LOVE

As we leave this year with John of the Cross, let us remember that each of his works begins with an active verb and all of them give the impression of starting an Exodus. We begin a journey through the desert to the Promised Land. Although God is drawing us, it is still a hard commitment for each of us. John has the mission of encouraging us to undertake this difficult enterprise. It will take time for growth, and we must make sure that we are giving our prime time to this journey. We cannot just leave it to secondary periods of each day. There is no easy access to perfect love. "The doctrine of the nights gives the lie to instant mysticism, to any theory of easy access to perfect love of God that would by-pass the cross" (Ernest Larkin). The nights are essential for growth, for all growth will take place in transition periods. The "nights" of each day, week, or month, or a lifetime, can create and strengthen our personality, since all renunciation is never negative but always a choice in love for a better, therefore, paschal, resurrected life.

1. Let us establish a program of action for ourselves following this year with John of the Cross.
2. Let us think of any obstacles we place in the way of growth and think of the potentialities for good that we also have.
3. We should remind ourselves of some of the big discoveries we have made about ourselves and what consequences they imply.
4. There is no resurrection without the cross.

CHALLENGES FOR TODAY
- Write a motto for yourself for the year ahead.
- Are you giving your best time to God?
- What causes your daily and weekly nights?

DAY 365 *SEPARATED BY A CLOUD OF UNKNOWING*

In our journey to God we will always be separated by a cloud of unknowing from a full knowledge of God. We can never confine God but must let God be who God wishes to be for us. This must not lead us to think God is absent but only distant. At each stage in our journey we must deepen our awareness of a sense of presence in absence. Darkness is a test of love which must be proved in confidence, patience, and ever deeper love-filled faith. At times we will continue to feel on our own, even rejected, and perhaps the only response we can offer is to accept the loneliness, give time to our spiritual lives, and live well and ethically.

1. John reminds us that the darkness we will inevitably find is also tranquil, serene, more lovely than the dawn.
2. Only by entering darkness can we find illumination.
3. Loneliness can remind us just how much we miss the one we love.
4. The cloud of unknowing makes us aware of the absolute otherness of God.

CHALLENGES FOR TODAY
- What do you want to continue from what you have learned this year?
- Who can support you in times of darkness?
- What was the most painful awareness you gained this year?

AUTHORS QUOTED IN THE DAILY REFLECTIONS

Allison Peers, E. *The Ascent of Mount Carmel*, 1958.

Allison Peers, E. *The Living Flame of Love*, 1962.

Brenan, Gerald. *St. John of the Cross: His Life and Poetry*, 1973.

Cheryl, J. *Song of Songs*, 2005.

Collings, Ross. *John of the Cross*, 1990.

Crisógono de Jesús. *The Life of St. John of the Cross*, 1958.

Cristiani, Leon. *St. John of the Cross: Prince of Mystical Theology*, 1962.

de Nicolás, Antonio T. *St. John of the Cross: Alchemist of the Soul*, 1989.

Egan, Harvey. *Christian Mysticism: the future of a tradition*, 1984.

Foley, Marc. *The Ascent of Mount Carmel: Reflections*, 2013.

Fr. Gabriel of St Mary Magdalen. *St. John of the Cross, Doctor of Divine Love and Contemplation*, 1954.

Fray Pablo de Santa Maria, quoted in E. Allison Peers, *The Ascent of Mount Carmel*, 1958, p. 44.

Kavanaugh, Kieran and Otilio Rodriguez. *The Collected Works of St. John of the Cross*, 1991.

Kavanaugh, Kieran. "Introduction," *John of the Cross: Selected Writings*, 1987.

Keating, Thomas. *Open Mind, Open Heart*, 1986.

Maritain, Jacques. "Introduction," in Fr. Bruno, *St. John of the Cross*, 1932, p. xxv.

Muto, Susan. "Seeking Deep Silence," *Spiritual Life* 52 (2006): 43-44.

O'Keefe, OSB., Mark. *Love Awakened by Love: The Liberating Ascent of Saint John of the Cross*, 2014.

Payne, Steven. "The Tradition of Prayer in Teresa and John of the Cross," in *Spiritual Traditions*, Robin Maas and Gabriel O'Donnell, eds. 1990, pp. 235-258.

Ruiz Salvador, Federico. *God Speaks in the Night*, 1991.

Slattery, O.Carm. Peter. "Naming Our Future," in *St. John of the Cross*, Peter Slattery, ed. 1994.

Stein, Edith. (Teresa Benedicta of the Cross, OCD.). *The Science of the Cross: A Study of St. John of the Cross*, 1960.

Symons, Arthur. "The Poetry of Santa Teresa and San Juan de la Cruz," *The Contemporary Review*, 75 (1899): 542-55.

Thompson, Colin. *St. John of the Cross: Songs in the Night*, 2003.

Trueman Dicken. W. W. "Teresa of Jesus and John of the Cross," in *The Study of Spirituality*, Cheslyn Jones and others, 1986, pp. 363-376.

Welch, John. O.Carm. *When Gods Die*, 1990.

Welch, O.Carm. John. "Transformed Humanity and St. John of the Cross," in *St. John of the Cross*, Peter Slattery, ed. 1994, pp. 106-107, 109.

Wojtyla, Karol. —the future Pope John Paul II, *Faith According to Saint John of the Cross*, 1981.

OTHER BOOKS AND E-BOOKS BY LEONARD DOOHAN

THE CONTEMPORARY CHALLENGE OF JOHN OF THE CROSS
STUDIES OF THE MAJOR WORKS OF JOHN OF THE CROSS

This series presents introductions to each of the great works of John of the Cross. Each volume is a study guide to one of John's major works and gives all the necessary background for anyone who wishes to approach this great spiritual writer with appropriate preparation in order to reap the benefits of one of the most challenging figures in the history of spirituality. Each book is a complete introduction offering background, history, knowledge, insight, and theological and spiritual analysis for anyone who wishes to immerse himself or herself into the spiritual vision of John of the Cross.

While targeted to the general reader these volumes would be helpful to anyone who is interested in the spiritual guidance of this saint. These books give insight into the critical components of spiritual life and can be helpful for anyone interested in his or her own spiritual journey. They could be helpful for the many people involved in the spiritual guidance of others, whether in spiritual direction, retreat work, chaplaincy, and other such ministries. Throughout these books the reader is encouraged to develop the necessary attitudes, enthusiasm, spiritual sensitivity, and contemplative spirit needed to benefit from these spiritual masterpieces of John of the Cross. Attentive reflection on these studies will encourage readers to have a genuine love for John of the Cross and his approach to the spiritual journey.

These books give historical, regional, and religious background rarely found in other introductory books on John of the Cross. They each present an abbreviated and accessible form of John's great works. Later chapters in each book give John's theological and spiritual insights that could be used for personal reflection and group discussion. Sections abound in quotes and references from John's books and each sub-section can be used as the basis for daily meditation. The volumes complement each other, and together give the reader excellent foundation for reading the works of this great spiritual leader and saint.

Volume 1. John of the Cross: Your Spiritual Guide

This unique book is written as if John of the Cross is speaking directly to the reader. It is a presentation by John of the Cross of seven sessions to a reader who has expressed interest in John's life and teachings. This book introduces the great mystic and his teachings to his reader and to all individuals who yearn for a deeper commitment in their spiritual lives and consider that John could be the person who can guide them.

Table of contents
1. John's life as a contemporary life
2. John as a spiritual guide
3. John's vision of the spiritual life
4. Preparations for the spiritual journey
5. Major moments and decisions in the spiritual life
6. Necessary attitudes during the spiritual journey
7. Celebrating the goal of the spiritual journey

Volume 2. The Dark Night is Our Only Light: A Study of the Book of the *Dark Night* by John of the Cross

This introduction to the *Dark Night of the Soul* by John of the Cross gives all the necessary background for anyone who wishes to approach this great spiritual work with appropriate preparation in order to reap the benefits of one of the most challenging works in the history of spirituality. The book starts with the life of John of the Cross, identifying the dark nights of his own life. It provides the needed historical, religious, and personal background to appreciate and locate its content. It then presents readers with aids they can use to understand the work. With these preparations in mind the book moves on to present the stages of the spiritual life and the importance of the nights. A summary of John's own work brings readers in direct contact with the challenges of the message and its application today. The book ends with 20 key questions that often arise when someone reads this book.

Table of contents

Volume 3. The Spiritual Canticle: The Encounter of Two Lovers. An Introduction to the Book of the *Spiritual Canticle* by John of the Cross

The book starts with the life of John of the Cross, showing how he was always a model of love in his own life, and how, guided by his own experience he became a teacher and later a poet of human and divine love. The book provides the needed historical, religious, and personal background to appreciate and locate its content. The book then presents the links between John's *Spiritual Canticle* and Scripture's love poem, the *Song of Songs*. A summary of John's own work brings readers in direct contact with the challenges of the message and its application today. With these preparations in mind the book moves on to present the stages of the spiritual life and the importance of the journey of love. The book then focuses on key concepts in the *Spiritual Canticle*, applying each of them to contemporary situations. Finally it considers the images of God presented in the book and how they relate to the spiritual journey.

Table of contents

Volume 4. John of the Cross: The Living Flame of Love

The *Living Flame of Love* is the final chapter in John's vision of love. It describes the end of a journey that began in longings of love that became an experience of purification for the person seeking union. *The Living Flame of Love* picks up from the final stage of union in the love of spiritual marriage and describes, in great beauty, several aspects of this final stage in the union of love. All these ideas are part of John's wonderful vision of love. Many writers have emphasized the spiritual value of a life of love, but John's vision is more expansive and integrated than approaches presented by anyone else.

OTHER BOOKS OF INTEREST

THE CONTEMPORARY CHALLENGE OF ST. TERESA OF AVILA
An Introduction to her life and teachings

Leonard Doohan

This book is an introduction to the life and teachings of St. Teresa of Avila. It is a collection of notes and reflections taken from material I have presented in courses and workshops on St. Teresa over many years and in many countries to people from all walks of life who see Teresa's teachings on prayer as the vision and guidance they long for. This book on *The Contemporary Challenge of Saint Teresa of Avila,* is an introduction to her life and writings, and readers should use it as a companion to the careful and prayerful reading of Teresa's own writings. It is in no way a substitute for reading her works, in fact I have rarely quoted from her writings, insisting that readers must encounter them for themselves. I hope these notes and reflections will introduce readers to this giant in the history of spirituality and one of the greatest teachers of prayer that the world has ever known. This book is a companion to an earlier book, *The Contemporary Challenge of St. John of the Cross,* which was used extensively by individuals and groups as an introduction to St. John of the Cross' life and teachings. It was also used by many in formation programs. This current book on Teresa may well fulfill similar goals.

BOOKS ON SPIRITUAL LEADERSHIP

How to Become a Great Spiritual Leader: Ten Steps and a Hundred Suggestions

This is a book for daily meditation. It has a single focus—how to become a great spiritual leader. It is a book on the spirituality of a leader's personal life. It presumes that leadership is a vocation, and that it results from an inner transformation. The book proposes ten steps that individuals can take to enable this process of transformation, and a hundred suggestions to make this transformation real and lasting. It is a unique book in the literature on leadership.

This book is the third in a series on leadership. The first, *Spiritual Leadership: The Quest for Integrity* gave the foundations of leadership today. The second, *Courageous Hope: The Call of Leadership*, gave the contemporary characteristics and qualities of leadership. This third book focuses on the spirituality of the leader.

Courageous Hope: The Call of Leadership

This book's focus on leadership and hope is very appropriate given today's climate of distrust that many find results in a sense of hopelessness in their current leaders. Individuals and organizations are desperate for leaders of hope. Many books on leadership point to the need for inner motivation, but that inner motivation must be hope in new possibilities for a changed future. It is hope that gives a meaningful expression to leadership and enables the leader to be creative in dealing with the present. More than anything else it is a vision of hope that can excite and empower leaders to inspire others to strive for a common vision.

"Doohan strengthens our resolve. He restores our hope. And in an echo of Robert Frost, he is not only a teacher, but an awakener. May this book find you in a place where your will to grow is matched by an inner radiance to serve and help heal those around you... the reading will meet you there and the end result will be a gift to the world." **Shann Ray Ferch, PhD., MFA** Professor and Chair, Doctoral Program in Leadership Studies, Gonzaga University. Editor, International Journal of Servant Leadership.

"Read every word of this book. Leaders stuck in the past, afraid to face the future, afraid to take a risk because they might be wrong need an infusion of *Courageous Hope*. People are not looking for a simple, blind-faith hope. They are looking for leaders with a deeper understanding of hope as described in this book. **Mary McFarland, PhD.,** Professor, and Former Dean of undergraduate through doctoral programs in Leadership. International consultant in leadership and education.

"Ask people who were alive during the Great Depression what a huge difference Franklin Roosevelt made in their lives by giving them reasons to be hopeful. Ask people who were alive during the papacy of John XXIII what they loved most about him, and chances are they'll say that "good Pope John" gave them hope for the future. Read Courageous Hope and learn how to be that kind of leader yourself." **Mitch Finley,** Author of over 30 award winning books.

Spiritual Leadership: The Quest for Integrity

In eight clear and challenging chapters, the reader is invited to partake of a rich menu of reflections on the meaning of spiritual leadership and how it can transform one's role in the workplace, ensuring a collaborative environment of trust and confidence that energizes not only the culture of an organization, but also the effective accomplishment of its mission.

Leonard Doohan's highly readable book presents leadership as a call motivated by faith and love that results in a change of life, a conversion, and a breakthrough to a new vision of one's role in the world.

"Leonard Doohan's *Spiritual Leadership* is a profound and caring work . . . I highly recommend it to anyone interested in the spiritual meaning of servant leadership." **Larry C. Spears.**

"'The leader within,' . . . is well served by Leonard Doohan's book, *Spiritual Leadership.* It is a profound guidebook for leaders of the future, who live their values, who keep the faith." **Frances Hesselbein.** Chairman, Leader to Leader Institute

Dr. Leonard Doohan's new volume on Spiritual Leadership reaches beyond, or perhaps better, beneath the many current volumes on leadership which emphasize skill sets, techniques, and learned habits." **Robert J. Spitzer, SJ, PhD.** President and CEO, Magis Institute

BOOKS ON CONTEMPORARY SPIRITUALITY FOR CHRISTIAN ADULTS

Embrace the new enthusiasm in the Church and nurture your Christian commitment with weekly reflection.

A new spirit is stirring in the Church. We must overcome the failures of the past and prepare ourselves for a future of growth and responsibility. Let us rekindle spiritual insight, accept our spiritual destiny, and refocus on the essential teaching of salvation. While many have left the institutional churches, and sadly may never return, perhaps the challenge to renewal of Pope Francis may re-attract them to the essentials of Christian commitment. The Church will grow and benefit from an informed laity who deepens knowledge of the essential teachings of faith. I created a book with short sections, targeting areas of personal reflection valuable for individuals and discussion groups for this purpose. Read a section each week and gain a new strategy for nurturing your spiritual life.

Rediscovering Jesus' Priorities.

This book urges readers to look again at Jesus' teachings and identify the major priorities. It is a call to rethink the essential components of a living and vital Christianity and a challenge to rediscover the basic values Jesus proclaimed. Use the book for a short meditation and personal examination, as a self-guided retreat to call yourself to renewed dedication to Jesus' call, or for group discussion and renewed application of Jesus' teachings.

Ten Strategies to Nurture Our Spiritual Lives: Don't Stand Still—Nurture the Life Within You.

This book presents ten key steps or strategies to support and express the faith of those individuals who seek to deepen their spirituality through personal commitment and group growth. These ten key components of spirituality enable dedicated adults to bring out the meaning of their faith and to facilitate their spiritual growth. It offers a program of reflection, discussion, planning, journaling, strategizing, and sharing.

The One Thing Necessary: The Transforming Power of Christian Love.

This radical new interpretation of love as the touchstone of the Christian message, explores the human longing for meaning; the Scriptures; the relational model of the Trinity: the ideas of human vocation, destiny and community; the mystical spiritual traditions; and his own experiences to explain what love is, how we find it, and how it can change the world. Each of the seven chapters contains several quotes and focus points at the beginning and provocative questions at the end for reflection or discussion by adult religious educations and bible study groups.

"This book is all about love—and love as the one thing necessary. It is most certainly not about easy love or cheap grace. It is about the transforming power of Christian love. It is not only challenging but disturbing, a book written with conviction and passion."
Fr. Wilfrid Harrington, OP., Biblical scholar.

"[Doohan's] artful gathering and arranging of ideas reminds one of the impact of a gigantic bouquet of mixed flowers chosen individually and with great care." **Carol Blank**, Top 1000 reviewers, USA.

"Would that we heard more about this in our churches and religious discussions because, "this transforming power of Christian love will save the world" (p. 93). **Mary S. Sheridan**, "Spirit and Life."

The One Thing Necessary: The Transforming Power of Christian Love is available from www.actapublications.com or from amazon.com

Comment on the author's blog at
johnofthecrosstoday.wordpress.com

More about all books at
leonarddoohan.com

All books available at *Amazon.com*

CPSIA information can be obtained
at www.ICGtesting.com
Printed in the USA
LVHW062355220321
682188LV00017B/677